Women's Voices,
Women's Lives

NORTHEASTERN UNIVERSITY

1898–1998

Women's Voices, Women's Lives

DOCUMENTS IN EARLY AMERICAN HISTORY

EDITED BY
CAROL BERKIN AND LESLIE HOROWITZ

NORTHEASTERN UNIVERSITY PRESS
BOSTON

Northeastern University Press

Library of Congress Cataloging-in-Publication Data
Women's voices, women's lives : documents in early American history /
    edited by Carol Berkin and Leslie Horowitz.
        p. cm.
    ISBN 1-55553-351-5 (cloth : alk. paper). — ISBN 1-55553-350-7
(pbk. : alk. paper)
    1. Women—United States—History—17th century.   2. Women—United
States—History—17th century—Sources.   3. Women—United States—
History—18th century.   4. Women—United States—History—18th
century—Sources.   5. United States—History—Colonial period, ca.
1600–1775.   6. United States—History—Colonial period, ca.
1600–1775—Sources.   I. Berkin, Carol.   II. Horowitz, Leslie.
HQ1416.W67   1998
305.4'0973—dc21   98-11255

Designed by Janis Owens

Composed in Caslon 540 by Coghill Composition, Richmond,
Virginia. Printed and bound by Edwards Brothers, Inc., Ann Arbor,
Michigan. The paper is Glatfelter Offset, an acid-free sheet.

MANUFACTURED IN THE UNITED STATES OF AMERICA
02 01 00 99 98 5 4 3 2 1

To Edith Gaylord Harper, Sally Motyka, Kerry Candaele,
and Barbara Winslow, family by choice not chance

—CAROL

To the nieces, Jennifer, Elizabeth, and Rachel

—LESLIE

Contents

Acknowledgments

A SCHOLARLY PROJECT undertaken by two authors means more than twice as many acknowledgments, for there are hers, hers, and theirs to be made. We begin with "theirs." First, to John Weingartner, senior editor at Northeastern University Press, whose long-standing commitment to publishing works of feminist theory, women's history, and women's autobiography and biography has produced one of the finest lists in these fields. We are pleased to be included on that list and thank John for his support, patience, and enthusiasm. Our appreciation goes also to Ann Twombly, who guided the book from its awkward manuscript stages to its published form, improving it at every step along the way. We also thank Cindy Lobel, who took time off from work on her own dissertation to transcribe the seventeenth- and eighteenth-century documents in this collection. We are grateful to those scholars who answered our SOS calls and provided us with documents they had gathered in the course of their own research, especially Angelo Angelis, Bill Foster, Mary-Jo Kline, Simon Middleton, Mary Beth Norton, Susanah Shaw, Iris Towers, and Margaret Washington. And finally, our deepest respect goes to the scholars who preceded us in compiling collections of documents in early American women's history and collections that included sources from the colonial period. More than many, we appreciate the difficulties of your task and the value of your successes.

Each of the editors has been fortunate to have helpful colleagues and friends.

Carol Berkin: I want to thank Bert McCutcheon, Tammie McDaniels, John Woltjer, Bill Mendelsohn, Bill Walker, and Steve Kramer, a special group of historians and teachers who gather with me each June at the Advanced Placement Exam reading in San Antonio, Texas—and who this year patiently listened as I rambled on about the difficulties, frustrations, and pleasures of collecting documents for this volume. Their suggestions for topics and format were taken to heart, for they are expert teachers, practiced in the art of using primary sources in the classroom. Gratitude also goes to my graduate students, talented young scholars who have taught me much about history during our hours of conversation—and even more during our heated debates. Finally, my role in this collection, as in all of my history projects, ultimately was made possible by the willingness of my two children, Hannah and Matthew, to endure pizza, Chinese takeout, and cereal and milk for dinner on many occasions while their mom journeyed to earlier centuries.

Leslie Horowitz: I appreciate the support of my mother, Edna Horowitz, my sister, Andrea Horowitz, my brother, Marc Horowitz, and my nieces while I was in graduate school. Appreciation also goes to Mary Beth Norton, advisor, inspiration, and scholarly model over the last several years. For listening to me agonize over the frustrations of colonial sources, I thank Jackie Hatton, Nick Fowler, Marcia Butler, Anne Brophy, and Liette Gidlow. Very special thanks to Tom Volman, who made sure I ate while I was completing this project. And finally, to Colette, who had the good grace to stay up a tree for five days while we finished this project.

We gratefully acknowledge permission to use excerpts from the following materials:

Practitioner of Physick: A Biography of Abraham Wagner, 1717–1763 (Philadelphia: Schwenkfelder Library, 1954). Reprinted with the permission of Schwenkfelder Library.

Acknowledgments

The Adams Family Correspondence, vol. 2, edited by L. H. Butterfield (Cambridge: Belknap Press of Harvard University Press, 1963). Copyright © 1975 by the Massachusetts Historical Society. Reprinted by permission of Harvard University Press.

The letter from John Murray to Colonel Paul Dudley Sargent is reproduced courtesy of the Sargent House Museum, Gloucester, Mass.

The Diary of Landon Carter of Sabine Hall, 1752–1778, edited by Jack P. Greene (Charlottesville: University Press of Virginia, 1965). Reprinted with permission of the University Press of Virginia.

The Diary of Elizabeth Drinker, edited by Elaine Forman Crane (Boston: Northeastern University Press, 1991). Reprinted with permission of Northeastern University Press.

The deposition on the abortion and subsequent death of Sarah Grosvenor is reproduced courtesy of The Connecticut Historical Society, Hartford.

Archives of Maryland, edited by William Browne (Baltimore, 1883–1912). Reprinted with permission of the Maryland Historical Society.

Letters of Benjamin Rush, vol. 2, 1793–1813, edited by L. H. Butterfield (Princeton: Princeton University Press, 1951). Reprinted by permission of Princeton University Press.

The Book of Abigail and John: Selected Letters of the Adams Family, 1762–1784, edited by L. H. Butterfield, Marc Friedlaender, and Mary-Jo Kline (Cambridge: Harvard University Press, 1975). Copyright © 1975 by the Massachusetts Historical Society. Reprinted with permission of Harvard University Press.

Diary of the Reverend Jacob Elliot, 1763. Reproduced courtesy of The Connecticut Historical Society, Hartford.

"Huswifery," by Edward Taylor, in Thomas H. Johnson, "Edward Taylor: Puritan 'Sacred Poet,' " *New England Quarterly* 10, no. 2 (June 1937). Copyright held by The New England Quarterly. Reproduced by permission of the publisher and the author.

The Angel of Bethesda, by Cotton Mather, edited by Gordon W. Jones (Worcester, Mass.: American Antiquarian Society and Barre Publishers, 1972). Reprinted courtesy of the American Antiquarian Society.

"The Sentiments of an American Woman," by Esther DeBerdt Reed, *Pennsylvania Magazine of History and Biography* 18 (1894). Reprinted by permission of The Historical Society of Pennsylvania.

"Free Soil in Berkshire County," *New England Quarterly* 10 (December 1937). Copyright held by The New England Quarterly. Reproduced by permission of the publisher and the author.

"A Cherokee Women's Petition," in *The Cherokee Removal*, edited by

Acknowledgments

Theda Perdue and Michael D. Green (Boston: Bedford Books of St. Martin's Press, 1995). Copyright © 1995 by St. Martin's Press.

"On Educating Negro Women." Reprinted with permission from *The Negro in American History,* © 1969 by Encyclopedia Britannica Educational Corporation.

Women's Voices,
Women's Lives

Introduction

THIS COLLECTION is designed to provide an introduction to the lives of early American women, conveyed through their own words whenever possible rather than through commentary by the men around them. It is also designed to provide an introduction to the documentary sources from which historians reconstruct the lives of these women. The editors hope that, in the process of exploring women's experiences through primary materials rather than descriptive or analytical secondary sources, readers will come to appreciate the excitement of doing history—and the difficulty of doing it as well.

We have organized the documents in this collection into the six categories indicated by the chapter titles: sex and reproduction, marriage and family, women's work, religion, politics and the legal system, and a changing gender ideology. These categories were selected after a critical mass of documents had been collected; we did not want to find only what we had decided to seek. Like all categories imposed for the sake of clarity, these fail to do justice to the complex, overlapping, integrated, and contradictory experiences of our subjects. Yet if they are inadequate, they are not arbitrary: they represent central themes in the lives of colonial women and central themes in the history written about them. The reader will not find the categories equal in size or in richness of documentation. We would argue that these differences reflect the circumstances of colonial women's lives rather than our own judgments. For example, while politics and law may weigh heavily in the lives of modern women, the family was the core of the concentric circles of colonial white women's experiences.

In each category we have tried to include the voices of African American and Indian women as well as European, poor women as well as rich, women of the southern and middle colonies as well as New England. Our working premise—that race, class, and region crosscut gender in every woman's life—did not alter in the course of gathering and annotating the documents we have included in this collection.

The structure of the book is simple. Each chapter begins with an introduction to establish a context for the documents that follow, drawing on the remarkable scholarship of the last two decades. Each document carries a brief introduction as well, providing the reader with information about the author of the document and its typicality or special circumstances. The documents themselves are grouped under two broad rubrics: prescriptive and descriptive. Prescriptive (and proscriptive) materials are those that sought to define women's proper or normative place within society, setting the perimeters and parameters of women's lives. In many cases the authors of these documents are men, speaking as individuals or as representatives of social institutions. Taken as a whole, the collection is intended to offer a sampling of colonial female life rather than a mosaic or composite portrait.

Some observations about sources are in order. We hoped to create a collection in which colonial women would speak for themselves, about themselves. Historical realities did not always permit this. In the hierarchy of colonial America, race, class, and gender each played a part in defining the centers and margins of power and authority. In that world, husbands were expected to speak for their wives and children, masters and mistresses for their servants and slaves, and an increasingly dominant Anglo-European culture for Indians and African Americans. In such a world, free white men, usually of the elite, articulated the ideologies, encoded the norms and regulations, and enjoyed the privilege of commentary on the character, intellectual capacities, and social place of others. Thus, most of the prescriptive and proscriptive writings and even many of the descriptive ones—accounts of women's daily experiences—come from European men.

Historians can lament but cannot alter this reality. Scholars cannot hope to locate written documents from nonliterate societies such as the Eastern Woodland Indians, or to uncover diaries of early eighteenth-century slave women that comment on their life experiences. Yet, to an admirable degree, scholars have been able to reconstruct the circumstances of colonial women's lives. Through quantitative data, ethnographic work, archeology, and the examination of material culture, through the analysis of language, and through the interrogation of prescriptive literature, historians can provide us with details of lives we once thought lost to us.

Colonial women are not silent figures, of course. From court records and wills, from letters, diaries, daybooks, poetry, petitions, and newspaper advertisements, women can be heard, speaking directly to us. This material is subject to the realities of social class and race: elite women leave us more correspondence, more diaries, and more public statements. The affective lives of enslaved women, Indian women, female servants, and poor women come to us filtered through their masters and mistresses, employers, and benefactors—that is, ironically, through their female social superiors as well as the men of the era. Thus, in the end the gaps and silences in this collection confirm the reality in which colonial women lived, closed off by virtue of gender, class, and race from the resources that would have allowed them to comment and reflect on their internal and external worlds as those in power could do.

Finally, a word on the task of locating sources and recognizing their limitations. Finding early American women's sources often requires ingenuity and a certain temperamental doggedness. Richly descriptive and literate correspondence by women is often buried within collections bearing a husband's or father's name. Court records, rich with the voices of ordinary women who gave depositions as witnesses, do not provide a cast of characters at the top of the transcript; the researcher must read through many pages of testimony to discover if, indeed, one of the neighbors giving evidence is female. And once a source is located, the researcher must recognize its limitations. Court records, after all, offer women a chance to speak primarily in circumstances of deviance and disaster, not to describe the satisfactions of their lives. Newspapers, then as now, preferred to report the extraordinary rather than the ordinary. Formal language and expressions of personal affection or animosity are interwoven on the pages of documents such as wills and prenuptial agreements. And records of oral recollections of the illiterate include the perceptions and biases of the amanuensis. Many of the most revelatory materials are accidental inclusions in documents dealing with other matters. Prescriptive documents, such as sermons and legal statutes, often provide indirect or unintended evidence of widespread behavior and attitudes contrary to the norms and standards they assert. In the end readers, like the editors, must be gleaners rather than reapers of knowledge about colonial women's experience.

CHAPTER ONE

Sex and Reproduction

Historians probably can reconstruct the physical world and the physical experiences of many groups of colonial women far more richly than their intellectual or emotional lives. There are few sources from the cultures of the Eastern Woodland tribes because their oral traditions elude scholars. Women of the Huron, Iroquoian, and Creek tribes come to us more observed than observing in the rare written sources we do have, and most of those sources carry the bias of the missionary or the captive. Still, we make do with what we have; and from what were essentially field reports by Jesuits and other male European commentators we can garner some knowledge of reproductive and sexual practices and ceremonies among the Eastern Woodland Indians. These men often had an eye for detail, and if we take care to separate commentary from observation, we can gain some insight into native American women's lives. Similarly, poorer white women speak to us less directly than wealthy ones in both the seventeenth and eighteenth centuries. We would be hasty to assume that the meaning they made of their world, the perceptions they formed, and the expectations against which they measured their lives were identical to those recorded by the well-to-do in letters or diaries. Aspects of their lives are embedded in the documents left behind by record keepers and lawmakers, and modern-day historians have coaxed such documents into revealing general patterns. Demographic data help us chart the life cycle of seventeenth- and eighteenth-century white women, and similar though thinner sources on African American women in the eighteenth century yield knowledge about their life cycles. A range of quantitative sources suggest not only family size and the spacing of children, but the ages of menarche, marriage, and menopause.

The biological was, of course, also social. Thus it was interpreted through the prisms of religion, law, and custom—social lenses that varied greatly among the three races that shared the colonial world. The social contexts in which women grew to physical maturity, experienced sexual intimacy, participated in reproduction, nurtured their children, suffered illnesses, and went to their deaths can be examined through sources as disparate as trial and court records, diaries and letters, wills, church baptismal and burial records, laws and statutes, material artifacts such as birthing stools and tombstones, and a range of prescriptive literature from medical books and midwives' journals to sermons, obituaries, oral histories, folk legends, and myths.

The variety of women's physical experiences is striking. In the seventeenth-century Chesapeake colonies, for example, European women and men lived short and often spartan lives. Staking their claims in a region with a new and, for them, deadly disease environment, only the hardiest of these settlers could expect to live more than forty years. Here, where the demand for laborers in the tobacco fields translated into a great influx of young males, a skewed sex ratio of 3 to 1, sometimes 6 to l, made women a scarce commodity. And because home manufacture of vital items such as food, candles, and cloth and the reproduction of a family labor force were women's tasks, the competition for a wife was intense among these immigrant farmers. This meant that adult women, even those who arrived as indentured servants, had little trouble becoming brides, no matter what their sexual reputation, dowery, age, or appearance. And as English society provided women with few options other than dependence on

8

a husband, these Chesapeake women undoubtedly were glad of the opportunity to marry. The great demand for wives in Maryland and Virginia did not abate for several decades; thus, many daughters of former indentured servants found themselves married off at a shockingly young age. For some, puberty and marriage coincided, and virtual children became the wives of older, established men.

Whatever their ages, Chesapeake brides quickly became mothers. Indeed, many were pregnant before they wed. The cycle of pregnancy, birth, nursing, and weaning followed a remarkably even tempo, with two or two and a half years between children. If one husband died another was wed; and the cycle of reproduction continued. Indeed, remarriage was common in the seventeenth-century south because most marriages were ended within a decade by the death of the husband or wife. Complex families came together under one roof when widows remarried and produced children or widowers took new wives and became fathers once again.

Many of the children delivered live by Chesapeake women did not survive infancy; others died as youngsters. More than a third were dead before their twentieth birthdays. Mothers buried the stillborn, the neonates, the toddlers, and the young adults—and they themselves died of the same malaria or dysentery as the children. In this relentless cycle of reproduction, the white woman of the seventeenth-century Chesapeake might reasonably see her life as shaped by her anatomy and overwhelmed by biology.

For the white woman of New England the rhythms of life were no less influenced by reproductive roles. But there, where the environment was less dangerous and the sex ratio more balanced, women usually married in their early twenties. New England women could look forward—with pleasure, resignation, or dread—to decades together with their husbands, for the life expectancy was much higher there than in the southern colonies. To be fruitful, or fecund, was acclaimed by ministers as a womanly accomplishment, and the community generally concurred. Even without religious sanction, however, women who began a childbearing process in their twenties were likely to produce large families before menopause ended the reproductive cycle. Anne Hutchinson, the Massachusetts matron exiled for heresy, may have been radical in her theology, but in bearing more than thirteen children she was comfortably within the norm.

These demographic differences between the Chesapeake and New England faded in the eighteenth century. Improved survival rates in the south and increased risk of death from communicable diseases in the more urban north evened out the mortality figures. Natural increase in the Chesapeake balanced the sex ratio there. White women in most colonies, including New York and the Carolinas, began to marry later, typically in their early twenties. The serial marriages of seventeenth-century Maryland and Virginia became less common.

Even for Puritan women, raised under the watchful eyes of their parents, sexual experience frequently preceded marriage. Historians estimate that in the seventeenth century 15 to 20 percent of colonial women were pregnant before they became wives, and prebridal pregnancies remained common throughout the colonial period. Other sexual activity was not even linked to socially accepted reproduction. In the Chesapeake, court records speak of single women who lifted their skirts for any number of men without hesitation. From Georgia to the Maine frontier of Massachusetts bastardy was a common occurrence, despite threats of prosecution and sermons condemning it. The cramped and undifferentiated quarters in which the early colonists lived seemed to invite adultery and rape, as well as an early awareness of the nature of intercourse among children sleeping beside their parents each night. With parents, children, guests, and servants sleeping, eating, and dressing in the same room, it is not surprising perhaps that nonmarital and nonconsenting sex occurred. Court depositions tell us of servants who climbed into bed with their master's wife when he was away; of married women who seduced neighbors dropping in to warm themselves by the fire; and of darker episodes of incest, rape, and infanticide. All of these sexual experiences, although defined by the community as sins, crimes, or both, continued throughout the eighteenth century.

The African community remained small, even in the tobacco colonies, until the turn of the century. As economic conditions improved in England and the steady supply of indentured servants dried up, tobacco planters looked for new labor sources. By the 1680s the African slave trade was no longer dominated by competitor nations, and as English slaving increased, the price of a slave decreased. Mortality rates were dropping, and planters now considered the investment in a slave a reasonable risk—and potentially an excellent solution to the labor problem. By the 1720s forced immigration of thousands of African men and women had transformed the southern colonies into biracial communities.

The early generations of enslaved African women bore fewer children than the white colonists did. On small farms where men of African descent were not available, or in circumstances where an acceptable family life could not be sustained, black women appear to have curbed their reproductive activities. Whether because of limited opportunities or conscious decisions, children of enslaved women were more widely and often sporadically spaced. Black women may also have begun their families later than white women, perhaps because of delayed maturation due to diet and work or through the conscious use of birth control techniques. Yet, like white women of both the north and the south, many black women were sexually active before marriage. Their life expectancy, like their sexual activity, was similar to white women's in the south.

The experiences of Indian women were far from uniform. In many tribes sexual experimentation was not only common, as in white communities, but acceptable for young women as well as for young men. European observers have left us many shocked accounts of "promiscuous" women among the matrilineal and matrilocal tribes. Unregulated by fathers and not dependent on husbands for shelter and food, these women were liberated from the need for even a semblance of what Europeans termed modesty or chastity. Such circumstances were, no doubt, a French missionary's deepest fear and a Puritan minister's most scandalous nightmare.

Unlike the white settlers, the Indians directly acknowledged female physical maturation and female sexuality through ritual and ceremony. In some tribes girls were physically isolated during their first menstrual period. In many, women continued to remove themselves to "moon houses" during each monthly period. Among some Indians menstrual blood was considered dangerous and polluting;

among others it was a sign of heightened power within the woman, a power that deserved recognition and careful management.

Generally, Eastern Woodland Indians nursed their children longer than white women, sometimes not weaning them until the fifth or sixth year. This influenced the spacing of children, for Indians as well as colonists used breast-feeding as a birth control method. In some tribes, the spacing of children was also ensured by sexual abstinence for an extended period after the birth of an infant. Drug-induced abortion appears to have been sanctioned in cases where a woman became pregnant before her baby was weaned.

On the whole, childbirth was a social process in white society. There are accounts of births attended by every matron in the town, and in some cases, by every adult female, married or single. Rituals surrounded childbirth in these communities: birthing linens were brought out, refreshments served, bawdy jokes indulged, and the sociability continued until labor pains grew intense. Midwives attended the mother-to-be, and the baby might be delivered with the mother sitting on a "birthing stool" or held upright in the arms of a friend. There was no stigma attached to shouting out in pain during the delivery. In black communities, birth was similarly a collective female experience, where circumstances permitted. In Indian culture, however, childbirth was more often a solitary activity, undertaken in a special hut in nearby woods or outdoors under the trees. A midwife or relative could assist the mother-to-be if necessary. Indian culture viewed childbirth as one of the few opportunities for women to test and demonstrate their bravery and stoicism in the face of pain. It was a sign of weakness, therefore, to cry out.

Under English law a woman's body rarely belonged entirely to the woman herself. A married woman owed her husband sexual access; an indentured servant owed her master the right to prohibit anyone's access to her. Corporal punishment of wives was a legal and accepted practice in the colonies, and many men exercised the right—commonly viewed as an obligation—to administer physical punishment for their wives' alleged misbehavior in public or in private. Not all husbands did so, of course, but the option remained. Observers of Indian communities were quick to point out that the economic inde-

pendence of women in many agricultural tribes, together with matrilocal living arrangements, gave women greater autonomy in most areas,
including access to their bodies. Enslaved women and even free black
women had no legal protection against sexual abuse by white men.
Ownership of an African American woman included the right to pun-
ish or enjoy her body.

Colonial American governments, courts, and religious institutions
generated scores of prohibitions regarding sex, reproduction, and birth
control. Laws were passed defining extramarital sex as criminal, out-
of-wedlock birth as bastardy, and infanticide as murder. Sermons were
preached on virginity, adultery, and women's proper resignation to
the dangers and discomforts of reproduction. Medical books advised
women on what to eat when pregnant or nursing, how to cure illnesses
connected to breast-feeding or childbirth, and how to care for infants.
Midwives passed on an oral tradition regarding proper behavior during
pregnancy and birth. Tribal authority and custom together enforced
the rituals associated with Indian women's reproductive cycle,
prescribing puberty rites and proscribing certain behavior during
menstruation. Clearly, seventeenth- and eighteenth-century women,
whether white, black, or red, lived in a world that paid close and often
intrusive attention to the female body and its functions.

PRESCRIPTIVE DOCUMENTS

CONDEMNING INTERRACIAL SEX

"An Act Defining the Status of Mulatto Bastards," December 1662, in
William Hening, ed., *The Statutes at Large, Being a Collection of All the Laws of
Virginia, from the First Session of the Legislature in the Year 1619* (Richmond,
1809–1823), vol. 2, p. 170; and "An Act for Suppressing Outlying Slaves,"
April 1691, ibid., vol. 3, p. 87.

*English law and custom prescribed when sex was acceptable and with whom. By the
1660s legislation proscribing sexual intercourse between European and African colonists began to appear. While the first act quoted below simply outlaws sex between*

"christians" and "negro women," the second makes clear that the lawmakers condemned interracial offspring not only as evidence of sin but as abominations.

❦

[DECEMBER 1662] Whereas some doubts have arrisen whether children got by an Englishman upon a negro woman should be slave or Free, Be it therefore enacted and declared by this present grand assembly, that all children borne in this country shall be held bond or free only according to the condition of the mother, And that if any christian shall committ Fornication with a negro man or woman, hee or shee soe offending shall pay double the Fines imposed by the former act.

[APRIL 1691] For prevention of that abominable mixture and spurious issue which hereafter may encrease in this dominion, as well by negroes, mulattoes, and Indians intermarrying with English, or other white women, as by their unlawfull accompanying with one another, Be it enacted by the authoritie aforesaid, and it is hereby enacted, that for the time to come, whatsoever English or other white man or woman being free shall intermarry with a negroe, mulatto, or Indian man or woman bond or free, shall within three months after such marriage be banished and removed from this dominion forever, and that the justices of each respective countie within this dominion make it their perticular care, that this act be put in effectuall execution. And be it further enacted by the authoritie aforesaid, and it is hereby enacted, That if any English woman being free shall have a bastard child by any negro or mulatto, she pay the sume of fifteen pounds sterling, within one moneth after such bastard child shall be born, to the Church wardens of the parish where she shall be delivered of such child, and in default of such payment she shall be taken into the possession of the said Church wardens and disposed of for five yeares, and the said fine of fifteen pounds, or whatever the woman shall be disposed of for, shall be paid, one third part to their majesties for and towards the support of the government and the contingent charges thereof, and one other third part to the use of the parish where the offence is committed, and the other third part to the informer, and that such bastard child be bound out as a servant by the said Church wardens untill he or she shall attaine the age of thirty yeares, and in case such English woman that shall have such bastard child be a servant, she shall be sold by the said Church wardens, (after her time is expired that she ought by law to serve her master) for five yeares, and the money she shall be sold for divided as is before appointed, and the child to serve as aforesaid. . . .

PUNISHING FEMALE FORNICATORS

↦ ↤

"An Act for Suppressing of Immorality within this Province of New-Jersey,"
1704, in Bernard Bush, ed., *Laws of the Royal Colony of New Jersey, 1703–1745*
(Trenton, N.J.: Trenton State Library Archives and History Bureau, 1977),
vol. 2, pp. 21–22; and "An Act imposing a Duty on Persons convicted of
heinous Crimes; and to prevent poor and impotent Persons being imported
into this Province of New-Jersey; and for Amendment of the Law relating to
Servants," 1732, ibid., pp. 426–427.

*When New Jersey lawmakers decided in 1704 to establish the penalties for fornication
and adultery, they clearly hoped that the severity of the punishment would act as a
deterrent. They defined fornication as a female action although adultery could be
committed by a member of either sex. By 1732, however, male servants were included
in the category of possible fornicators—if a bastard child resulted.*

↜↝

[1704] And be it further Enacted by the Authority aforesaid, That all and
every person and Persons within this Province who shall be Lawfully Convicted of Fornication or Adultery, upon presentment indictment or information in the Supream Court, or the Court of General Quarter Sessions of the
peace of the County where such Fact shall be committed, every such Offence shall be by the said Court punished in manner following viz. Every
Woman Convict of Fornication as aforesaid, shall be fined by the said Court
for every such Fact in the Sum of five Pounds Money aforesaid besides Costs,
and if unable or unwilling to pay the same shall receive Thirty Lashes or
Stripes on the bare back; and every such Bastard, shall be also fined in the
Sum of five Pounds Money aforesaid, and give security to save the Town or
Precinct harmless from the Charge of such Bastard Child, and every Man
convicted of adultery as aforesaid shall be whip't at three several Courts and
each time receive Thirty Lashes on the bare back or pay the Sum of Thirty
Pounds Money aforesaid (and every Woman so Convicted of Adultery as
aforesaid shall be Whip't at three several Courts and each time shall receive
Thirty Lashes or Stripes on the bare back, or pay the Sum of Thirty Pounds
Money aforesaid), the said Sums and Penaltys herein before mentioned.

[1732] And, Be it further Enacted by the Authority aforesaid, That if any
bought White Man Servant of any Person or Persons inhabiting in this Province shall beget a Child on the Body of any bought White Maid Servant of

any other Person or Persons in this Province, and they the said Servants shall thereupon be duly convict of Fornication, in such Case the Master or Mistress of both shall pay each one half of the Charges that the Prosecution shall amount unto; and the Justices of the Court where such Conviction may happen shall adjudge such Man and Maid Servants respectively to serve so much longer to their respective Masters or Mistresses as they in their Discretion may think reasonable to make Satisfaction for such Offence. Provided always, That the Costs of the Prosecution aforesaid shall not amount to more than Forty Shillings, Proclamation Money, for each Person, to be divided in such Manner as the Court in which such Prosecution may happen shall see meet.

MASTERS AND WOMEN SERVANTS

↔↔

"Women Servants Got with Child By Their Masters After Their Time Expired To Be Sold By The Church Wardens For Two Years For The Good Of The Parish," in William Hening, ed., *The Statutes at Large, Being a Collection of All the Laws of Virginia, from the First Session of the Legislature in the Year 1619* (Richmond, 1809–1823), vol. 2, p. 167.

Virginia lawmakers knew that masters took sexual advantage of their female servants and sometimes got them pregnant. Some masters added insult to injury by demanding that the women serve additional time to compensate for lost productivity during pregnancy. Although this law is aimed at cynical masters, it also reveals a deep distrust of the women who bore the illegitimate children.

↜↝

Whereas by act of assembly every woman servant having a bastard is to serve two years, and late experience shows that some dissolute masters have gotten their maid with child, and yet claim the benefit of their service, and on the contrary if a woman got with child by her master should be freed from that service it might probably induce such loose persons to lay all their bastards to their masters; It is therefore thought fit and accordingly enacted, and be it enacted henceforeward that each woman servant got with child by her master shall after her time by indenture or custom is expired be by the churchwardens of the parish where she lived when she was brought to bed of such bastard, sold for two years, and the tobacco to be imployed by the vestry for the use of the parish.

Sex and Reproduction

↦↤

"Indeed Young Man I Must Deny"
(New York: Gilfert, 1795).

Many colonial brides were no longer virgins when they took their wedding vows. In fact, quite a few were pregnant with the couple's first child. Once a man publicly proclaimed his intention to marry a woman, usually by publishing banns in the church, many families considered sexual intercourse an acceptable next step. In the song below, the young woman resists all her suitor's advances until he pledges marriage. Then she considers it foolish to "deny."

↜↝

When first young Harry tole his tale,
I smil'd and turned the deafen'd Ear,
Or if he met me in the vale,
I laughe'd his doleful sigh to hear
I danc'd and sung as if for life nor thought [he]
meant me for his wife, and when he woo'd I
Us'd to cry, Indeed Young Man I must deny,
Indeed young Man I must deny I must deny
I must deny I must deny
Indeed young man, I Must Deny
One Day upon the Village green
To dance the Lads and Lasses met
In evry face gay mirth was seen,
Yet Harry seem'd to Pine and fret
He look'd and sigh'd yet fear'd to speak
As if his Heart was like to Break
He ask'd a kiss, I cried O Sie
Indeed Young Man I must Deny
He pull'd my sleeve, I turn'd my head
As if I was inclin'd to stay
While bluches on my cheeks were spread
Which he Observing, kiss'd away,
To Yonder Church lets go he cried
And there be made my charming bride
I though 'twas folly to be shy
And Own's I could no more deny.

In the Best Interest of Children

↔ ↩

William Cadogan, "An Essay upon Nursing and the Management of Children, From Their Birth to Three Years of Age," 10th ed. (Boston: Cox and Berry, 1772).

During the eighteenth century, women's control over childbirth and infant care was slowly eroded by the entry of male physicians into obstetrics. Genteel women employed male doctors rather than midwives to deliver their babies, and older traditions of childbirth as an exclusively female experience gave way to innovations that included the father in the process. Non-elite women, however, continued to rely on local midwives for prenatal care, birthing, and advice on the care of neonates and infants.

↜↝

It is with great pleasure I see at last the preservation of children become the care of Men of Sense: It is certainly a matter that well deserves their attention, and I doubt not, the Public will soon find the good and great effects of it. . . . In my opinion, this business has been too long fatally left to the management of women, who cannot be supposed to have any proper knowledge to fit them for such a task, not withstanding they look upon it to be their own province. What I mean is, a philosophic knowledge of Nature, to be acquired only by learned observation and experience, and which therefore the unlearned must be incapable of. They may presume upon the examples and transmitted customs of their great grandmothers, who were taught by the physicians of their unenlightened days; when Physicians as appears by late discoveries, were mistaken in many things. . . .

The feeding of Children properly is of much greater importance to them than their cloathing. We ought to take great care to be right in this material article, and that nothing be given them but what is wholesome and good for them, and in such quantity as the body calls for towards its support and growth, not a grain more. . . .

When a child sucks its own Mother, which, with very few exceptions, would be best for every child and every Mother, Nature has provided it with such wholesome and suitable nourishments; supposing her a temperate Woman, that makes some use of her limbs, it can hardly do amiss. The Mother would likewise, in most hysterical nervous cases, establish her own health by it though she were weak and sickly before, as well as that of her offspring. For these reasons I could wish that every woman that is able, whose fountains are not greatly disturbed or tainted, would give suck to her child. I am very sure, that forcing back the milk, which most young women must have in great abundance, may be of fatal consequence: Sometimes it endangers life and often lays the foundation of many incurable diseases. . . . the reasons that are given for this practice are very frivolous, and drawn from false premises; that some women are too weak to bear such a drain, which would rob them of their nourishment. This is a very mistaken notion; for the first general cause of most peoples diseases is not want of nourishment as here imagined, but two great a fulness and a tendency of humours.

RELYING ON MALE EXPERTISE

↦↤

Nicholas Culpepper, "The English Physician" (Boston, 1708).

Advice manuals and medical books were readily accessible to the colonial elite of the eighteenth century. In "The English Physician," Culpepper offers cures for a wide variety of problems, some medical, others cosmetic.

↜↝

AGAINST THE FALLING EVIL:

Take the Roots of Peony beaten to powder, 1 drachm in wine, Ale or Broth, given in a Morning some days before and after the full of the moon; it cures the falling sickness, if not too far spent; for it drives away all passions from the Brain, heart and spleen: also, it helps the windiness of the matrix, suffocation of the mother & stopping of the Courses; & will ease deliverance to women in Labour.

A PULTESS FOR A SORE BREAST:

Take new Milk and grate white bread into it, then take Mallows and Red Rose Leaves, 1 handful of each then chop them small, and boyl them together till it be thick, then put some honey and turpentine, mix them, then spread it on a cloth and apply it.

FOR AN AGUE IN THE BREAST:

Take good aqua vitae and Linseed Oil, and warm them together on chafing dish of coals, dip them in cloths made fit for the Breasts, and lay them there as hot as may be suffered Morning and Evening.

TO BRING LONG AND GREAT BREASTS TO LITTLE PROPORTION:

Take hemlocks, shred them and boyl them in white-wine, then make a plaster of them and apply them to the breasts.

TO HEAL ULCERS IN THE BREASTS . . . VERY GREVOUS:

Take Oyl of Sulfer & touch them, then make this Ointment, Take the Yolks of New eggs, 2 ounces, Turpentine, Butter, Barley Flower, & Honey of Roses half an ounce of each; incorporate them all in a mortar, & therewith dress them till they be whole.

TREATING "FEMALE PROBLEMS"

↔ ↩

"Specimen book of remedies from the practice of Abraham Wagner," 1740, excerpted in Andrew S. Berky, *Practitioner of Physick: A Biography of Abraham Wagner, 1717–1763* (Philadelphia: Schwenkfelder Library, 1954), pp. 112–114.

Like Nicholas Culpepper, Dr. Abraham Wagner shared his medical wisdom, based on his experiences as a popular physician in eighteenth-century America. Although there is no reference to inducing abortion, Wagner's suggestions for curing a "cessation of menses" may have been understood by his readers as a birth control formula.

↜↝

SICKNESSES PECULIAR TO WOMEN

A. Cessation of Menses   This condition causes many kinds of grief and distress, none of which will be eased unless a cure is effected, such as stomach pains, shortness of breath, headaches, toothaches, melancholia, convulsions, consumption, etc.

Causes are an overabundance of blood and thickened blood, fright, horror, unhealthy foods, chilling of the body and the feet and legs, prolonged cold water baths, going around in cold and dampness with bare feet, etc.

In the cure one must attempt to purify and thin the blood in order to make it flow; get rid of the cause and establish a nourishing diet and a well-ordered life.

The first can be acomplished by bitter digestive salts . . . and through laxative medicaments . . . which will prepare the body. After this, at the time when menses is to occur, one gives elixir proprietatis, elixir uterin, essence of myrrh, etc. Warm footbaths are helpful to draw down the blood and letting a vein in the foot during the beginning of the treatment will be helpful.

B. Death of the Foetus in the Uturus   If a pregnant woman or a woman in labor has not for some time noticed any movement on the part of the child, beyond what feels like a heavy pressure that falls on the same side to which the mother turns, when she feels sudden chills and trembling, when she becomes unconscious, experiences terror without cause, notices a pressure on her back, when the appearance and color of her lips is pale and wan, the breasts become soft and flabby, the lower part of the abdomen as well as the hands and feet become cold . . .

If the foetus remains in the uterus without labor pains . . . the dead child can remain in the mother for many weeks without any evil effects. In this case it is best to wait and let nature itself complete the abortion rather than to remove it through medicaments or force it out by hand. If however, the water has broken . . . one must attempt to remove the foetus in order to save the mother. The strongest medicaments have never been succesful.

REMEDIES FOR SORE AND INFECTED NIPPLES

↔↔

Elisha Cullen Dick, "Doctor Dick's Instructions for the Nursing and Management of Lying-In Women: With some Remarks concerning the Treatment of New Born Infants" (Alexandria, D.C.: Thomas and Wescott, 1798).

One of the most frequent complaints recorded by eighteenth-century American white women was soreness or infection of the nipples as a result of nursing. In this guide for mothers, the author urges at least three weeks of preparation before the baby is born and begins to suckle. The author's remedies will probably strike the modern reader as intrusive, involving as they do the manipulation of the breast by an assistant.

↔↔

TO GUARD AGAINST SORE NIPPLES

A very frequent and painful complaint, which, in its consequences, is commonly an important one, is for Nipples. This happily will be found, almost universally to be within the reach of the means of prevention.

About 10 days, or a fortnight before the expected time of confinement, pains should be taken to form the nipples, and to render them less sensible to the frequent and irritating applications of the Childs Mouth. For which purpose, let them be drawn out by the mouth of an assistant at least once everyday for the 1st week: and for the remainder of the time before delivery twice a day: after every operation of this sort, especially if there appear any considerable tenderness in the nipples, let them be bathed with a little new milk and spirit carefully combined. In summer, this application may be made as cool as the natural temperature of the liquid, and in winter, it should be brought up to about the summer standard. If the nipples are elongated or drawn out with difficulty, and show a disposition speedily to retract and disappear, rings made of bee wax, and adapted to their size, should be applied round them, and kept steadily on for the 1st five or six days before delivery; and afterwards as much longer as circumstances shall appear to make necessary. If upon thus using the nipples before confinement, they discover a propensity to crack, as it is generally termed, it will be found useful to sprinkle over them lightly, while in a state of moisture, with the milk and spirit a little finely powdered gum arabic: The powder, adhering to the surface, will form a kind of artificial skin, and will be found a useful protector of the natural one. This precautionary treatment, will gradually prepare the nipples for the reception of the child, and correct their natural irritability. It will moreover tend to prevent another complaint, formidable in its progress, and generally the result of inattention in the beginning.

Sore nipples naturally excite a reluctance in the patient to frequent application of the child, and the consequence is often a morbid retention of the milk, producing hard inequalities in the breast; which, by continuence, bring an inflamation and abscesses. It May generally be observed, that what are commonly called gatherings in the breasts, have been preceeded by sore nipples; and in such cases may justly be considered as their consequences: It is therefore highly incumbent on the patient to attend particularly to the advice contained in the foregoing section. If however, from neglect of it or otherwise, any partial swellings, or small hard tumors should appear, the breast should be immediately well drawn by the mouth of an assistant, for the purpose of relieving it as much as possible, from the pressure of the Milk, and the operation should be frequently repeated, to prevent a further accumulation. It will sometimes be found, that these tumors will readily disappear upon drawing the breast two or three times at short intervals especially if the part be gently rubbed at the same time in a direction toward the nipples, with a soft warm hand previously moistened with a sweet oil. If the obstruction should resist these methods, the vapour of hot water may be applied five or six times a day; which, together with an application of thick molasses in the intervals will generally prove successful.

DESCRIPTIVE DOCUMENTS
꩜

THE EXPERTISE OF INDIAN WOMEN
꩜

Adrien Van der Donck, *A Description of the New Netherlands*, 2d ed. (Amsterdam, 1656), trans. Jeremiah Johnson, excerpted in *Collections of the New-York Historical Society*, 2d ser., 1 (1841), p. 200.

While eighteenth-century medical reformer William Cadogan considered it folly to leave pregnancy, childbirth, and infant care in the hands of uneducated women, the seventeenth-century Dutch commentator Adrien Van der Donck considered Indian women to be expert in all matters relating to birth. According to Van der Donck, Indian women knew which medicines to administer and when to do so, their prenatal care was exemplary, and death in childbirth was unknown. Along with this near-perfect picture of reproduction among the Indians of the region, Van der Donck also accepted the view popularly held among white settlers that Indian women suffered no pain in childbirth. In searching for an explanation of this phenomenon, the Dutchman did not consider examining Indian cultural values.

+~+

Whenever a native female is pregnant, in wedlock or otherwise, they take care that they do no act that would injure the offspring. During pregnancy they are generally healthy, and they experience little or no sickness or painful days, and when the time of their delivery is near, (which they calculate closely,) and they fear a severe accouchement [delivery], or if it be their first time, then they prepare a drink made of a decoction of roots that grow in the woods, which are known by them, and they depart alone to a secluded place near a brook, or stream of water, where they can be protected from the winds, and prepare a shelter for themselves with mats and covering, where, provided with provisions necessary for them, they await their delivery without the company or aid of any person. After their children are born, and if they are males, although the weather be ever so cold and freezing, they immerse them some time in the water, which, they say, makes them strong brave men, and hardy hunters. After the immersion they wrap their children in warm clothing and pay them great attention from fear of accidents, and after they have remained several days in their secluded places, again return to their homes and friends. They rarely are sick from child-birth, suffer no inconveniences from the same, nor do any of them die on such occasions. Upon this subject some persons assign, as a reason and cause for their extraordinary deliveries, that the knowledge of good and evil is not given to them, as unto us; that therefore they do not suffer the pains of sin in bringing forth their children; that such pains are really not natural, but the punishment which follows the knowledge of sin, as committed by our first mother [Eve], and is attached to those only; others ascribe the cause of the difference to the salubrity of the climate, their well-formed bodies, and their manner of living.

A SPEEDY TRAVAIL

↔ ↔

Roger Williams, *A Key into the Language of America* (London, 1643).

Roger Williams's intellectual curiosity led him to attempt the first dictionary of the Narraganset language. In the excerpt below, Williams provides phrases relating to childbirth and infant care. In his commentary, he remarks on the ease with which Indian women bore their children. Unlike Van der Donck, however, Williams recognized that cultural factors, including the gendered division of labor and gender expectations, explained the ease and speed of an Indian woman's "eéchaw."

Kato eneéchaw.	She is falling into Travell.
Neéchaw.	She is in Travell.
Paugcótche nechaúwaw.	She is already delivered.
Kitummâyi-mes-néchaw.	She was just now delivered.

Obs. It hath pleased God in wonderfull manner to moderate that curse of the sorrowes of Child-bearing to these poore Indian Women: So that ordinarily they have a wonderfull more speedy and easie Travell, and delivery than the Women of Europe: not that I thinke God is more gracious to them above other Women, but that it followes, First from the hardness of their constitution, in which respect they brave their sorrowes the easier.

Secondly from their extraordinary great labour (even above the labour of men) as in the Field, they sustaine the labour of it, in carrying of mighty Burthens, in digging clammes and getting other Shelfish from the Sea, in beating all their corne in Morters: &c. Most of them count it a shame for a Woman in Travell to make complaint, and many of them are scarcely heard to groane. I have often knowne in one Quarter of an houre a Woman merry in the House, and delivered and merry again: and within two dayes abroad, and after foure or five dayes at worke, &c.

Noosâwwaw.	A Nurse.
Noònsu Nonánnis.	A sucking Child.
Wunnunògan.	A Breast.
Wunnunnóganash.	Breasts.
Munnúnnug.	Milke.
Aumaúnemun.	To take from the breast, or Weane.

OTTAWAN MENSTRUAL TABOOS

Father Gabriel Sagard, *The Long Journey to the Country of the Hurons*, ed.
George M. Wrong, trans. H. H. Langton (Toronto:
Champlain Society, 1939), p. 67.

Although English society surrounded childbirth with ceremonies and rituals (created mostly by women), it did not mark a girl's transition to womanhood and established no ceremonial taboos regarding menstruation. Many Indian societies, however, did acknowledge the onset of the menses as a female rite of passage and viewed menstruation as evidence of the power of women's life force. That the French priest Gabriel Sagard, writing in 1632, viewed menstruation as a "sickness" reveals more about his own culture than about the Ottawas or Hurons.

↜

The [Ottawa] women live very comfortably with their husbands, and they have this custom, like all other women of wandering peoples, that when they have their monthly sickness [menstruation] they leave their husbands, and the girl leaves her parents and other relatives, and they go to certain isolated huts away from their village; there they live and remain all the time of their sickness without any men in their company. The men bring them food and what they need until their return, if they have not themselves taken provisions enough as they usually do. Among the Hurons and other settled tribes the women and girls do not leave their house or village for such occasions, but they cook their food separately in little pots during that period and do not allow anyone to eat their meats and soups; so that they seem to copy the [Biblical] Jewish women who considered themselves unclean during these periods. I have not been able to find out whence they derive this custom of separating themselves in such a manner, although I think it a very proper one.

GIVING BIRTH IN THE ABSENCE OF FAMILY AND FRIENDS

↦ ↤

The Journal of Esther Edwards Burr, 1754–1757, ed. Carol F. Karlesen and Laurie Crumpacker (New Haven: Yale University Press, 1984), pp. 188–190.

Esther Edwards Burr joined together two distinguished families by her marriage: her father was the dynamic minister Jonathan Edwards; her husband was Aaron Burr, president of Princeton College. Although there were no complications in her delivery, both she and her newborn son, Aaron, became ill soon afterward. As a member of Philadelphia's elite society, Burr was able to set aside more than two weeks following the birth of Aaron for her "laying in" period; poorer women, servants, and slaves had to return to their normal activities much sooner.

↜

[MARCH 26, 1756] I am my dear Fidelia yet alive and allowed to tell you so—I have been able to write nothing from the time of my confinement till now which is the 26. day of March and 7 weeks since I was delivered of a Son.

I have but a short time to write and but little strength, tho' I have good will enough to write a quire of paper. I shall endevour to say as much as I can in as few words as possible for reasons that I shall give—I conclude you have received long since a Letter from Mr Burr informing you that I was unexpectedly delivered of a Son the sixth of Febry. Had a fine time altho' it pleased God in infinite wisdome so to order it that Mr Burr was from home as you will see by looking back to the last page.

It seemed very gloomy when I found I was actually in Labour to think that I was, as it were, destitute of Earthly friends—No Mother—No Husband and none of my petecular friends that belong to this Town, they happening to be out of Town—but O my dear God was all these relations and more than all to me in the Hour of my distre[ss]. Those words in Psalms were my support and comfort thro' the whole. . . . I had a very quick and good time—A very good laying in till about 2 weeks, then I had the Canker very bad, and before I had recovered of that my little Aaron (for so we call him) was taken very sick so that for some days we did not expect his life—he has never been so well since tho' he is comfortable at present.

I have my self got a very bad Cold and very soar Eyes which makes it very difficult for me to write at all. Sometimes I am almost blind.

A Child Is Stillborn

↦ ↤

Abigail Smith Adams to John Adams, July 16, 1777, in Lyman H. Butterfield, ed., *The Adams Family Correspondence* (Cambridge: Belknap Press of Harvard University Press, 1963), vol. 2, p. 282.

In 1777, while her husband was attending the Continental Congress in Philadelphia, Abigail Adams gave birth to a stillborn daughter. Abigail preferred not to discuss the cause of the child's death in this letter to John, fearing that the letter might fall into the hands of Loyalists or the British and be made public.

↜↝

Join with me my dearest Friend in Gratitude to Heaven, that a life I know you value, has been spaired and carried thro Distress and danger altho the dear Infant is numbered with its ancestors.

My apprehensions with regard to it were well founded. Tho my Friends would have fain perswaded me that the Spleen [or] the Vapours had taken hold of me I was as perfectly sensible of its discease as I ever before was of its existance. I was also aware of the danger which awaited me; and which tho my suffering[s] were great thanks be to Heaven I have been supported through, and would silently submit to its dispensations in the loss of a sweet daughter; it appeard to be a very fine Babe, and as it never opened its Eyes in this world it lookd as tho they were only closed for sleep. The circumstance which put an end to its existance, was evident upon its birth, but at this distance and in a Letter which may possibly fall into the Hands of some unfealing Ruffian I must omit particulars. Suffice it to say that it was not oweing to any injury which I had sustaind, nor could any care of mine have prevented it.

My Heart was much set upon a Daughter. I had had a strong perswasion that my desire would be granted me. It was—but to shew me the uncertanty of all sublinary enjoyments cut of[f] e'er I could call it mine.

A FATHER REPORTS A DIFFICULT DELIVERY

↦↤

John Murray to Colonel Paul Dudley Sargent, October 1, 1789, in *The Selected Writings of Judith Sargent Murray*, ed. Sharon M. Harris (New York: Oxford University Press, 1995), p. xxiv.

The presence of a male doctor during childbirth became steadily more common among the prosperous classes of the new nation, especially when complications developed in the pregnancy. As the letter below indicates, the essayist and educational reformer Judith Sargent Murray underwent a painful and life-threatening labor, which ended in the death of the infant and serious complications for the mother. Dr. Plummer, like many of the physicians of the era, employed forceps in the delivery, an instrument midwives did not use when they officiated.

↜↝

The first saturday in August our suffering friend was taken ill. She continued to suffer more than any language can describe till the wednesday night following. She was then, with the assistance of Doctor Plummer, and his Instruments, delivered of a Male child weighing very near fifteen pounds, whose spirit returned to the God who gave it, a few hours before it was born. We now flattered ourselves the worst was over, but alas, never did woman suffer more than she has suffered since. Near three weeks we were obliged to have three nurses, and four weeks were obliged to have two. I am not able to make you acquainted with her complaints. Sufficient to say, that for many weeks her life was dispared of, and day and night she suffered the most excruciating tortures. She is not yet able to sit on any seat but one which she is often obliged to use. With great difficulty she can walk from there to her bed which she can neither enter nor leave without assistance, and pain, and God only knows whither she will ever be well. However, I am incouraged to hope. I am willing to hope. She would do better now was it not for the [swelling?] in her legs. Her leg is larger than her father's thigh, but Doctor Plummer assures us she will, in time have all her complaints behind her.

A New England Midwife Records Her Career

↦ ↤

Diary of Martha Ballard, excerpted in Charles Elverton Nash, *The History of Augusta: First Settlement and Early Days as a Town* (Augusta, Me.: Charles E. Nash and Sons, 1908), pp. 240–244, 263.

With the publication of Laurel Ulrich's award-winning study, A Midwife's Tale, *Martha Ballard became the most famous midwife in American history. The excerpts printed below suggest the range of experiences this frontier midwife shared with her patients, from the tragic to the joyous. They also demonstrate the range of services she provided, from delivering babies, to postnatal care and advice, to preparing the bodies of mothers or infants for burial.*

↜

[1785] August 19. James Moore called me . . . to go to Simmion Clark's wife, she being in travail; was safely delivered of a daughter at 11 o'clock, evening.

September 10. Mrs. Hodges was safely delivered of a daughter at 6 o'clock this morning. I returned home at ten.

September 13. I was at Chamberlain's all day; she was delivered six o'clock, afternoon, of a daughter.

September 22. I was called to Mr. Leighton's, his wife being in travail. Left home at ten, forenoon; arrived there at two, afternoon. Found her safely delivered of a son, the operation by Solomon Leighton's wife.

October 21. Ephraim Town came here about day for me to go to Mr. Dexter's. We left here at 7 o'clock; arrived at Dexter's at afternoon; found his wife very ill. I removed the obstruction and delivered her safe of a fine daughter about the middle of the night. It stormed severely as I was on my journey.

OCTOBER 31. I was called at 10 o'clock in the morn in haste to Captain Jobe Springer's wife in travail, who was safely delivered at 2 o'clock, soon after my arrival there of a daughter. Left them both comfortable.

NOVEMBER 11. I was called at 5 o'clock this morn to Henry Babcock's, his wife being in travail. Arrived there about day-light— found her put to bed. The operation performed by Mrs. Smith. Mrs. Babcock, I found in severe pain, Her complaints so great, and she very desirous I should inquire into the cause. I complyd, and found her greatly ingered by some mishap. Mrs. Smith does not allow that she was sensible of it; however her fix. Mrs. Babcock's distress was so severe we were apprehensive she was expiring; sent for Doctor Coleman. But Dr. Williams fortunately came in and prescribed remedies which afforded some relief. I left him there and returned home at 10 P.M.

NOVEMBER 12. I am at home. Doctor Williams called here on his return from Mr. Babcock's. Informs me that she is some more comfortable; he has hopes she may recover.

[1787] AUGUST 20: . . . Mr. Hinkly brot me to Mr. Westons. I heard there that Mrs. Clatons Child departed this life yesterday & that she was thot Expireing. I went back with Mr. Hinkly as far as there. Shee departed this Life about 1 pm. I asisted to Lay her out. Her infant Laid in her arms. The first such instance I ever saw & the first woman that died in Child bed which I delivered.

LANDON CARTER OPPOSES BREAST-FEEDING AS BIRTH CONTROL

↦↤

The Diary of Landon Carter of Sabine Hall, 1752–1778, ed. Jack P. Greene (Charlottesville: University Press of Virginia, 1965), vol. 1, pp. 511–515.

Landon Carter believed his daughter-in-law was breast-feeding her baby as a birth control measure. In the journal entries below, this wealthy Virginia planter accused the ailing woman of selfishness, charging her with endangering the welfare of an infant for her own "pleasure."

⌇

[1770] 14 SUNDAY

. . . Mrs. Carter taken ill yesterday and was to be seen so before, though she would not own it. And the poor little baby Fanny is every time to share her

Mama's disorder by sucking her, and this because she should not breed too fast. Poor children! Are you to be sacrificed for a parent's pleasure?

I have been a parent and thought it murder and therefore hired nurses or put them out.

15 MONDAY

Mrs. Carter and little Fanny very ill and [y]et this child is to continue to suck the poison; she can't live, it is said without the baby and it is certain she can't live with it. Of course, the death of the child is inevitable from such an absurd way of reasoning: I hope my Lord and my God clear of this death. . . .

20 SATURDAY

. . . Last night, I thank god, little Fanny missed her terrible ague; it was thought she had a fever; but it is common for the flesh to feel warm on the period of the ague when it leaves them, especially if that is obtained by the bark, which I fancy this was. Note: the day before the child only took 3 doses of 6 grains each with rhubarb in them and yesterday 3 doses of 10 grains each without rhubarb; and if my advice is followed she shall take 2 doses this day with a small quantity of rhubarb, this for 2 days and then some drops of Elixer Proprietatis to prevent any ill effects of the bark and carry off what remains of the bile; but unless they wean her, still sucking from a morbid breast will in spite of fate bring on a return. Poor baby. . . .

LONG AND ANXIOUS DAYS

‹›‹‹

The Diary of Elizabeth Drinker, ed. Elaine Forman Crane (Boston: Northeastern University Press, 1991), vol. 1, pp. 116–125.

Elizabeth Drinker was a wealthy eighteenth-century Quaker matron. With several children afoot by 1765, the Drinker household was subject to what seemed like an endless stream of childhood illnesses and accidents, both minor and serious. Drinker was more fortunate than most mothers, for her wealth allowed her to draw upon the assistance of numerous servants and Philadelphia's best doctors. Nevertheless, Drinker's anxiety over the well-being of her children comes through in these excerpts from her diary.

˜

[JUNE] 17 [1765]. . . . Sally, who has been unwell several days past, grew worse this Afternoon, Complains of her Throat, and has a Fever, which increas'd as night came on. I sent to AJs for Nurse who did not come till 11 o'clock.—A James and Patty Accompanied her. the Child bad all night, vomited, freaquently—this has been a tedious long and anxious Day.

30

[JUNE] 20 [1765]. Sally so bad this Morning that we thought it best to consult Docter Evans, who with Docr. Redman, who before attended her, concluded in the Evening to cap on a Blister [to bring the inflammation to the surface of the skin], and a large one it was, which we laid on her back, Betsy Jervis sat up with us.

[JUNE] 21ST [1765]. Sally continues much the same. the Blister drawn and runs finely. her disorder the Doctors call an Apthea Fever, something of the nature of the Melignent sore Throat—her Mouth having several soars in it. . . .

[AUGUST] 15 [1765]. Sally fell this Morning against a Tub. and cut the back part of her Head. and I am afraid she has fractur'd the Bone—we stop'd the Blood with Turlington. . . .

[AUGUST] 20, 1765. . . . We gave Nancy a Clyster [enema], composed of Worm-wood, and Tansey, made into a strong Tea; to a Gill of it: put a table Spoon full of Lynseed Oyl, and a little Venice-Treacle;—it is gave with a design of killing the little Worms, that she is troubled with. . . .

A FAMILY GENEOLOGY

↔↔

"History of the Payne Family," *Proceedings of the Massachusetts Historical Society* 13 (1875), pp. 405–418.

Tobias Payne constructed the geneology excerpted below as part of an autobiographical sketch. In the rich details of his family's births, deaths, marriages and remarriages, careers, and migratory patterns, Payne personalizes the life cycle patterns studied by historians.

↔↔

I shall now say something of my own father, William Payne, the only child of my grandfather Tobias Payne.

He was born, the 22nd January, 1668, about eight months before his father's death. In 1685 he went to college, where he continued until 1689; after which he lived with his stepfather, Mr. Richard Middlecott, to learn merchants' accounts, till 1691. He went to England in 1692 and returned the next year to merchandize; but, meeting with continual loss, he applied himself to public business, and in 1698 received a commission from Gov. Stoughton for the impost. In 1699 [he] received a commission from my Lord Bellomont for collector, in which office he continued till 1710. In 1714 he had a commission from Governor Tailer for the same. In 1716 he was Commissioner of the Excise, after which he was in no business at all, but lived on the income of his estate until his decease, which was [on] the 10th of June, 1735, in the 66th year of his age—leaving a widow, three sons, five daughters, one daughter-in-law, a widow, and five grandchildren, all living.

In October, 1694 he was married to Mrs. Mary Taylor, daughter of James Taylor, Esq., of Boston, who died in childbed, the 6th of January, 1700. By her he had four children, viz.

William, born Nov. 25, 1695

Tobias, born June 25, 1697

Sarah, born Jan., 1699

Mary, born Jan. 6, 1700

In May, 1703, he was married again to Mrs. Margaret Stuart, an orphan, the only child of William and Margaret Stuart of Ipswich. Her mother was the daughter of a dissenting minister in yorkshire in the reign of King Charles the Second, whose father and mother died when she was young, which occasioned her going to live with her sister in Limerick, where she was married to my grandfather, Mr. William Stuart, of whom I can give no further account than that he was a Scotchman and a good liver. They both came to New England in 1684 and settled at Ipswich, where my grandfather kept a shop till his decease, which was in August, 1693. By him my grandmother had one child, viz. my mother, Margaret Stuart, born in Limerick, in May, 1683. After my grandfather's decease my grandmother was again married to Colonel Gedney of Salem, anno 1696, with whome she lived till her decease, being the 15th of October, 1697.

By her my father had eight sons and four daughters.

Sarah, born June 15, 1704, dec'd 1705

William, born Sept. 19, 1706, died

William, born Jan. 26, 1708

Edward, born Mar. 17, 1709, died

Ann, born June 8, 1711

John, born Feb. 9, 1713

Edward, born Oct. 7, 1714 died

Margaret, born May 22, 1716

Richard, born Apr. 4, 1718

Thomas, born Apr. 23, 1720

Edward, born Feb. 4, 1722

Jane, born Feb. 17, 1724.

My eldest brother, William Payne [was] born 25 Nov., 1695 [and] deceased Feb., 1705.

My brother, Tobias Payne, lived with my father till he was 18 years of age; then [he] went to sea with his uncle, Capt. Christopher Taylor, with whom he sailed about a year, and was taken by the pirates; after which he resided some time at Barbados, where my uncle Haggat put him in [as] master of the sloop. Some time after he returned to New England and married Mrs. Sarah Winslow, daughter of Kenelm Winslow of Marshfield, by whom he had one child, viz.

Mary Payne, born———

He sailed hence as captain of a ship, till his decease about the Virgin Islands, anno 1733.

Mary Payne was married in October, 1724 to Mr. Jonathan Sewall, a merchant, son of Major Sewall of Salem, with whom she lived till his decease, being in November, 1731, and had six children by him, viz.

Margaret Sewall, 6 Oct., 1725

———

———

Jonathan Sewall, Aug., 1728

———

Jane Sewall, Nov., 1731
Sarah Payne.

My sister, Sarah Payne, was married the 26th of December, 1734, to Mr. John Colman, Jr., a distiller, son of John Colman, Esquire, of Boston, with whom she now lives and has had five children.

Sarah Colman, July 1736
John Colman, 18 Jan., 1738
William Colman, Aug., 1739
Benjamin Colman, July, 1748
William Colman, Aug., 1744

My brother, William Payne [was] deceased May, ———

My sister, Ann Payne, now lives a maiden.

My brother, John Payne, lived two years as an apprentice to Mr. Jonathan Sewall, viz., till his decease; then he wrote in the Registrar's office with Mr. Boydell till his decease being [in] 1740; after which he continued in said office under Mr. Jonathan Belcher while he held said office . . . then under Mr. Auchmuty while he held the said office . . . then under Mr. Belcher again, in which place he continues at this day.

My brother, Edward Payne, deceased June. . . .

My sister, Margaret Payne, was married the 7th [of] October, 1741, to Mr.

John Phillips of Boston, who was formerly married to my cousin, Sarah Cooke, with whom she now lives and has no children.

My brother, Richard Payne, served seven years as an apprentice to Mr. Joseph Sherburne, to learn the brazier's trade.

My brother, Thomas died [as] a child.

Sister Jane now lives [as] a maiden.

Edward, the youngest son, born the 4th [of] Feb., 1722, lived as an apprentice with Mr. Benjamin Colman, merchant, in Boston, from April, 1736 to May, 1743. In August following [he] opened a store on the Long Wharf at the desire of Brother John Phillips, who proposed to put a stock into my hands to trade with on our joint accounts, but, his stock being chiefly employed in a distilling house with Brother Colman, he could not furnish me with the stock I expected. . . .

During my abode at Gloucester I was married to Rebecca Amory of Boston (daughter of Thomas and Rebecca Amory), born the 25th of June, 1725, by whom I had three children born in Gloucester, viz.

Mary, Sarah twins, born Dec. 1, 1757

Rebecca, born Aug. 28, 1759.

FEIGNING PREGNANCY

↦ ↤

The Diary of Landon Carter of Sabine Hall, 1752–1778, ed. Jack P. Greene (Charlottesville: University Press of Virginia, 1965), vol. 1, pp. 371–372.

Enslaved women, like men, found myriad ways to protest and resist the conditions of their servitude. Members of both sexes ran away for short periods of time, but women could also feign pregnancy or pregnancy-related problems to deprive the master of their work. As the diary entries below demonstrate, women used pregnancy as a weapon of resistance even when the risk of punishment was clear.

↜↝

[THURSDAY, MARCH 22, 1770] Guy came home yesterday and had his correction for run away in sight of the people. The 2 Sarahs came up yesterday pretending to be violent ill with pains in their sides. They look very well, had no fever, and I ordered them down to their work upon pain of a whipping. They went, worked very well with no grunting about pain but one of them, to wit Manuel's Sarah, taking the advantage of Lawson's ride to the fork, swore she would not work any longer and run away and is still out. There is a curiosity in this creature. She worked none last year pretending to be with child and this she was full 11 months before she was brought to bed. She has now the same pretence and thinks to pursue the same course but as I have full warning of her deceit, if I live, I will break her of that trick. I had two before of this turn. Wilmot of the fork whenever she was with child always pretended to be too heavy to work and it cost me 12 months before I broke her. Criss of Mangorike fell into the same scheme and really carried it to a great length for at last she could not be dragged out. However by carrying a horse with traces the lady took to her feet run away and when caught by a severe whipping has been a good slave ever since only a cursed thief in making her children milk my cows in the night.

DEVIANT SEX
↔ ↔

Fornication, rape, and adultery cases from the seventeenth century. William and Mary Watts's case, 1649 (Lower Norfolk Country Order Book, 1646–1650, 113a), and Katherine Watkins's case, 1681 (Henrico County Deed Book, 1677–1692), quoted in Warren M. Billings, *The Old Dominion in the Seventeenth Century* (Chapel Hill: University of North Carolina Press, 1975), pp. 161–163; Daniell and Faith Black's case, September 1664 (Ipswich Quarterly Court), in *Records and Files of the Quarterly Courts of Essex County, Massachusetts, Vol. 3, 1662–1667* (Salem, Mass.: Essex Institute, 1913), pp. 192–195.

The Virginia and Massachusetts cases excerpted below provide evidence of sexual appetites and activities that colonial society judged deviant: interracial intercourse, rape, adultery, and lesbianism. While William Watts's case was simple, Katherine Watkins's claim of rape was challenged by several witnesses who insisted that she had seduced the mulatto man in question. And as the Black case unfolded, it was said that Faith Black not only committed adultery but had sexual relations with another woman.

↔

WILLIAM WATTS'S CASE:

William Watts and Mary (Mr Cornelius Lloyds negro Woman) are ordered each of them to doe penance by standing in a white sheete with a white Rodd in theire hands in the Chappell of Elizabeth River in the face of the congregation on the next sabbath day that the minister shall make peninnce service and the said Watts to pay the court charges.

35

KATHERINE WATKINS'S CASE:

The examination of Katherine Watkins, the wife of Henry Watkins of Henrico County in Virginia. . . . The said Katherine aforesaid on her Oath and examination deposeth, That on fryday being in the Month of August about five weeks since, the said Katherine mett with John Long (a Mulatto belonging to Capt. Thomas Cocke) at or neare the pyney slash betweene the aforesaid Cockes and Henry Watkins house, and at the same tyme and place, the said John threw the said Katherine down (He starting from behinde a tree) and stopped her Mouth with a handkerchief, and tooke up the said Katherines Coates and putt his yard into her and ravished her; Upon which she the said Katherine Cryed out (as she deposeth) and afterwards (being rescued by another Negroe of the said Cockes named Jack White) she departed home, and the said John departed to his Masters likewise, or that way; after which abuse she the said Katherine declares that her husband inclinable to the quakers, and therefore would not presecute, and she being sicke and her Children likewise, she therefore did not make her complaint before she went to Lt. Col. Farrars (which was yesterday, Morning) and this day in the Morning she went to William Randolphs' and found him not at home, But at night met with the gentlemen Justices aforesaid at the house of the aforesaid Cocke in Henrico County in Virginia aforesaid before who she hath made this complaint upon oath. . . .

The deposition of John Aust aged 32 yeares or thereabouts Deposeth, That on fryday being the twelvth of August or thereabouts he came to the house of Mr. Thomas Cocke, and soe went into his Orchard where his servants were a cutting downe weeds, whoe asked the deponent to stay and drinke, soe the doponent stayed and dranke syder with them, and Jacke a Mulatto of the said Thomas Cocke went in to draw syder, and he stay'd something long whereupon the deponent followed him, and coming to the doore where the syder was, heard Katherine the wife of Henry Wakins say (Lord) Jacke what makes the refraine our house that you come not oftner, for come when thou wilt thou shalt be as well come as any of My own children, and soe she took him about the necke and Kissed him, and Jacke went out and drawed Syder, and she said Jack wilt thou not drinke to me, who sayd yes if you will goe out where our Cupp is, and a little after she came out, where the said Thomas Cockes Negroes were a drinking and there dranke cupp for cupp with them (as others there did) and as she sett Negroe dirke passing by her she tooke up the taile of his shirt (saying) Dirke thou

36

wilt have a good long thing, and soe did several tymes as he past by her; after
this she went into the roome where the syder was and then came out againe,
and between the two houses she mett Mulatto Jacke a going to draw more
syder and putt her hand on his codpiece, at which he smil'd, and went on his
way and drew syder and she came againe into the company but stay'd not
long but went out to drinking with two of the said Thomas Cockes Negroes
by the garden pale, And a while after she tooke Mingoe one of the said
Cocke's Negroes about the Necke and fling on the bedd and Kissed him and
putt her hand into his Codpiece, Awhile after Mulatto Jack went into the
Fish roome and she followed him, but what they did there this deponent
knoweth not for it being near night this deponent left here and the Negroes
together, (He thinking her to be much in drinke) and soe this deponent went
home about one houre by sunn. . . .

The Deposition of William Harding aged about 35 yeares . . . That he
came to the house of Mr. Thomas Cocke to speake with his brother where
he see Katherine the wife of Henry Watkins, and soe spoke to one there and
sayd, that she said Henry Watkins wife had been drinking; And that this
deponent see the said Katherine Watkins turne up the taile of Negroe Dirks
shirt, and said that he would have a good pricke, whereupon this deponent
sayd is that the trick of a quaker, who made him anser, that what hast thou
to say to quakers. . . .

The Deposition of Mary Winter aged about 22 years . . . That Mr. Thomas
Cockes Negroes and others being in company with them a drinking of syder,
Then came in Katherine Watkins the wife of Henry Watkins and went to
drinking with them, and tooke Mulatto Jack by the hand in the outward
roome and ledd him into the inward roome doore and then thrust him in
before her and told him she loved him for his Fathers sake for his Father was
a very hansome young Man, and afterwards the said Mulattoe went out from
her, and then she fetched him into the roome againe and hugged and kist
him. . . .

Humphrey Smith aged 26 yeares, deposeth . . . That he heard John Aust
say (about September last past) what Matter is it what I swore to and likewise
the deponent saw Katherine's Mouth (the wife of Henry Watkins) torne and
her lipps swel'd, And the Handkerchief that she said the Mulatto Stopt her
Mouth with very much bloody And the deponent heard the Mulatto confess
that he had beene to aske the said Watkins wife forgiveness three tymes, and
likewise the Mulatto sayd that Henry Watkins (the last tyme he went) bidd
him keepe off his plantation or else he would shoote him. . . .

37

DANIEL AND FAITH BLACK'S CASE:

Complaint of Dannell Black against his wife Faith Black: "For her keeping company with Juadeth Trumbell and John Hoow and for keeping of John Hoows hous and espachelley one night above the rest the saide faith Back was seen wallking with Juadath trumbell About the daye Light sehuttin in withing a Lettell Spacese earch of the other and being not seen from that tyme tell mednight or aboute that tyme and then Goodey Back came to Goodman wakeles house shee came to the dore and knocked att the dore soe sauft that no one could not heare her att Last shee went the back side of the house and takin up a clow Boord and knocken Against the house wakned the woman and the woman ris and opned the dore and lett her in and Asked whare shee had been that tym of night shee Answared she had ben att Goodman Clarkes eaten of fish Goodey wakley Asking why shee did nott goe home to her husband and to her one house shee Answered and sd that shee did not Care for goein home And Lickwise att other severell tymes being seene att John Howes hous and sum tymes in bed with John Hoow was seen to bee and allsoe her husband being A Pore man and one that hath nothing to Live by but his Labor had but one Cow and for the want of the milchen of her Lost the Profet of her by his wifes carlesnes whare upon hee was Provocked severell tymes and often to theretten her and tell her that hee would complaine of her to the Court her Father And the rest of her frinds with John How togeather hearing of this made A Complant to Mr. Symons," etc.

Goodwife Black complained that her husband had called her baud, swearing and cursing at her, threatening to kill her and knock her brains out. He told her to go and shift for herself and pulled off her stockings, turning her out of doors and not suffering her to come in, so that she was forced to go in the snow to Goodman Carall's, which was half a mile from her home.

John How testified that he heard Danil Black "wish god to dam his soul if he ded not Bett his wif Brains outt."

Edmon Bridges and John How testified that he forced his wife out so that she was obliged to go half a mile up to the knees in snow to get relief.

Obidia Bridgis deposed that Danill Black and his wife were at deponent's father's house, and she was very ill. There were several people in the house and Thomas Lovekin was desired by "my seester black" how his finger was that he had cut off. Danill Black seeing this, told his wife that he vowed that he would make her know sorrow for that. Some hours after, he asked his wife to go up with him to Mosis Pangren's and she refused, but he went and brought down a bottle of sack, drank some of it with his wife and so fell out with her. Deponent came between them and prevented his striking her, and Black replied "you Rog I will ron you thorow," having his knife drawn in his hand. Deponent and Edmon Bridges also deposed that they heard Black at Wenham tell his wife to go bring a sickle out of a field of corn when it was very wett weather and when she had not been abroad a great while on account of a great sickness, and when she refused to go, he abused her so that they had to send for the constable to quiet him. . . .

Elizabeth Perkins, sr., and Agnes Ewens were ready to depose as follows, if called: That they did not desire to testify, but what had brought them forth was the busy prattling of some other, probably the one whom they had taken along with them to advise a young woman, whose simple and foolish carriages and words, having heard of, they desired to advise better. This had come to the ears of Dan. Black, who had them summoned as witnesses. They desired to be excused from testifying because what was told them was a private confession which they had never to that day divulged, and the woman had never offended since that time but had lived gravely and soberly. The testimony was briefly that Mary, wife of John Howe, confessed to them and to Mary, wife of Dan. Clarke, that Goody Black lay with her one night in her husband's absence, and her husband coming home, etc.

Zacheus Curtis and Luk Wakelin deposed that they heard John How say that Daniell Blacke was a jealous fellow, etc.

Luke Wakelin and Katherine Wakelin testified that John How had often given Judah Trumbole counsel not to keep in the company of Goodwife Black for fear trouble would come to him, etc.

Daniel Black, complained of by John How for abuse, was bound, July 23, 1664, by Samuel Symonds to appear at the next Ipswich court.

John Danfed deposed that after working at the plains one day, he called at John How's and saw Goodwife Blake there by the loom-side shelling pease and heard her say that she would be at John How's in spite of her husband's teeth.

INFANTICIDE

↦↤

"Ordeal of Touch in Colonial Virginia, 1680," *Virginia Magazine of History and Biography* 4 (1896–1897), pp. 185–195.

In 1679 the magistrates of Accomac County, Virginia, began their investigation before a jury into the suspicious death of a "bastard child." On March 16 the magistrates examined each member of the Carter family: Paul Carter, a paint stainer; Sarah Carter; and Sarah's daughter, Mary, who had given birth to the infant. What unfolds in the testimony and depositions below is a complicated, surprising, and gripping story of a young woman, her lovers, and her accomplices in the murder of her unwanted child.

༁

The examination of Sarah the wife of Paul Carter taken in open Court by his Magesties Justices of the peace for Accomack County, March the 16th, 1679.

QUEST[ION]. Whether or noe had ye daughter a bastard child borne of her body?

ANSWERE. She had a bastard childe borne of her body, borne in the night about two hours before day.

QUEST. How long was your daughter in Labour?

ANSWERE. About two hours or two hours & a halfe.

QUEST. Was the child borne dead or alive?

ANSWERE. Dead and never had any sign of life in it.

QUEST. Who assisted at the birth of the child?

ANSWER. Her self and husband.

QUEST. Who receaved the child and assisted the woman to bed?

ANSWER. That she herself cut her blew apron and put the child in it and a blanket and laid in a couch, and then she her self laid her daughter in the bed.

QUEST. Where was y[ou]r husband when you assisted [you]r daughter to bed?

ANSWR. That he went out of the house imediately.

QUEST. What child bed linnen did you provide ag[ains]t the child was borne?

ANSWER. That she provided one sute w[hi]ch the child was buried in.

QUEST. What did you do with the childe untill day?

ANSWER. That she laid it drest in the bed betwixt her daughter untill sun rise and then she buried it.

QUEST. Where did you first bury the childe?

AN. In the old house.

QUEST. Who digged the grave where the child was buried?

ANS. That she her own self, and that her husband was absent and knew not where twas buried.

QUEST. How long did the child ly in the old house where it was first buried untill it was removed?

40

ANS. From the 13th of Jan[ua]ry to the latter end of February.

QUEST. Why did y'u remove the child from the place where it was first buried?

ANS. Because she thought it was most convenient for those p'sons that were to come to viewe the body.

QUEST. Why did you deny that y[ou]r daughter was with child or had a childe when y'u were brought before ye Justices?

ANS. To conceale her daughter's shame.

QUEST. How long time did you know y[ou]r daughter was wth child before she was delivered?

ANS. About two months and a halfe before it was borne. . . .

QUES. Did y'u ever examine who got y[ou]r daughter wth childe?

ANS. That she did examine her and she owned no father but James Tuck.

QUEST. Did y'u never see betwixt y[ou]r husband and daughter any unusual familiarity or incivillity?

ANS. That one time being to catch her mare for going to mill she came to the old house and there saw her husband hugg and kiss her daughter and took up her daughters coates up to her knees, and that she rebuked him for it and charged him wth debauching her daughter, and Paul her husband said he did her daughter no harm and so went away.

QUEST. Why did y'u send for no help having neighbours neer y'u to y[ou]r daughters delivery?

ANSWER. Her labour took her in a stormy night and could not send for help, but thought her husband and self sufficient.

QUEST. Why did y'u bury the child in the old house and not in the usual place that people commonly bury in?

ANSWERE. It was her folly so to doe thinking it would be safest there.

Accomack.

Be it remembered that upon the sixteenth day of March, in the 31st of his Ma[gis]ties Reign &c., It is pr'sented to this Worship[fu]ll Court that Sarah, wife of Paul Carter of the country afores'd . . . not haveing the feare of God before her eyes, but being lead & instigated by the devill out of meere malice pr'pensed and forethought as is vehemently suspected, sometimes in the months of January or February last past after the birth of a bastard child begotten by the said Paul on the body of Mary daughter of the said Sarah, did together wth the said Paul villanously murder and destroy the s'd bastard child, and after the said murder comitted as afore'sd together, wth the said

Paul did privilly bury the s'd bastard child in an old house thereby to hide and conceale the same, and for the further perpetration of the said crimes as afores'd together with the said Paul did sometime after privily take up and remove the body of the said bastard child into a garden place, and there also privily buried the same, for all w'ch crimes so committed as aforesaid the said Sarah is here pr'sented to this worship'll Court that further proceedings may be thereupon had according to the lawes in that behalfe provided.

Wee the Jury vehemently suspect Sara the wife of Paul Carter by circumstance to be guilty of the death of the bastard child in the pr'sentment within mentioned, and did bury the s'd child in an old house and did after take up the said child and bury it in the garden.

Rob't Hutchinson, foreman.

The examination of Mary the daughter of Sarah Carter taken in open Court by his Mag[i]stys Justices of the peace for Accomack County this 16th day of March anno Dom., 1679.

QUEST. Was it in the day or the night that you were delivered of y[ou]r bastard child?

ANSWERE. In the night.

QUEST. How long were you in labour?

ANSWER. An hower or two or thereabout.

QUEST. About what time was the childe borne?

ANSWER. Some time in the month of February.

QUEST. Whether was the childe borne alive or dead?

ANSWER. That it was borne alive & she heard it give one shreek and no more at the birth.

QUEST. Was the child alive or dead when y'r mother laid it at y'r breast?

ANSWER. That is was a little alive.

QUEST. What other means was there used beside the breast?

ANSWER. That she saw her mother bring out water & sugar to the fire side and offered it to the childe and it would not take it.

QUEST. Where was y'r father in law when ye childe was borne?

ANS. He was pr'sent & assisted at her labour and after it was borne went out of the house, and her mother tooke it from her and laid it in the couch.

QUEST. Did y'r father & mother ever tell you where it was buried and who assisted at the buriall?

ANSWER. That her father made the grave and her mother put it in as they informed her, and that they tould her they buried it in the old house.

QUEST. Whether or no did you tell y'r father or mother that you were w'th child before delivery?

ANSWERE. That about two months before her delivery her mother found out that she was w'th child and she told her father about a month before her delivery.

QUEST. Who do y'u thinke is the father of y'r bastard child?

ANSW. She does verily beleeve that her father in law Pa: Carter is the father, he haveing frequently to doe w'th her, and that once in the old house her Mother found him w'th her in his armes with his hands under her coates, and thinks that her mother comeing hindred them of any further action: but that James Tuck had once to doe with her.

QUEST. Whether did y'r father & mother give y'u notice of the removall of the child?

ANSWERE. That her mother told her she would remove the child before she did remove it, and her father was also knowing of the removall of it.

QUEST. What child bed linnen did y'r Mother p'vide?

ANSWER. One sute of child bed linning and that her father in law had a peice of scotch cloth to make into child bed linning.

The examination of Mary daughter of the said Sarah.

Saith. That Mr. James Tuck did at furst use violence towards her & after she was consenting and that the said Paul her father in Law did doe in like manner and that both of them lay w[ith] her and that she did keep it from her Mother untill her Mother did discover the same in maner as aforesaid and that both her Mother and Father in Law assisted her at the birth of the child and that she supposed the child to be born alive and that it lay between her Mother & herself all night and that in the morning it was dead and that she thinks her father and Mother buried it & that she thought in her conscience Paul was Father thereto. These examinations taken before us the day and yeare aforesaid and further the said Paul and Sarah being examined whether it was buried in the place where it was then laid it being in a garden very shallow, they answered it was first buried in the old house and after removed to the place aforesaid.

Cha: Scarburgh,	John West,
Richard Hill,	Wm. Custis.

Accamack:

Be it remembred that upon the sixteenth day of March in the 31st yeare of his Ma[gis]ties Reigne &c., It is pr'sented to this Worshipfull Court that

Paul Carter of the County aforesaid, painter stainer, not haveing the feare of God before his eyes but being lead and instigated by the divell, did beget a bastard child on the body of Mary, daughter of Sarah wife of the said Paul, and being further lead & instigated as aforesaid out of meere malice pre-pensed and forethought did sometimes in the monthes of January or February last past (as is vehemently suspected) after the birth of the said bastard child, I have villainously murder & destroy the said bastard child, and after the said murder comitted as afore[sai]d did privily bury the said bastard child in an old house thereby to hide and conceale the same, and for the further perpetracon of the said crimes afores'd did some time after privily take up & remove the body of the said murdered bastard child into a garden place, and there allso privily buried the same, for all w[hi]ch crimes soe comitted as aforesaid the said Paul Carter is here pr'sented to this Worsh'pll Court that further proceedings may be thereupon had according to the Lawes in that behalfe provided.

Foreman Mr. Rob[er]t Hutchinson, John Stretton, Henry Read, Wm. Marshall, Richard Hinman, John Bagwell, Barth. Meers, Isaac Metcalfe, Rob[er]t Watson Occahannock, Jno Bells, Tho: Bagwell, Arthur Robins.

Wee the jury vehemently suspect Paul Carter by circumstance to be guilty of the death of the bastard child in the wthin pr'sentment menconed, and that he was the person that dug the grave in the old house where the said child was first buried, as by his confession appeares.

Rob[er]t Hutchinson, foreman.

The deposicion Madam West the 35 yeare of her age. Was at the house of Paul Carter the first day of March, and did view the body of a bastard child borne of the body of Mary the daughter of Sara Carter, and when Paul Carter did touch the body of the dead child Mary Andrews clapt Paul Carter upon the back saying fie, Paul, fie, this is your child, he answered and said I doe not gain say it, but it is when y[ou]r depon't was coming from the house and taking my leave y[ou]r depon't saith were not y[o]u a wicked man to ly with y[ou]r wifes child, he answered I was a wicked man for so doeing and I must goe to God and not to man for forgiveness.

MARCH THE 17TH 1679.
Matilda West.

Sworn in open Court.
Test: Jno. Washbourne, Cl. Cu. Accomk

The deposicon of Mary Mickell the 50 yeare of her age. Was at the house of Paul Carter the 1st day of March, & did view the body of a bastard child borne of the body of Mary the daughter of Sara Carter, and when Paul Carter did touch the body of the dead child Mary Andrews clapt Paul Carter upon the back saying fie, Paul fie, this is your child, he answered and said I doe not gain say it but it is.

MARCH THE 17TH, 1679.
Mary Mikell.

Be it remembred that upon the sixteenth day of March . . . It is pr'sented to this Worsh'pll Court that Mary the daughter of Sarah, wife of Paul Carter of the County aforesaid . . . had a bastard child borne of her body begotten by the said Paul, w'ch said bastard child as is vehemently suspected in the monthes of January or February last past was murdered and destroyed, and that the said Mary not haveing the feare of God before her eyes, but being lead & instigated by the divill, did most wickedly consent to abett and conceale the said murder, for w'ch said fact the said Mary is here pr'sented to this worshipfull court that further proceedings may be thereupon had according to the lawes in that behalfe provided.

Wee the Jury find according to the within pr'sentment, that Mary the daughter of Sarah wife of Paul Carter had a bastard child borne on her body alive begotten by Paul Carter, and that after the death of the said bastard child she did conceale that she had a child.

Robt. Hutchinson, foreman.

At a Gen[era]ll Court held at James City 27th of April 1680 . . .

Whereas its vehemently suspected that Paul Carter hath contrary to all good manners and behaviour accompanyed wth Mary the naturall daughter of Sarah the wife of him the s'd Paul, Its therefore by this Court ordered that his Ma[gis]ties Justices of the peace of the county of Accomack doe take effectual order for the removall of the s'd Mary from the house & being of the s'd Paul Carter father in Law to her the s'd Mary, & place the s'd Mary in some convenient part of the County of Accomack to the intent . . . the s'd Paul Carter and Mary, the natural daughter of Sarah the wife of the s'd Paul may not cohabit, as likewise that the s'd Paul be constrained from accompanying w'th the said Mary, the afores'd Justices are desired and required to compell the s'd Paul to finde good security for his due performance of this order and for his future good behaviour. . . .

Whereas there was an order from the . . . Govern[o]r and Councill dated the 27th of April, 1680, this day p'duced to the Court wherein it was ordered that his Magssties Justices of the peace for this County of Accomack should take effectual order for the removall of Mary the natural daughter of Sarah the wife of Paul Carter for sev. reasons . . . the s'd order menconed as allso to cause the s'd Paul to finde good security for the due p'formance of their Honrs. Shereff of the county forthwth take the s'd Paul into safe custody and him to detaine untill he hath fully satisfied every p'ticular part and clause of the s'd order according to the true sence and intent thereof.

AN ABORTION TRAGEDY

↦ ↤

Deposition on the abortion and subsequent death of Sarah Grosvenor, *Rex v. John Hallowell et al.*, 1742, Superior Court Record books, #9, 113, 173, 175, and Windham County Superior Court Files, box 172, Connecticut State Library, Hartford.

When Sarah Grosvenor realized she was pregnant, she sought John Hallowell's help in inducing an abortion. Something went wrong—and Hallowell's later efforts to extract the fetus, which he insisted was dead but the mother suspected was still alive, ended in Sarah Grosvenor's death. The deposition below, given by Grosvenor's friend Abigail Nightingale, recounts Dr. Hallowell's botched procedure with forceps.

↜↝

Abigail Nightingale's deposition:
On [Sarah's] going down [to her cousin John's], [Hallowell] said he wanted to Speake with her alone; and then they two went into a Room together; and then sd. Hallowell told her it was necessary that something more should be done or else she would Certainly die, to which she replyed that she was afraid they had done too much already, and then he told her that there was one thing more that could easily be done, and she asking him what it was; he said he could easily deliver her. but she said she was afraid there was life in the Child, then he asked her how long she felt it; and she replyed about a fortnight; then he said that was impossible or could not be or ever would; for that the trade she had taken had or would prevent it; and that the alteration she felt Was owing to what she had taken. And he farther told her that he verily thought that the Child grew to her body to the Bigness of his hand, or else it would have Come away before that time. and that it would never Come away but Certainly Kill her, unless other Means were used. On which

she yielded to his making an Attempt to take it away; charging him that if he could percieve that there was life in it he could not proceed on any Account. And then the Doctor openning his portmantua took an Instrument out of it and Laid it on the Bed, and she asking him what it was for, he replyed that it was to make way; and that then he tryed to remove the Child for Some time in vain putting her to the Utmost Distress, and that at Last she observed he trembled and immediately perceived a Strange alteration in her body and thought a bone of the Child was broken; on which she desired him (as she said) to Call in some body, for that she feared she was a dying, and instantly swooned away.

CHAPTER TWO

Marriage and Family

M UCH OF a seventeenth- or eighteenth-century woman's life was
spent within the realms of marriage and motherhood. In Anglo-
European society, an adult woman was defined by her relationship to
the institution of marriage: she was either a miss or a madam—a maid
(and later a spinster) or a wife (then perhaps a widow). Her sense of
accomplishment and her reputation within the community were measured according to a female ideal of the "notable housewife," with its
central demands that a woman be a helpmeet to her husband, a fertile
wife, a competent mother, and an economical and productive household manager. These demands could not be met outside marriage and
without the creation of a family. In short, the only arena in which a
white colonial woman could hope to be fully acknowledged was
within marriage.

As institutions, marriage and the family served important legal
ends. They provided mechanisms for the identification of legitimate
heirs and for the inheritance of property. They ensured the maintenance of individuals socially defined as dependent, such as women
and children, through private rather than public resources. As social

institutions, they regulated behavior, including reproduction, instilled and reinforced community values, and provided vocational training. The many critical social functions performed by the family prevented colonists from viewing it as a private institution. New England's Puritans spoke of the family as a microcosm of civil society, a "little commonwealth" upon which the larger society was modeled and upon which it relied for survival. Thus, the community intervened whenever necessary to preserve the family and uphold the assigned duties and obligations of both wife and husband.

Colonists were given ample guidance in what to seek in a mate and ample instruction in the respective rights, duties, and obligations of husband and wife. From the pulpits, ministers exhorted women to obey their husbands, to practice economy in their households, to be fruitful and multiply. Husbands were told to acknowledge their wives publicly, support and protect them, be faithful to them, and provide them moral guidance. English etiquette books and marriage manuals were available in the colonies, especially in the eighteenth century, along with cookbooks and books on family health and household remedies. All were infused with the prevailing gender assumptions of the day: a wife was to submit to her husband's will and judgment; she was to make herself agreeable to him; she must shun idleness and demonstrate her housewifely skills; she was to bear and nurture his children. By the middle of the eighteenth century, however, prosperous women had begun consulting the prescriptive literature for advice on gentility rather than notable housewifery. Feminine rather than female behavior became the goal, with an emphasis on making the home attractive, developing refined social skills, and creating a pleasing persona through delicacy and charm rather than household efficiency. Still, for the majority of white colonial women, the bustling, competent, obedient, and fecund wife remained the ideal.

Women in every colony recognized the importance of acquiring a husband and, when circumstances allowed, selecting one. A woman's economic condition, her social standing, her place of residence, and the quality of her affective life depended on her husband; marriage to a lazy, incompetent, conniving, or simply unfortunate man meant a lifetime of hardship no matter how resourceful or intelligent a woman might be. Marriage to a violent man threatened her safety; marriage to an unfaithful man humiliated her. Although there were courtship rituals in every generation and for every social class, most colonial white women did not hold romantic love as the standard for the selection of a mate. Instead, women (and especially their fathers) looked for a man of comparable or better social standing, without obvious vices, with a reputation as a responsible member of the community and, among some groups, devotion to a church or faith. Romantic love was not always viewed with suspicion, but the ideal match was a matter of respect and responsibility rather than impassioned love.

There is no way to know whether colonial marriages were any more contentious, violent, or satisfying than marriages in other eras. The letters of Abigail Adams and her husband or of Margaret and John Winthrop, the love poems of Anne Bradstreet, and the correspondence of women such as Eliza Lucas Pinckney of South Carolina and Sarah Jay of New York offer ample evidence that marriage could be a source of happiness and deep affection. Court records recounting adultery, wife and husband beating, and desertion offer a less positive view. We do know that the colonists had few options for ending an unsatisfactory marriage. Death ended most marriages; desertion, others. In cases of abuse or continued disruption of the community by marital discord, legal separation might be granted. Absolute divorce was extremely rare. The most common means of escaping a violent husband or an oppressive wife, or of renouncing the economic responsibilities of marriage, was abandonment. Advertisements for runaway wives and requests for legal separations after years of desertion appeared regularly in colonial newspapers. Disease, disaster, and old age were more likely than the courts to release a woman from an unsatisfactory union.

Colonists spoke of marriage as a system of mutual obligations and duties. Thus, although marriage constricted women's financial autonomy, it also demanded that men support their wives. As *feme covert* a woman lost the right to sue or be sued, to alienate property or purchase it, to sign contracts, or to earn or dispense wages. Once a child was born, a husband acquired the right to use any property his wife brought into the marriage. Yet the wife was legally entitled to support by her husband—after his death as well as during his lifetime. The dower, a widow's one-third share of her husband's estate, was among the most protected forms of inheritance, and women actively pursued legal recourse if their husbands failed to honor it. The courts in most colonies established procedures to keep a husband from disposing of property without his wife's knowledge and consent, and also permitted prenuptial agreements through which a bride's father or a widow about to remarry could protect wealth from a husband's control. However, the rationale of these protections was not so much respect for the rights of women as the need to prevent dependent members of society from becoming a drain on public resources.

Marriage also defined the acceptable context for reproduction. Childbearing was laudable within marriage—but it was a crime or sin outside it. Colonial regulations regarding bastardy abound, suggesting the frequency of this social problem as well as the level of concern about it. The local laws restricting marriage among indentured servants usually were accompanied by others detailing the punishment for servants who produced illegitimate children. Most colonies had formal procedures in place to investigate out-of-wedlock births. Respectable women were appointed to interrogate the mother during labor in order to extract the father's name. The search for the father rested on economic as much as moral considerations because communities did not want to bear the burden of supporting the infant or mother. Given the shame and the possible penalties for bearing illegitimate children, it is not surprising to find records of infanticide investigations and trials in every colony. In cases of suspected infanticide, a panel of women was appointed to examine the body of the infant carefully and to interrogate the mother as well as any witnesses, relatives, or suspected accomplices. The report these women provided to the court weighed heavily in determining if criminal proceedings would follow.

Only a small percentage of white colonial women did not marry or bear children. Reviled as "thornbacks"—too prickly to be lived with—or cherished as spinster sisters or daughters who helped care for family members, most unmarried women earned their keep by performing the same domestic duties as their married friends and relatives. Wealth, of course, mitigated a spinster's circumstances. Women in comfortable circumstances might well consider freedom from the risks of childbirth and the burdens of child care as a benefit, and as *femes sole*, or women alone, they enjoyed full control over their land, slaves, or other property. For the majority of women, however, marriage and motherhood were the unquestioned path; a reputation as a "notable housewife" or, in the late eighteenth century, a "republican woman" encompassed their social aspirations.

Black women's experiences and expectations were shaped either by the institution of slavery or, in the case of free black women by the racial discriminations encoded in law and custom. Slave marriages were social, if not legal, realities. On plantations, marriage ceremonies sometimes followed African traditions; sometimes plantation owners insisted on orchestrating the ceremonies. A rough analogy can be made between these slave marriages and the common-law marriages of white settlers in the borderlands or backcountry areas of the southern and middle colonies. Here, where courts and ministers were scarce, the legitimacy of a marriage depended on a public declaration of intent to satisfy the obligations of husband and wife.

Within the constraints of the slave system, married couples attempted to assume the gendered duties of wife and husband. Whenever possible, African American men supplemented the family's diet by fishing and hunting, and women performed domestic chores such as cooking and gardening. Much energy was devoted to coping with the contingencies arising from slavery. Because husband and wife frequently lived on different plantations, the children's connection to their fathers was often cemented by naming patterns favoring paternal family names over maternal ones. Broad and sometimes fictive kinship relations usually were established to compensate for the possible disruption of family life by the sale of fathers or children. These support networks also helped parents respond to the work requirements placed upon the mother or to the sexual abuse of a woman by a white master or overseer. Child care could be relied on from aunts, older siblings, elderly grandparents, and available friends and neighbors. This "extensive" rather than intensive mothering tradition of the plantation—in which all adult women were assumed to have competence and authority to tend to, teach, and chastise all plantation children—was not entirely foreign to seventeenth-century white women in New England, whose household production duties kept them from devoting long stretches of time to child care.

Marriage patterns and customs in Indian society diverged greatly from those of white society, largely because the institution's purposes and functions were so different. Many Indian societies were both matrilineal and matrilocal—that is, both lineage and residence patterns revolved around the mother. Unlike the English and European systems, family systems in these societies did not require laws and sexual proscriptions to help men identify their legitimate heirs. And because women were not economically dependent on men, marriage did not provide women with their most viable source of support in exchange for obedience and service. The results were gender and sexual norms that never failed to shock English and European observers.

There are few sources to tell us how individual Indian women felt about marriage and motherhood. Yet marriage was the primary rite of passage for them just as it was for white colonial women. Because a marriage joined two clans as well as two individuals, important clan members rather than the couple or their parents usually decided on the desirablity of a union. Despite this, Indian women were rarely forced to marry a man they found unacceptable. Few tribes restricted female sexual behavior before marriage, and sexual experimentation—discreetly conducted—was condoned. Divorce was a simple procedure in most communities because there were no complex inheritance issues or religious injunctions. The dissolution of a marriage did not threaten a woman with poverty or the loss of her children, and in matrilocal and agriculture-based societies, dependency was not a factor at all. That divorce was a viable option does not suggest that marriage was taken lightly. Several tribes required couples to test their commitments before starting a family. The tests varied: some urged premarital cohabitation to discover sexual compatibility; others required a period of celibacy after marriage to determine emotional compatibility. The goal was the same: to dissolve a bad match before children were born. Once children arrived, the resolution of custody issues should a marriage dissolve depended on whether the tribe was patrilineal or matrilineal. In most Algonquin tribes, for example, the children already belonged to the mother's clan and remained with them if divorce occurred.

Individual women's experiences of marriage and motherhood depended on many factors. Yet some generalizations can be made. More than Indian or African American women, white colonial women entered into intimate relationships with men that were shaped by elaborate and overlapping legal, economic, and ideological prescriptions and proscriptions. More than whites or Indians, black women lacked control over critical aspects of their relationships with husbands and children, because they had to construct their marriages and their motherhood within the contingencies of enslavement or racial discrimination. And Indian women witnessed the erosion of their society's values and behavioral norms, as the colonizers impinged on the Indians' physical space, challenged their political independence, and attacked their norms and expectations in the cultural battles between native and immigrant societies.

PRESCRIPTIVE DOCUMENTS

A MARRIED WOMAN'S IDENTITY

Samuel Chase, *Baron and Feme, A Treatise of the Common Law Concerning Husbands and Wives* (London, 1700).

English law established several categories of dependent citizens, including male minors and married women. In declaring married women sub potestate viri, *subject to the power of a man, lawmakers argued they were simply confirming the laws of nature. In theory, a married woman, or* feme covert, *lacked free will and thus was not responsible for her actions; yet, as New Englander Samuel Chase explained in the following treatise on coverture, occasions did arise when it was necessary to "[make] bold with the law of nature" and treat a wife as if she was, indeed, a responsible adult. As Chase also pointed out, even subject groups had rights under English law. A wife was entitled to support from her husband, through alimony during his lifetime and through dower after his death. A widow's claim on a portion of her husband's*

54

property was vigorously protected in colonial society, although the terms of that claim varied over time and by colony. Of course, by honoring a widow's "thirds" local governments avoided the need to expend scarce resources in support of impoverished women and their children.

＋～＋

Coverture is *tegere* in Latin, and is so called for that the wife is *sub potestate viri.* The law of nature has put her under the obedience of her husband, and has submitted her will to his, which in the law follows, *cue ipsa in vita sua contradicer e tradicere non potuit,* and therefore will not bind her by acts joining with her husband, because they are judged his acts and not hers; she wants free will as *minors* want judgment, and yet the law of the land for necessity sake makes bold with this law of nature in a special kind, and therefore allows a fine levied by the husband and his wife, because she is examined of her free will judicially by an authentical person trusted by the law, and by the King's Writ, and so taken in a sort as a sole woman, as also when she comes in by receipt. . . .

A feme covert in our books is often compared to an infant [an underaged male], both being persons disabled in the law. . . . And yet a feme covert is a favorite of the law, and therefore the law gives her *rationabile Estoveriun,* til dower is assigned: and its said in some of our books an action lies not by the executors against her for her *paraphernalia.*

''TEACH THE YOUNG WOMEN TO LOVE THEIR HUSBANDS''

↔ ↤

Cotton Mather, *Ornaments for the Daughters of Zion* (Boston, 1692).

Cotton Mather was one of the leading ministers and opinion-makers of the Massachusetts Bay Colony. Like most devout Puritans, Mather believed that the family was the prototype of the well-ordered society, a "little commonwealth" in which lines of authority and obligation were clear and harmony was established through the obedience of the dependent and the responsible behavior of the powerful. In this popular and influential treatise, Mather exhorts women to love, honor, and obey their husbands, to be faithful and thrifty wives, and to foster godliness in their households.

＋～＋

I. As for her love to her husband, I may say, 'Tis even strong as death, many waters cannot quench it, neither can the floods drown it. She can like Sarah, Rebeckah, Rachel, freely leave all the friends in the world for his company; and she looks upon that charge of God unto his ministers, teach the young women to love their husbands, as no less profitable, than highly reasonable. . . .

II. But her love to her husband, will also admit, yea, and produce the fear of, a cautious diligence never to displease him. . . . While she looks upon him as her guide, by the constitution of God, she will not scruple with Sarah to call him her lord; and though she does not fear his blows, yet she does fear his frowns, being loath in any way to grieve him, or cause an head-ache in the family by offending him. . . . In every lawful thing she submits her will and sense to his, where she cannot with calm reasons convince him of inexpediences; and instead of grudging or captious contradiction, she acts as if there were but one mind in two bodies. . . .

IV. But she is for plenty as well as peace in her household; and by her thriftiness makes an effectual and sufficient reply unto her husband, when he does ask her, as he must, whether he shall thrive or no? She is a Deborah, that is, a bee for her diligence and industry in her hive. . . .

V. And this thriftiness is accompanied by such fidelity to her husband, as that she will not give a lodging to the least straggling or wandering thought of disloyalty in his bed. . . . She is a dove, that will sooner die than leave her mate. . . .

VI. But her fidelity is no where more signalized, than in her sollicitude for the eternal salvation of her husband. . . . Truly, tho' a woman may not speak in the church, yet she may humbly repeat unto her husband at home what the minister spoke in the church, that may be pertinent to his condition. Thus every Paul may have women that labour with him in the gospel. . . .

A Guide for Helpmeets
↦ ↤
Benjamin Wadsworth, *The Well-Ordered Family* (Boston, 1712).

Like Cotton Mather, New England educator and author Benjamin Wadsworth believed that the well-ordered family was the model for the well-ordered society. And like Mather he believed that both were hierarchical. Those with power, however, were not entitled to be arbitrary or tyrannical. Thus Wadsworth placed the responsibility for family harmony on the husband as well as the wife, insisting that a man forgo any violence against his wife, be solicitous of her feelings and of her health, be faithful to her, and provide generously for her material needs. A woman's obligation was to be her husband's "helpmeet," turning her energies toward the success of his household, obeying his wishes and commands, and providing him both physical and emotional comfort and support. In Wadsworth's vision, the imbalance of power and autonomy in a marriage should never prevent a couple from realizing a mutually supportive and loving relationship.

٭✧٭

THE DUTIES OF HUSBANDS AND WIVES

Tis their duty to cohabit or dwell together with one another. . . . If one house can't hold them, surely they're not affected to each other as they should be. Indeed men's necessary Occasions often call them abroad. . . . But they should not separate nor live apart, out of disgust, dislike, or out of choice. . . .

They should have a very great and tender love and affection to one another. This is plainly commanded by God. . . . If therefore the *Husband* is *bitter against his Wife,* beating or striking of her (as some vile wretches do) or in any unkind carriage, ill language, hard words, morose, peevish, surly behavior . . . he breaks the Divine Law. . . . The same is true of the *Wife* too. If she strikes her Husband (as some shameless, impudent wretches will) . . . she dishonours and provokes the glorious God. . . .

They should be chaste, and faithful to one another. . . . They must have nothing to do with any but their *own.* . . . As for Christians, their Bodies as well as Souls belong to Christ, and that by special dedication. Tis therefore a most vile aggravated wickedness in those that call themselves Christians (tis bad in any, but worse in them) to commit *fornication* or *adultery.* . . .

The Husband and Wife *should be helpful to each other.* The Lord said, it is not good that the man should be alone, I will make *an help meet for him.* The Wife should be a meet help to her Husband; he also should do what he can, to help forward her good and comfort.

As to Outward Things. If the one is sick, pained, troubled, distressed; the other should manifest care, tenderness, pity, compassion, & afford all possible relief and succour. . . . Husband & Wife should bear one anothers burthens, sympathize with each other in trouble; affording to each other all the comfort they can. They should likewise unite their prudent counsels and endeavours, comfortably to maintain themselves, and the Family under their joint care. . . . The Husband should indeavour, that his Wife may have Food and Raiment suitable for her. . . . The Wife also in her place should do what she can, that they may have a comfortable support. The Apostle requires that *wives be faithful in all things, keepers of the home,* and *that they guide the house, give none occasion to the adversary to speak reproachfully:* he condemns those that are Idle, wandring from house to house, and not idle only, but tatlers also, and busie bodies, speaking things which they ought not. . . .

Husband and Wife *should be patient one towards another.* . . . You therefore that are Husbands & Wives, dont aggravate each others faults; dont aggravate every error or mistake, every wrong or hasty word, every wry step, as though it were a wilful designed intollerable crime. . . .

Wives are part of the House and Family, and ought to be under the Husband's Government: they should *Obey their own Husbands.* Though the Husband is to rule his Family and his Wife yet his Government of his Wife should not be with rigour, haughtiness, harshness, severity; but with the greatest love, gentleness, kindness, tenderness that may be. Though he governs her, he must not treat her as a Servant, but as his own *flesh:* he must love her as himself. He should make his government of her, as easie and gentle as possible; and strive more to be lov'd than fear'd; though neither is to be excluded. On the other hand, Wives ought readily and chearfully to obey their Husbands. *Wives submit your selves to your own Husbands, be in subjection to them.* . . .

Children, Fear Your Mothers

↔↩

Benjamin Wadsworth, *The Well-Ordered Family* (Boston, 1712).

Benjamin Wadsworth stressed the obligations and responsibilities of children as well as parents. In this excerpt, he makes clear that children owe their mother the same degree of respect as their father, despite her secondary position in the family hierarchy. Late eighteenth-century white women, lauded in the prescriptive literature as the family's moral center, might have been surprised to read that mothers once were in danger of being disregarded or treated with disrespect by their daughters and sons.

↩↪

The Duties of Children to their Parents

Children should fear their Parents. God requires that *every person* should *fear* his Parents, not only his *Father,* but also his *Mother.* Yes, the *Mother* is here mention'd first possibly because Persons are more apt to disregard their *Mothers,* tho they stand in some aue of their *Fathers.* But the great God of Heaven bids *Children fear their Parents,* if therefore they fear them not, they rebel against God. . . .

Persons are often more apt to *depise a Mother* (the weaker vessel, and frequently most indulgent) than *Father;* yet if any man does despise his Mother, God calls him a *fool* for it; God counts him, and will treat him, as a vile, scandalous, wicked Person.

BENJAMIN FRANKLIN GIVES ROMANTIC ADVICE

↔ ↔

Benjamin Franklin to ———, June 25, 1745, in *The Papers of Benjamin Franklin, Vol. 3, January 1, 1745, through June 30, 1750* (New Haven: Yale University Press, 1961), pp. 30–31.

Benjamin Franklin, printer, diplomat, politician, and author of prescriptive litera-ture, earned a reputation as a man with a practical bent—and a lifelong interest in women. This letter to a friend gives evidence of both. In it, Franklin advocated mar-riage as an antidote to the unsettled life and unbridled passions of bachelorhood. But if his friend preferred love affairs to marriage, Franklin was ready to offer practical observations on that course of action as well. His sophisticated, secular approach to marital infidelity would have appalled the Puritan divine Cotton Mather; his objecti-fication of women would probably appall many modern readers.

↜↝

My dear Friend,

I know of no Medicine fit to diminish the violent natural Inclinations you mention; and if I did, I think I should not communicate it to you. Marriage is the proper Remedy. It is the most natural State of Man, and therefore the State in which you are most likely to find solid Happiness, Your Reasons against entering into it at present appear to me not well-founded. The cir-cumstantial Advantages you have in View by postponing it, are not only un-certain, but they are small in comparison with that of the Thing itself, the being *married and settled.* It is the Man and Woman united that make the compleat human Being. Separate, she wants his Force of Body and Strength of Reason; he, her softness, Sensibility, and acute Discernment. Together they are more likely to succeed in the World. . . .

But if you will not take this Counsel and persist in thinking a Commerce with the Sex inevitable, then I repeat my former Advice, that in all your Amours you should *prefer old Women to young ones.* You call this a Paradox and demand my reasons. They are these:

1. Because they have more Knowledge of the World, and their Minds are better stor'd with Observations, their Conversation is more improving, and more lastingly agreeable.

2. Because when Women cease to be handsome they study to be good. To maintain their Influence over Men, they supply the diminution of Beauty by an Augmentation of Utility. . . .

3. Because there is no Hazard of Children, which irregularly produc'd may be attended with much Inconvenience.

4. Because thro' more Experience, they are more prudent and discreet in conducting an Intrigue to prevent Suspicion. The Commerce with them is therefore safer with regard to your Reputation. And with regard to theirs, if the Affair should happen to be known, considerate People might be rather inclin'd to excuse an old Woman, who would kindly take care of a young Man, form his Manners by her good Counsels, and prevent his ruining his Health and Fortune among mercenary Prostitutes.

5. Because . . . regarding only what is below the Girdle, it is impossible of two Women to tell an old one from a young one. And as in the dark all Cats are grey, the Pleasure of corporal Enjoyment with an old Woman is at least equal, and frequently superior; every Knack being, by Practice, capable of Improvement.

6. Because the Sin is less. The debauching a Virgin may be her Ruin, and make her for Life unhappy.

7. Because the Compunction is less. The having made a young Girl *miserable* may give you frequent bitter Reflection; none of which can attend the making an old Woman *happy*.

8thly & lastly. They are so *grateful!!*

Thus much for my Paradox. But still I advise you to marry directly; being sincerely Your affectionate Friend.

Benjamin Franklin

THE DANGER OF BIGAMY

↦ ↤

Susan M. Kingsbury, ed., *Records of the Virginia Company of London* (Washington, D.C., 1935), vol. 4, p. 487; and William H. Whitmore, ed., *The Colonial Laws of Massachusetts* (Boston, 1890), pp. 101–102.

Divorce was rarely granted in white colonial society, but desertion and abandonment proved to be an effective way to end an unsatisfactory marriage. Men and, more rarely, women who wanted to escape their spouse or children could simply vanish, resettle in a new community, and perhaps marry again. Colonial authorities showed their concern about the possibility of bigamy by insisting that couples make a public announcement of their intention to wed and observe a waiting period between this public notice and the ceremony. Below are examples of such colonial legislation from the seventeenth century: the first passed in Virginia, the second in Massachusetts.

⤙↭⤚

[VIRGINIA, 1624] Whereas to the great contempt of the majesty of God and ill example to others, certain women within this colony have of late contrary

60

to the laws ecclesiastical of the Realm of England contracted themselves to two several men at one time, whereby much trouble does grow between parties: and the Governor and Council of State, thereby much disquieted: to prevent the like offense in others hereafter, it is by the Governor and Council ordered in court, that every Minister give notice in his church to his parishioners, that what man or woman soever shall hereafter use any word or speech tending to contract of marriage unto two several persons at one time (though not precise and legal, yet so as may entangle and breed scruple in their consciences) shall for such their offense undergo either corporal punishment (as whipping etc.) or other punishment by fire or otherwise, according to the quality of the person so offending. Given at James City this 24th of June 1624.

[MASSACHUSETTS, 1647] Whereas divers persons, both men and women, living within this jurisdiction, whose wives and husbands are in England, or elsewhere, by means whereof, they live under great temptations here, and some of them committing lewdness and filthiness here among us, others make love to women and attempt marriage, and some have attained it, and some of them live under suspicion of uncleanness, and all to the great dishonor of God, reproach of Religion, Common-wealth and Churches; It is therefore ordered by this Court and Authority thereof, for the prevention of all such future evils, that all such married persons as aforesaid, shall repair to their said relations by the first opportunity of shipping, upon the pain or penalty of twenty pounds, except they can show just cause to the contrary to the next County Court or Court of Assistants, after they are summoned by the Constable there to appear, who are hereby required so to do, upon pain of twenty shillings for every such default wittingly made; Provided this order do not extend to such as are come over to make way for their families, or are in a transient way, only for traffic or merchandize for some small time.

MANSTEALING

↦↤

Records of the Colony of Rhode Island, and Providence Plantations (Providence, R.I.: A. Crawford Greene and Brothers, 1856), p. 174; and Bernard Bush, ed., *Laws of the Royal Colony of New Jersey, 1703–1745* (Trenton, N.J.: Trenton State Library Archives and History Bureau, 1977), vol. 2, p. 21.

Marrying or promising marriage to a woman without the consent of her parents was, like bigamy, considered a threat to the social order. Both seduction and elopement were thus subject to legislation. Colonists referred to marriage without parental permission as "manstealing," a term that reminds us that children, especially daughters, were the property of their fathers. The laws quoted below addressed this issue in Rhode Island and New Jersey.

†∾†

[RHODE ISLAND, 1647] It is agreed, and by this present Assembly enacted, that the taking away, deflouring or contracting in marriage a maid under sixteen yeares of age, against the will of, or unknown to the Father or Mother of the Maid, is a kind of stealing of her; and that the penaltie shall be eyther five years' imprisonment or satisfaction of her parents.

[NEW JERSEY, 1719] Whereas of late years several Young Persons have been by the Wicked Practices of evil disposed Persons, and their Confederates, inticed, inveigled and deluded, led away and Clandestinely Marryed, which has often been to the Ruin of the Parties so marryed, as well as the great Grief of their Parents and Relations. In order therefore to prevent the like, as much as may be, for the future, *Be it Enacted by the Governour, Council and General Assembly of this Province, and it is hereby Enacted by the Authority of the same,* That from and after the Publication of this Act, no Lisence shall be given to Marry any Person under the Age of One and Twenty years, until such Person have had the Consent of his or her Parent or Parents, Guardian or Guardians, or Person or Persons under whose Care and Government he or she shall be, signified by a Certificate in Writing, under the hand of the Parent or Parents, Guardian or Guardians of him and her intended to be Married; or in case any the said Persons intending to be Married have no Parent or Guardian, then by a Certificate in Writing under the Hand of the Person or Persons under whose Care and Government the said person intending to be Married, at that time, shall be; which Certificate shall be filed in the Secretary's Office of this Province, and Registred in a Book to be kept for that purpose, for doing of which it shall be lawful for the Secretary of this Province, or his lawful Deputy, to receive the Sum of three Shillings as a Fee or Reward.

REGULATING THE MARRIAGES OF SERVANTS AND SLAVES
↔↩

Warren M. Billings, ed., "Some Acts Not in Henings Statutes," *Virginia Magazine of History and Biography* 83 (1975), pp. 37–38; and William Browne, ed., *Archives of Maryland*, vol. 53 (Baltimore, 1883–1912), pp. 533–534.

Both race and legal status were critical factors in determining marriageabilty. By the middle of the seventeenth century, colonial governments were taking steps to prevent interracial marriages, particularly those involving Anglo-European women and men of African descent. But colonial authorities were also concerned about protecting a master's property rights, which included control over the sexual life and marital relations of white indentured or bound servants. By the 1640s Virginia legislators had spelled out the penalties for clandestine marriages between servants or between a freeman and a woman servant. Because pregnancy deprived a master of the full value of a servant's labor, the Virginia authorities also established penalties for nonmarital sexual relations. Note that in the Maryland law of 1664, children of slaves are declared to follow the condition of their fathers rather than their mothers.

᠇᠊

[VIRGINIA, APRIL 1652] *Act the 27th [con]cerninge secrete [ma]rriges of Servants. Altered.*

Whereas many greate abuses, and much Detriment hath beene found to arrise both against the Law of god, and Likewise to the Service of manye masters of ffamelyes in the Collonye occassioned through secret marriages of servants, theire masters and mistresses not beinge any wise made privye thereto, as alsoe by the Committinge of ffornication, for the preventinge of the like abuses heereafter, Bee it Enacted, and Confirmed by this present grand Assembly that what man Servant soever hath since January 1640, or heereafter Shall secretlye marrye with any maid, or wooman Servant without the Consent of her master or mistress if shee be a Widdowe, he or they soe offendinge Shall in the first place serve his or theire time, or times with his or theire master or mistress Afterward shall serve his or their master or mistress one Compleate yeare more for such offence Committed, And the maid or Wooman Servant soe marryinge without Consent as aforesaid shall for such her offence Double her time of Service with her master or mistress, And a ffreeman Soe offendinge shall give satisfaction to the master or mistress by Double the Vallew of her Service, and Pay a fine of five hundred pounds of tobacco to the Use of the parrish where such offence shall be Committed, And it is Alsoe further Enacted, and Confirmed by the present grand Assemblye that if any man Servant shall Committ the Act of ffornication with any maide or wooman Servant he shall for his said offence, Besides the punishment of the law apppointed in like Cases, give satisfaction for the losse of her service, by one whole yeares Service when he shall be free from his master. . . .

[MARYLAND, 1664] An Act concerning Negroes and Other Slaves:
Be it enacted by the Right Honorable the Lord Proprietary by the advice

and consent of the upper and lower house of this present General Assembly that all Negroes or other slaves already within the Province and all Negroes and other slaves to be hereafter imported into the Province shall serve Durante Vita and all children born of any Negro or other slave shall be slaves as their fathers were for the term of their lives and forasmuch as divers freeborn English women forgetfull of their free condition and to the disgrace of our nation do intermarry with Negro slaves by which also divers suits may arise touching the issue of such women and a great damage does befall the Masters of such Negroes for prevention whereof for deterring such freeborn women from such shameful matches be it further enacted by the authority advice and consent aforesaid that whatsoever freeborn woman shall intermarry with any slave from and after the last day of this present Assembly shall serve the master of such slave during the life of her husband and that all the issue of such freeborn women so married shall be slaves as their fathers were and be it further enacted that all the issues of English or other freeborn women that have already married Negroes shall serve the Masters of their parents til they be thirty years of age and no longer.

GROUNDS FOR DIVORCE

↦↤

Records of the Colony of Rhode Island, and Providence Plantations (Providence, R.I.: A. Crawford Greene and Brothers, 1856), pp. 231–232; and J. Hammond Trumbell, ed., *The True-Blue Laws of Connecticut and New Haven* (Hartford: American Publishing Co., 1876), pp. 216–217.

Absolute divorce was rarely permitted in any of the English colonies. When couples flagrantly defied the ideal of a well-ordered family, when husbands abandoned their wives or one partner inflicted physical abuse, colonial governments might grant a divorce a mensa et thoro, that is, a legal separation. In such a case neither party was free to remarry. New England's leadership, however, proved more willing than most colonial authorities to dissolve a seriously flawed marriage so that the injured party could pursue the marital ideal under better circumstances. Rhode Island, for example, granted absolute divorce to a colonist married to a proven adulterer. While still an independent colony, New Haven granted divorce to any woman whose husband proved impotent.

↜↝

[RHODE ISLAND, 1650] Ordered, that no bill of divorce shall stand legall in this Colony butt that which is sued for, by the partie grieved, and not to be by law conferred for any other case but that of Adulterie; and that to be proved by the partie grieved, eyther by the man against the woman, or the woman against the man; and that neither partie shall procure devorce by accusing themselves of the same fact, except the contrarie partie be greeved, and sue to ye Generall Assemblie for divorce; then it being so granted, each partie shall be [as] free from each other as they were before they came together.

[COLONY OF NEW HAVEN, 1655] And if any man marrying a woman fit to bear children, or needing and requiring conjugal duty, and due benevolence from her husband, it be found (after convenient forbearance and due trial) and satisfyingly proved, that the husband, neither at the time of marriage, nor since, has been, is, nor by the use of any lawful means, is like to be able to perform or afford the same, upon the wife's due prosecution, every such marriage shall by the court or magistrates, be declared void, and a nullity, the woman freed from all conjugal relation to that man, and shall have liberty in due season, if she see cause, to marry another, but if in any such case, deceipt be charged and proved, that the man before marriage knew himself unfit for that relation, and duty, and yet proceeded, sinfully to abuse an ordinance of God, and in so high a measure to wrong the woman, such satisfaction shall be made to the injured woman, out of the estate of the offender, and such fine paid to the jurisdiction, as the court of magistrates shall judge meet. But if any husband after marriage, and marriage duty performed, shall by any providence of God be disabled, he falls not under this law, nor any penalty therein. And it is further declared, that if any husband shall without consent, or just cause shown, willfully desert his wife, or the wife her husband, actually and peremptorily refusing all matrimonial society, and shall obstinately persist therein, after due means have been used to convince and reclaim, the husband or wife so deserted, may justly seek and expect help and relief, according to 1. Cor. 7. 15. And the court upon satisfying evidence thereof, may not hold the innocent party under bondage.

PROTECTING DOWER RIGHTS

↦↤

"An act to enable feme-coverts to convey their estates, and for confirming and making valid all conveyances and acknowledgements heretofore made by feme-coverts," April 24, 1760, *Colonial Records of the State of Georgia* (Atlanta: Chas. P. Byrd, 1910), vol. 18, pp. 417–420.

Most colonies discovered that to protect a widow's dower rights, they had to protect a wife's interest in her husband's property transactions. An irresponsible or foolish husband might sell property his wife had brought to the marriage or property acquired during the marriage, thus reducing her economic security in widowhood. In England, the protective procedure was "fine and recovery," but this proved impractical in the colonies. Colonial governments instituted a simpler process of separate, private examination of a wife to discover if she approved of a proposed sale of property. How effective this safeguard was is questionable. Few wives were likely to challenge their husbands' decisions, even in the privacy of a judge's chamber. And many husbands simply ignored the requirement, selling property without informing their wives at all. In the following document, the New Jersey government reaffirmed that separate examination was an acceptable substitution for fine and recovery.

⊷

1. WHEREAS, the usual method of conveying lands and tenements in England by feme-coverts, is by fine or recovery, which methods have not been practised in any of his majesty's American colonies.

And whereas, instead thereof it has been customary in the conveyances of lands by husband and wife, to acknowledge her consent before a judge or justice, being first privately examined by the said judge or justice, whether she acknowledged the same voluntarily and freely; *Be it therefore enacted,* That all alienations and conveyances whatsoever, which have at any time heretofore in this province been made, either by husband and wife, having jointly signed a deed of conveyance before witness, or by the acknowledgment of the wife of her consent to such a sale of lands and tenements, before any of the then justices or magistrates, shall in such cases be valid in law, and good and effectual against the husband and wife, their heirs and assigns, and against all other person or persons whatsoever claiming under the said husband and wife, or either of them, to all intents and purposes, as if the same had been done by fine or recovery, or by any other way or means in the law.

2. *And whereas* it is necessary to secure the property of future purchasers of lands and tenements, as well as to prevent husbands disposing, without the consent of the wife, what of right did or would belong to them: *And whereas* also the method practised in England in these cases would prove exceedingly troublesome and very expensive to the inhabitants of this province: *Be it therefore enacted,* That from and after the passing of this Act, . . . where a feme-covert has or may have any right in part, or the whole of the lands and tenements to be conveyed, and the said feme-covert doth willingly consent to part with her right . . . the said feme-covert shall become a party

with her husband in the said deed of conveyance, and sign and seal the same before the chief justice or assistant judges, or one of his majesty's justices of the peace for the parish where such contracts shall be made, declaring before the said judge or justice that she has joined with her husband in the alienation of the said lands and tenements of her own free will and consent, without any compulsion or force used by her said husband to oblige her so to do. . . .

DESCRIPTIVE DOCUMENTS

EUROPEANS DESCRIBE INDIAN COURTSHIP AND MARRIAGE

John Lawson, *A New Voyage to Carolina* (London, 1709), pp. 185–188; and "A Narrative of the Captivity of John M'Cullough, Esq.," in Archibald Louden, ed., *A Selection of Narratives of Outrages Committed by the Indians in Their Wars with the White People* (reprint, New York: Garland, 1977), vol. 1, pp. 347–348.

Over the two centuries of Anglo-American colonial history, travelers, traders, priests, ministers, and government officials set down their observations on the Indian cultures they encountered. Their motives were many, their perspectives decidedly biased, their choice of subjects idiosyncratic. The modern reader's tendency may be to discount these observations entirely. Yet, if read with care and awareness of their limitations, these documents offer a glimpse into the experiences of Indian women. The first excerpt comes from an early eighteenth-century travel account; the second, from a captivity narrative.

When any young Indian has a Mind for such a Girl to his Wife, he, or some one for him, goes to the young Woman's Parents, if living; if not, to her nearest Relations, where they make Offers of the Match betwixt the Couple. The Relations reply, they will consider of it; which serves for a sufficient Answer, till there be a second Meeting about the Marriage, which is generally brought into Debate before all the Relations (that are old People) on both Sides, and sometimes the King with all his great Men, give their Opinions therein. If it be agreed on, and the young Woman approve thereof (for these Savages never gave their Children in Marriage without their own Consent) the Man pays so much for his Wife; and the handsomer she is the greater Price she bears. Now, it often happens, that the Man has not so much of their Money ready as he is to pay for his Wife; but if they know him to be a good Hunter, and that he can raise the Sum agreed for, in some few Moons, or any little time they agree, she shall go along with him as betrothed, but he is not to have any Knowledge of her till the utmost Payment is discharged; all which is punctually observed. Thus they lie together under one Covering for several Months, and the Woman remains the same as she was when she first came to him. I doubt our Europeans would be apt to break this Custom, but the Indian Men are not so vigorous and impatient in their Love as we are. Yet the Women are quite contrary, and those Indian Girls that have conversed with the English and other Europeans, never care for the Conversation of their own Countrymen afterwards. . . . Although these People are called Savages, yet Sodomy is never heard of amongst them, and they are so far from the Practice of that beastly and loathsome Sin, that they have no Name for it in their Language.

↜

OF MATRIMONY.

When a man takes the notion of marriage, (that is only those who are of some note amongst them) he informs his mother, or some other female relative, of his intention of entering into the matrimonial state, requesting her to make a choise for him. She then mentions half a dozen or more whom she knows to be industrious; out of which he makes choise of two or three of the number—making a preference of one out of the whole; he then gives his mother or other female relative—a shroud, or piece of broadcloth about a yard and a half square; they are of different colors; some red, some black, and some blue, which the women double up and tie around their waist for a petticoat, a blanket or pair of leggins; and sometimes a shirt: if they are good hunters, and become pretty wealthy, they will sometimes send the whole as a present to the intended bride. The present is offered to the woman whom he first made choise of, and so on, alternately, if the first refuses to accept of it, the one that takes it is informed what part of the house he lies in: some time in the night, after they all retire to bed, the modest bride slips away to him and creeps down behind him—where she lies till about an hour or two before day; then she rises and goes home, pounds a mortar full of corn, bakes it into cakes, puts them into a basket, carries them to the groom's house and sets them down at his bed head; then goes home again: he rises up by daylight, takes some of the cakes, and his gun,—if he has good luck, and kills a deer soon, it is reckoned a good omen; he takes it on his back, and carries it to the bride's house, throws it down at the door, and goes his way home, which completes the nuptials. The modest bride appears shy and bashful for a few days—and only goes to the groom at nights, after the family retires to bed: still observing to bring the groom his provisions every morning, (that is, if she has any to spare.) In a few days she becomes more familiar, and at last contents herself to live along with him. . . .

JOHN ROLFE'S MOTIVES FOR MARRIAGE

↦ ↤

John Rolfe to Sir Thomas Dale, 1614, in Ra[l]ph Hamor, *A True Discourse of the Present Estate of Virginia, and the successe of the affaires there till the 18th of June, 1614 . . .* (London, 1615), pp. 61–68.

John Rolfe achieved notice when he successfully transplanted a strain of mild, and therefore marketable, Caribbean tobacco to the new mainland colony of Virginia. His fame today, however, rests on his brief marriage to Pocahontas, who died while visiting England. In this letter to the governor of the colony, Rolfe cites his desire to convert the Powhatan princess to Christianity as a motive equal to his physical and emotional attraction to her. By Rolfe's account, Pocahontas was equally concerned with the religious opportunities the marriage offered.

᙭

Let therefore this my well advised protestation, which here I make betweene God and my own conscience, be a sufficient witnesse, at the dreadfull day of judgment (when the secret of all mens harts shall be opened) to condemne me herein, if my chiefest intent and purpose be not, to strive with all my power of body and minde, in the undertaking of so mightie a matter, no way led (so farre forth as mans weaknesse may permit) with the unbridled desire of carnall affection: but for the good of this plantation, for the honour of our countrie, for the glory of God, for my owne salvation, and for the converting to the true knowledge of God and Jesus Christ, an unbeleeving creature, namely Pokahuntas. To whom my hartie and best thoughts are, and have a long time bin so intangled, and inthralled in so intricate a laborinth, that I was even awearied to unwinde my selfe thereout. . . . Likewise, adding hereunto her great apparance of love to me, her desire to be taught and instructed in the knowledge of God, her capablenesse of understanding, her aptnesse and willingnesse to receive anie good impression, and also the spirituall, besides her owne incitements stirring me up hereunto. . . . What should I doe? shall I be of so untoward a disposition, as to refuse to leade the blind into the right way? Shall I be so unnaturall, as not to give bread to the hungrie? or uncharitable, as not to cover the naked? Shall I despise to actuate these pious dueties of a Christian? Shall the base feare of displeasing the world, overpower and with holde mee from revealing unto man these spirituall workes of the Lord, which in my meditations and praiers, I have daily made knowne unto him? God forbid. . . . If I should set down at large, the perturbations and godly motions, which have striven within mee, I should but make a tedious and unnecessary volume. But I doubt not these shall be sufficient both to certifie you of my tru intents, in discharging of my dutie to God, and to your selfe, to whose gracious providence I humbly submit my selfe, for his glory, your honour, our Countreys good, the benefit of this Plantation, and for the converting of one unregenerate, to regeneration; which I beseech God to graunt, for his deere Sonne Christ Jesus his sake.

SABINA SMITH FOLLOWS HER FATHER'S WISHES

↔ ↤

William Byrd to Sabina Smith, July 2, 1717; and Sabina Smith to William Byrd, July 4, 1717, in *The Secret Diary of William Byrd of Westover*, ed. Maude H. Woodfin and Marion Tinling (Richmond: Dietz Press, 1942), pp. 302–303.

Although daughters of the eighteenth-century colonial elite expected to play an active role in the selection of their future husbands, most continued to look to parents for guidance in such a serious decision. Few young women would defy a father who expressed strong opposition to a suitor—and Sabina Smith was no exception. Although William Byrd insisted that his motives were not mercenary, Sabina Smith's father may have been unconvinced. Whatever her feelings toward the ardent William, Sabina preferred to marry a man approved by her family.

↜↝

[From William Byrd] Tis astonishing that my Invisible Character shou'd not shew itself upon the application of your Elixir: but I have now taken effectual care to express what I said. If you cou'd look into my heart, you'd beleive that I love you without any mean Regard to your Fortune; I bless my Stars my circumstances are not so low, nor my Avarice so high as to require it. But if Sabina were mistress of no more than the Linnen that covers her agreable person, she wou'd be altogether as enchanting, and I as passionate as now. She may please to remember, that I sigh't for her at a time when her Fortune cou'd be no part of the Temptation. I beseech you dont do that

Injustice to your own Charms, as to imagin, I cou'd have any other Reason but them for my Inclination. Alas when a heart is fir'd wth so generous a Flame as mine, twill detest all low considerations. But to give you the plainest argument that my tenderness has no motive but your most engageing Person, I declare, that I wou'd even marry you tho your Geoler shou'd be so hard hearted as to deny his Consent. and then t'is a plain case, you wou'd not be worth one spendid shilling If an act so very heroique be not sufficient to convince you I must pronounce you more unbeleiveing than a free think[er]. I know not what the discerning Sabina may Judge of this offer, but I vow I think in this covetous age, tis a handsome thing to love a Damsel well enough, to marry her with nothing but her good Qualitys. However I wou'd not desire this unless I knew my own Fortune sufficient to make you easy without any addition from yours. as violent as my Passion is for you, I wou'd not ask you to descend in your circumstances below the Post of your Education for my sake: but wou'd be always ready to sacrifice the dearest & most darling of my Inclinations to your happiness. This is true so help me Love, and Heaven. Adieu.

[From Sabina Smith] I must acknowledge the very civil offer which you had the goodness to make me, but can't in conscience accept of it. I thank you nevertheless for your great Generosity, which is all a poor Damsel can do under my Circumstances of Obedience. I need not urge to Veramour [Byrd's pen name] the duty of the 5th Commandmant, which by the good leave of Constitution I will religiously observe. Neither ought you to preach up Rebellion against a Parent, in one that I'm confident you wou'd not teach to rebel against a Husband. I don't question but Veramours circumstances are sufficient to recommend him to a good Fortune in a more regular way. When a Man is in condition to go to market fairly, tis surely as unpardonable to steal a Wife, as any other valuable thing. But if you shou'd be averse to proceed in the forms with me, the utmost I can do, is to wish you may have all the happy terms you desire with some Nymph more deserving. However I am so much obliged to you for the over-value you are pleas'd to set upon my qualifications, that I shou'd be ungratefull if I did not wish you happy in marriage as well as in every other concern of life. Adieu.

REJECTING SUITORS

↦ ↤

Eliza Lucas to Colonel George Lucas [1740?], in *The Letter Book of Eliza Lucas Pinckney*, ed. Elise Pinckney and Marvin R. Zahniser (Chapel Hill: University of North Carolina Press, 1972), pp. 5–8.

The young women and men of the eighteenth century played a more active role in the choice of their marital partners than had their seventeenth-century ancestors. Nevertheless, parents—especially fathers—often promoted "suitable" candidates for their children. Daughters might reject a father's choice, but they usually welcomed parental advice on what they considered the most important decision in their lives. Few young women were as independent-minded—or frank—as Eliza Lucas of South Carolina. Of course, few young women had been left to manage three plantations at the age of fifteen while their father was called off to naval service. Intelligent, well educated, rich, and a successful planter by eighteen, Miss Lucas saw no need to marry for financial security, and she rejected two men recommended to her by her father. Soon afterward, she selected her own husband, the widowed political leader and scholar Charles Pinckney.

Hond. Sir

Your letter by way of Philadelphia which I duly received was an additional proof of that paternal tenderness which I have always experienced from the most Indulgent of Parents from my Cradle to this time, and the subject of it is of the utmost importance to my peace and happiness.

As you propose Mr. L. to me I am sorry I can't have Sentiments favourable enough of him to take time to think on the Subject, as your Indulgence to me will ever add weight to the duty that obliges me to consult what best pleases you, for so much Generosity on your part claims all my Obedience, but as I know tis my happiness you consult [I] must beg the favour of you to pay my thanks to the old Gentleman for his Generosity and favourable sentiments of me and let him know my thoughts on the affair in such civil terms as you know much better than any I can dictate; and beg leave to say to you that the riches of Peru and Chili if he had them put together could not purchase a sufficient Esteem for him to make him my husband.

As to the other Gentleman you mention, Mr. Walsh, you know, Sir, I have so slight a knowledge of him I can form no judgment of him, and a Case of such consiquence [sic] requires the Nicest distinction of humours and Sentiments. But give me leave to assure you, my dear Sir, that a single life is my only Choice and if it were not as I am yet but Eighteen, hope you will [put] aside the thoughts of my marrying yet these 2 or 3 years at least. . . .

MARY RUSH SEEKS HER FATHER'S ADVICE

↦↤

Benjamin Rush to Mary Rush, April 1, 1803, in *Letters of Benjamin Rush, vol. 2, 1793–1813*, ed. L. H. Butterfield (Princeton, N.J.: Princeton University Press, 1951), pp. 861–862.

Like other elite young women of the new United States, Mary Rush entered into a courtship of her own choosing. Nevertheless, she consulted with both her mother and her father as the relationship grew more serious. Dr. Benjamin Rush, a reform-minded advocate of women's education, offered this thorough and measured advice to his daughter, speaking frankly about the limitations on her dowry and about his prospective son-in-law's failure to comply with all the usual steps in the courtship protocol.

෴

My beloved Daughter,

I have received and read with uncommon emotions your sister's letter of the 11th of last month, and have seldom been more at a loss in deciding upon any subject than I am to write an answer to it. In addition to what your Mama has said in her two last letters upon the subject now under consideration, I have only to add that we are highly gratified with the excellent character of the gentleman who has done you the honor to prefer you to all your sex, and are much pleased with the candor he has discovered in his account of his situation and prospects in life. Mr. McIlvery of Montreal, who is now my patient, in speaking of the officers of the 49th Regiment, has more than once accidentally introduced Mr. Manners' name and spoken of him as a gentleman of great worth and of "highly polished and attracting manners." Under all these prepossessing circumstances, your parents unite in declaring our willingness to adopt him as a son from his character as a man. The objection which would have arisen to his unsettled mode of life is obviated by your sister's saying he purposes to leave the army after the expiration of a year. We are further reconciled to your separation from us (although the surrender of your society so necessary to our comfort in the approaching evening of our lives would be extremely painful to us), provided his and your interest and happiness can be best promoted by it. Our only fears arise from the scanty resources upon which you must depend for several years for the support of a family should you come together. As most of your father's children are still young and uneducated, and a great part of his estate locked up in unproductive property, it will not be in his power to give you more than six or seven hundred pounds at your marriage, and perhaps no more afterwards before his death. Recollect, my dear girl, how much a gentleman brought up as Mr. M. has been may be disposed from his habits and compelled by the rank of his connections to live beyond his income. Consider further, however much Mr. M. may esteem and love you, he has offered you his hand *without* the consent or knowledge of his father, that it is possible he may have destined him to a more wealthy and advantageous alliance, and that his whole family may complain of your having interfered in their plans of domestic establishments. Think seriously and coolly, my dearest Mary, of these suggestions of parental love, and do not fail at the same time to look up to Heaven for direction in the present difficult crisis of your life. Our prayers shall be joined with yours that you may be disposed to act wisely and prudently, and that your happiness here and hereafter may be the result of your deliberations. We earnestly request the assistance of Mr. Cuthbert and your sister's advice in determining your conduct. One thing we think we have a right to insist upon, and that is that you form no engagement with Mr. M. until his father's approbation be obtained to the proposed connection of our respective families. Mr. M.'s dependence upon him for a settlement, and your proper and kind reception by his family render this step indispensably necessary.

Adieu! my ever dear and beloved child. All the family join in love to you, Mr. Cuthbert, your sister Maria, and Master James, with your affectionate father, BENJN: RUSH

LIVING SINGLE

↔↔

"The Jolly Orange Woman" (Worcester, Mass., 1781).

It is difficult to know how many women remained single by choice during the colonial period. Some "spinsters"—as unmarried women were called—remained single because of special circumstances that affected the sex ratio. In New England, for example, border conflicts with Indians and warfare with French forces in Canada sometimes reduced the eligible male populations. By the eighteenth century, young men from the older areas of New England were migrating west in search of new land, reducing the pool of eligible husbands in the coastal towns and cities. Later, throughout the new republic a small but significant percentage of women chose the single life over marriage, preferring what one young woman called her "liberty" to the confining, and time-consuming duties of marriage and motherhood. Few middle-class or genteel women would speak as bluntly as the pleasure-loving, independent-spirited, and cynical woman in the following anonymous poem, which may well have been written by a man.

↔↔

A Hearty buxom Girl am I,
    Came from Dublin city.
I never fear'd a Man, not I,
    Though some say more's the pity;
Well, let them say so once again,
    I've got no cause to mind 'em;

74

I always fancy pretty Men,
    Whenever I can find 'em.
I'll never marry, no indeed,
    For marriage causes trouble;
And after all the priest has said,
    'Tis merely hubble bubble.
The Rakes will still be counted Rakes,
    Not Hymen's chains can bind 'em,
And so preventing all mistakes,
    I'll kiss where'er I find 'em.
The game of Wedlock's all a chance,
    Cry over or cry under,
Yet many folks to Church will dance,
    At which I often wonder.
Some fancy this, some fancy that,
    All hope the joy design'd 'em;
I'll have my whim, that's tit for tat,
    Wherever I can find 'em.
But what a silly Jade am I,
    Thus idly to be singing,
There's not one here my fruit to buy,
    Nor any to be flinging;
In pretty Men all pleasure dwells,
    All hope the joy design'd 'em.
So now I'll wheel to Saddler's Wells,
And there I'm sure to find 'em.

Happy Marriages

↔ ↔

Anne Bradstreet, "To My Dear and Loving Husband," *Works of Anne Bradstreet in Prose and Verses*, ed. John W. Ellis (Charleston: A. E. Cutter, 1887), p. 394.

Unlike marriages marked by infidelity, physical violence, or evasion of responsibilities, happy marriages—or their details—do not make their way into court records. Evidence of affection and respect can be found in wills and tombstone inscriptions, but the most compelling evidence comes from the diaries, letters, and other written exchanges between married couples. The seventeenth-century Puritan poet Anne Bradstreet left this tribute to a long relationship with a loving companion.

If ever two were one, then surely we;
If ever man were loved by wife, then thee;
If ever wife was happy in a man,
Compare with me, ye women, if you can.
I prize thy love more than whole mines of gold,
Or all the riches that the East doth hold.
My love is such that rivers cannot quench,
Nor aught but love from thee give recompense.
Thy love is such I can no way repay;
The heavens reward thee manifold, I pray.
Then while we live in love let's so persevere
That when we live no more we may live ever.

FRIENDSHIP AND RESPECT

Letters of Abigail Smith Adams and John Adams, 1762, 1764, 1778, in *The Book of Abigail and John: Selected Letters of the Adams Family, 1762–1784*, ed. L. H. Butterfield, Marc Friedlaender, and Mary-Jo Kline (Cambridge: Harvard University Press, 1975), pp. 17, 45, 228–229.

Perhaps the most famous love letters of the eighteenth century are those written by Abigail Smith Adams and John Adams of Massachusetts. Separated frequently by John's diplomatic missions abroad and his political career at home, the couple generated a rich correspondence during nearly forty years of marriage. The love and loyalty they felt for each other and the intimacy they nurtured are evident from the earliest days of courtship.

JOHN ADAMS TO ABIGAIL SMITH, OCTOBER 4, 1762:

Miss Adorable

By the same Token that the Bearer hereof *satt up* with you last night I hereby order you to give him, as many Kisses, and as many Hours of your Company after 9 O'Clock as he shall please to Demand and charge them to my Account: This Order, or Requisition call it which you will is in Consideration of a similar order Upon Aurelia for the like favour, and I presume I have good Right to draw upon you for the Kisses as I have given two or three Millions at least, when one has been received, and of Consequence the Account between us is immensely in favour of yours, John Adams

JOHN ADAMS TO ABIGAIL SMITH, SEPTEMBER 30, 1764:
My dear Diana

. . . Oh my dear Girl, I thank Heaven that another Fortnight will restore you to me—after so long a separation. My soul and Body have both been thrown into Disorder, by your Absence, and a Month or two more would make me the most insufferable Cynick, in the World. I see nothing but Faults, Follies, Frailties and Defects in any Body, lately. People have lost all their good Properties or I my Justice, or Discernment.

But you who have always softened and warmed my Heart, shall restore my Benevolence as well as my Health and Tranquility of mind. You shall polish and refine my sentiments of Life and Manners, banish all the unsocial and ill natured Particles in my Composition, and form me to that happy Temper, that can reconcile a quick Discernment with a perfect Candour.
Believe me, now & ever yr. faithful   Lysander

ABIGAIL ADAMS TO JOHN ADAMS, NOVEMBER 12–23, 1778
. . . my Soul is wounded at a Seperation from you, and my fortitude all dissolved in frailty and weakness. . . . The affection I feel for my Friend is of the tenderest kind, matured by years, [sanctified?] by choise and approved by Heaven. Angles [angels] can witness to its purity, what care I then for the Ridicule of Britains should this testimony of it fall into their Hands. . . .

A TRIBUTE TO A LOVING WIFE
↔↩

Epitaphs of Gloucester and Mathews Counties in Tidewater Virginia through 1865
(Richmond: Virginia State Library, 1959), p. 55.

Although tombstone inscriptions, like obituaries and wills, are generally formulaic, the inscription below suggests a genuine sense of loss on the part of Judith Page's husband. If the description of her character and behavior is not exaggerated, this young woman who died after childbirth could justly lay claim to the titles "helpmeet" and "goodwife."

↳↲

To the sacred and most pious memory of his most beloved wife, Judith, cut down in the very flower of her age, this monument of grief was erected by the Honourable Mann Page Esquire. She was a most worthy daughter of the very illustrious Ralph Wormeley of County Middlesex, Esquire, formerly also a most deserving Secretary of Virginia. She was a most excellent and

choice lady who lived in the state of most holy matrimony for four years and
as many months. She left one survivor of each sex, Ralph and Maria, true
likenesses together of Father and Mother. She also had a third named Mann,
who, scarcely five days surviving, under this silent marble was enclosed with
his Mother. On the third day after his birth she exchanged mortality for
immortality. Alas, grief! She was a most affectionate wife, the best of Mothers, and an upright mistress of her family, in whom the utmost gentleness
was united with the most graceful suavity of manners and conversation. She
died on the 12th day of December in the year one thousand seven hundred
and sixteen and the twenty-second of her age.

The Struggle to Be United

↔↔

Petition of Jemima Hunt, December 9, 1811, quoted in "Petition To the
Honorable, the Speaker and House of Delegates of the General Assembly of
Virginia," *Journal of Negro History* 13 (January 1928), pp. 88–89.

Enslaved African American married couples lived under the shadow of possible sud-
den, permanent separation. A separation might occur when a master died and his
estate was divided among his children, when financial problems prompted a master
to sell a portion of his property, or when a planter made a wedding gift of a number
of slaves to a daughter or son. When a wife and husband belonged to two different
masters, the risks increased. Marriages between free and enslaved blacks added prob-
lems with a different authority, the state. This early nineteenth-century petition in-
volves a free black woman who contracted to purchase her enslaved husband from his
master. After many years she completed the schedule of payments. In the meantime,
however, Virginia had passed legislation forbidding emancipated slaves from remain-
ing within the state. If the Virginia government denied her petition, this woman would
be left with two painful options: to uproot her family and leave Virginia with her
husband or to remain behind when he left the state as a free man.

↔↔

The petition of Jemima Hunt (a free woman of color) of the county of
Southampton, humbly sheweth that some time in the month of November,
in the year 1805, your petitioner entered into a contract with a certain Benjamin Barrett of said County for the purchase of Stephen, a Negro man slave,
the property of said Barrett, and husband to your petitioner, for the sum of
ten pounds annually for ten years, and the said Barrett farther bound himself
to take the sum of ninety pounds if paid within five years and at the expira-

tion of that time to make a complete bill of sale for the said Negro Stephen, which will appear by reference being made to the obligation entered into between the said Barrett and your petitioner. Your petitioner further states that she has paid the full amount of the purchase money and has obtained a bill of sale for the said Negro Stephen; who (being her husband) she intended to emancipate after she had complied with her contract. But in some short time after, as your petitioner has been informed, an act of Assembly was passed, prohibiting slaves, being emancipated after the law went into operation, from residing in the state. Your petitioner farther states that she has a numerous family of children by the said Stephen, who are dependent upon the daily labor of herself and husband for a support, and without the assistance of her husband Stephen, they must suffer or become burthensome to their county.

Therefore, your petitioner humbly prays that the legislature would take her case into consideration and pass a law to permit the said negro Stephen to reside in the State after emancipation, and to enjoy all the privileges that other free people of colour are entitled to and as in dutybound your petitioner will ever pray, etc.

Seventy persons signed the above petition.

In "Mutual and Particular Love"

↦↤

The Will of Marten Cornelissen and Maeycke Cornelis, 1676–1677, *Early Records of the Colony and County of Albany and the Colony of Rensselaerswyck* (Albany: State University of New York Press, 1916–1919), vol. 3, pp. 359–361.

Dutch law placed fewer restrictions on married women than English law. In the colony of New Netherland, a married woman retained her separate legal identity and thus could make contracts, buy and sell property, earn wages, sue, and be sued. Under Dutch law marital property was owned jointly and both wife and husband participated in determining the distribution of the marital estate. Joint wills, therefore, were common; they continued for several decades even after the conquest of the colony by the English because the Duke of York permitted the Dutch colonists to retain their own laws, religious practices, and social customs. The joint will excerpted below reflects the widely held Dutch assumptions that a wife and husband contributed equally to the creation of their estate and that female and male children should have equal inheritances. It also demonstrates the affection and respect possible in a colonial marriage.

In the name of God, Amen. Know all men by the contents of this present public instrument that in the year after the birth of our Lord and Savior Jesus Christ 1676/7, on the 12th day of the month of January, before me, Adriaen van Ilpendam, notary public residing in New Albany . . . came and appeared the worthy Maerten Cornelisz, born in the city of Ysselsteyn, and his wife Maeycke Cornelis, born at Barrevelt, both dwelling at the Claverrack . . . both being sound of body, standing and walking, having perfect use and command of their faculties, reason, memory and understanding; which appearers, considering the shortness and frailty of human life, the certainty of death and the uncertainty of the time and hour thereof, and wishing therefore to dispose of their worldly goods to be left behind while through God's grace they still are able, as they do of their own free will and inclination, without persuasion or misleading of any persons, have now ordained and concluded this their last will and testament in form and manner following: First and foremost commending their immortal souls, whenever they may be separated from their bodies, to the gracious and merciful hands of God, their Creator and Redeemer, and their bodies to a Christian burial, at the same time revoking, anulling and canceling hereby all and every such testamentary disposition and bequest as they before the date hereof either jointly or severally . . . they, the testators, out of mutal and particular love, which during their marriage estate they have steadily borne and do now bear toward each other, declare that they have reciprocally nominated and instituted, as by these presents they do, the survivor of the two their sole and universal heir to all the property, whether personal or real, claims, credits, money, gold and silver, coined and uncoined, jewels, clothing, linen and woolens, household furniture etc., nothing excepted, which the one dying first shall leave behind as well here in this country as elsewhere, to do therewith as with his or her own property, without contradiction or opposition of any persons; which they do for the reason that they (through God's blessing) have obtained most of the estate by great labor and diligence during their marriage with each other. Likewise [they will] that no persons whatever, whether magistrates, orphan masters, friends, or others shall have the right to demand of the survivor any accounting or inventory of the estate, much less security or sureties, so long as he or she remains in his or her widowed estate; and if so be that the survivor again enter into wedlock, he or she shall be holden to settle a just half of the estate (as the same may be found) on the children left behind, that all of them, share and share alike, may receive their legitimate portion of the father or mother's estate, provided that the survivor shall receive the income and profits thereof until the children shall arrive at their majority or marriage estate, til which time the survivor shall be holden to bring them up in the fear of the Lord and (so far as he or she can) to have them taught reading and writing, together with some handicraft whereby under God they may earn their living with honor. . . .

Determining a Woman's Estate

↔↩

Agreement between Francis Plummer and Beatrice Plummer, November 25, 1670, *Probate Records of Essex County, vol. 2, 1665–1674* (Salem: Essex Institute, 1917), pp. 319–322.

Unlike the will of Maeycke and Marten Cornelissen, the agreement between Francis Plummer and Beatrice Cantlebury Plummer took care to distinguish property and debts rightfully belonging to him, to her, and to their heirs. It was equally explicit in defining what Beatrice Plummer was entitled to in her widowhood. As this was Beatrice Plummer's second marriage, the agreement spelled out her separate control over the estate left to her by William Cantlebury. It also exempted Francis Plummer and his heirs from any liability for debts William Cantlebury had incurred during his lifetime.

⤙⤚

Agreement, dated Nov. 25, 1670, between Francis Plummer of Newbury and Beatrice, his wife, confirming the contract made before marriage that if Plummer should die before the said Beatrice, the latter was to have all the estate that was properly hers before marriage, and also to have the new room, half the orchard, half the apples, and her thirds of the land of said Francis during her life, also firewood out of said Francis Plummer's twenty acres near the little river and the garden as it is now enclosed, If said Beatrice deceased before him, that she should have power to dispose of what estate was hers before marriage to any of her relatives, and if anybody claimed any debts due from William Cantlebury, deceased, said Beatrice's estate was to pay such debts and not the estate of said Plummer, her now husband. Witness: Richard Dole and Anthony Somerby.

An inventory of the goods to belong to Beatrice, the wife of Francis Plumer or to her heirs: a horse & mare & cattell soe many as was prised to him at 35li. to be paid within one year after the decease of either the said Francis or Beatrice; two Ruggs, four blancketts, two paire of sheets of cotten & linnen, pr. of fine sheets of six yards a peice in them, one feather bed, one brass kettle, an Iron kettle, a paire of sheets more, one chest with a coffer with wearing linnen in them, petticoats, wascoats, two pillows, foure platters, a basen, pewter pint pott, a paire of old curtaines & vallens.

The house and land at Salem that was William Cantleburyes is the proper estate of the said Beatrice, and Francis Plumer has no interest in it as shown by the marriage contract between the said Francis Plumer and Beatrice; besides four cattell and four sheep, and also what is due by bills from Joseph Plumer, Daniell Thurston and Robt. Long, also Francis Plumer agreed not to require anything for keeping his wife's grandchild for the time past to this day.

DATED NOV. 25, 1670
Francis (his mark) Plumer.

Witness: Richard Dole, Anthony Somerby.

A PRENUPTIAL AGREEMENT
↦ ↤

Articles of Agreement between William Berry and Margaret Preston, Calvert County, Maryland, January 8, 1669, in J. Hall Pleasants, ed., *Archives of Maryland*, vol. 57 (Baltimore, 1940), pp. 468–469.

A woman with property of her own, either inherited from her father or a former husband or earned while she was a feme sole, *could protect that property by signing a premarriage agreement before she fell under the rules of coverture. Only a small minority of colonial women took advantage of this sophisticated procedure, however, and most were widows. Of course, their insistence on a prenuptial contract did not necessarily indicate distrust or lack of affection. Many simply wished to protect the interests of existing children. Others, particularly those with experience in the pitfalls of marital financial relations, felt it prudent not to let love or physical attraction keep them from ensuring their economic security. It appears that Margaret Preston was one of these cautious women.*

↜↝

Articles of agreement, made and agreed upon between William Berry of the one part and Margaret Preston, both of Patuxent River in the County of Calvert, of the other part, witnesseth that the abovesaid Margaret Preston and William Berry have fully and perfectly concluded and agreed, that the said Margaret doth reserve for her own proper use and behoof, before she doth engage herself in marriage to the said William Berry, the value of one hundred pounds sterling, to be at her the said Margaret's own disposal, in such goods as shall be hereafter mentioned: viz.

Plate, to the value and worth of forty pounds sterling.

The little Negro girl called Sarah, born in Richard Preston's house, valued to ten pounds sterling. If the said girl should die, the said William Berry [agrees] to make the same good to the said Margaret by another Negro or the value.

A good mare to ride on, value seven pounds sterling.

A chamber or room to be well furnished with bedding and furniture, with other household stuff to the value of forty-three pounds sterling.

And for a further testimony that the above mentioned articles are fully and perfectly concluded and agreed upon by the parties aforesaid, the said William Berry both binds himself, his heirs, executors, and administrators to the true performance of all and every [one] of the above mentioned articles, to the full value as is aforementioned, whensoever the said Margaret Preston shall make demand of the same for her own proper use. But if it shall be so ordered after the aforementioned William Berry and Margaret Preston be married that the said William shall die first, that then the abovesaid goods (or the value) do remain firm to and for the said Margaret's own proper use, as she shall think fit to bestow, over and above her proportion of the estate which by the said William Berry shall be left her. For the true performance of this agreement the abovesaid William Berry hath hereunto set his hand and seal this ninth day of the tenth month, called December, in the year one thousand, six hundred, sixty, and nine.

RECORDING SEXUAL CONQUESTS

↦ ↤

The Secret Diary of William Byrd of Westover, 1709–1712, ed. Louis B. Wright and Marion Tinling (Richmond: Dietz Press, 1941), pp. 296–297, 377, 461.

William Byrd was a prosperous Virginia planter of the early eighteenth century. He is remembered for his political views, his agricultural experiments—and for his frank, detailed, and often crude record of his sexual activities. The excerpts from his diary below suggest Byrd's patronizing attitude toward his wife in sexual and emotional terms. In his recollections of "flourishing" and "rogering" his wife, Byrd reveals his belief that sexual domination was an effective component in maintaining a man's authority over his wife.

JULY 30, 1710   I rose at 5 o'clock and wrote a letter to Major Burwell about his boat which Captain Broadwater's people had brought round and sent Tom with it. I read two chapters in Hebrew and some Greek in Thucydides. I said my prayers and ate boiled milk for breakfast. I danced my dance. I read a sermon in Dr. Tillotson and then took a little [nap]. I ate fish for dinner. In the afternoon my wife and I had a little quarrel which I reconciled with a flourish. Then she read a sermon in Dr. Tillotson to me. It is to be observed that the flourish was performed on the billiard table. I read a little Latin. In the evening we took a walk about the plantation. I neglected to say my prayers but had good health, good thoughts, and good humor, thanks be to God. . . .

FEBRUARY 5, 1711   I rose about 8 o'clock and found my cold still worse. I said my prayers and ate milk and potatoes for breakfast. My wife and I quarreled about her pulling her brows. She threatened she would not go to Williamsburg if she might not pull them; I refused, however, and got the better of her, and maintained my authority. About 10 o'clock we went over the river and got to Colonel Duke's about 11. There I ate some toast and canary. Then we proceeded to Queen's Creek, where we all found all well, thank God. We ate roast goose for supper. The women prepared to go to the Governor's the next day and my brother and I talked of old stories. My cold grew exceedingly bad so that I thought I should be sick. My sister gave me some sage tea. . . . I neglected to say my prayers in form but had good thoughts, good humor, and indifferent health, thank God Almighty. . . .

JANUARY 1, 1712   I lay abed till 9 o'clock this morning to bring my wife into temper again and rogered her by way of reconciliation. I read nothing because Mr. Mumford was here, nor did I say my prayers, for the same reason. However I ate boiled milk for breakfast, and after my wife tempted me to eat some pancakes with her. Mr. Mumford and I went to shoot with our bows and arrows but shot nothing, and afterwards we played at billiards till dinner, and when we came we found Ben Harrison there, who dined with us. I ate some partridge for dinner. In the afternoon we played at billiards again and I won two bits. . . . in the evening . . . I took a walk about the plantation and at night we drank some mead of my wife's making which was very good. I gave the people some cider and a dram to the negroes. I read some Latin in Terence and had good health, good thoughts, and good humor, thank God Almighty. I said my prayers.

A Wife Commands Her Husband

Diary of the Reverend Jacob Elliot, 1763, Woodward Papers, Connecticut
Historical Society, Hartford, Conn.

*Colonial court records contain some accounts of women who were abusive toward
their husbands rather than victims of abuse. This selection from the diary of a minister
in Lebanon, Connecticut, provides a vivid account of life with an abusive, disgrun-
tled, demanding, and jealous wife. The Reverend Mr. Elliot may be exaggerating his
own innocence, patience, and forbearance, of course, but there can be no question that
his wife rejected the model of a submissive and obedient helpmeet.*

Nov. 24. Another V. quarrel, after having plagued my heart out all the morning, in directing and dictating about all my affairs, charging me with, and
often twitting me for, being too honest, neglecting my business much, trusting too much to other folks, not overseeing my own business, nor forseeing
things, events, and dangers as I might and ought, and reflecting as if [I were]
incapable of it, etc., till I could bear no longer. I showed some heat and anger
(God forgive me) and earnestly begged of her to forbear and not insist upon
them things anymore, for it was more than flesh and blood could bear. Or, if
she did not, I would complain to her friends and expose her—upon which
she flew into the utmost rage and fury again, calling me a cursed Devil,
kicked at me, and struck me with her fist again, and took up a powder horn
to strike me over the head with. But, defending myself, I warded off the
blows, etc. But she protested she would expose me to all the parish, have
nothing more to do with me, nor hear me again, as long as she lived, etc. But
after a while, on my tamely submitting to hear all the bad stories about first
wife, Betty Higley etc., and crying with her, and not carrying to her as before,
ever since I saw her etc., and bearing the greatest insults from her, her passion at last subsided.

Decem. 19. Another most V.Q. [venged quarrel], after long preaching to me
upon the old score about doing nothing about settling with Jacob and 1000
bugbears raised about her and Josie being left destitute etc. etc. till I could
bear no longer (and it is marvelous I have borne so much). I with some zeal
earnestly begged and entreated her to forbear and not trouble me and herself
with those things—I intended to take care about them as soon as I could
conveniently etc.—on which she flew into her usual, most violent, and un-

curbed passion, and with utmost rage and fury and malice cried out "God damn you, leave your devilling, begone out of the house or I will." Upon which I said, "you may go, and you will for I shan't." This she took in a great dudgeon, flung the child into my arms, and went quick out of the room. Patty went after her, but could not find her for a while [and] at last found her in the study closet. Then she came in again, and after Jacob and Patty were gone to bed, protested she would never lie with me again as long as she lived. (Though before they went off, [she] asked Patty for the key of the little chamber, to lie there; I said she should not have it.) Then [we] had a long parley, whether she or I should lie up-chamber. I said I would not and she should not, but earnestly advised her out of compassion to herself and the child, if she had none for me, to go to bed in the study, and I offered to warm it for her, or she might warm it herself, but she refused. And so we sat debating the case for an hour or two, except great part of the time she, as sullen and surly as a mad bull, would say nothing at all. At last she said that if I would give her my word that I would not come to bed at all to her, she would go to bed (for if I did she would get out again, for she would never have anything more to do with me, for I was no husband to her etc.), to which I (like a fool, for peace sake) consented and submitted, and accordingly warmed the bed for her, and she went to bed in state with the child. . . . After I sat a while, she bid me go and sit in the kitchen. I told her I hoped she would allow me the liberty of my own fire and not be so cruel to the poor old man as to make him sit in the kitchen such a cold night (and as cold as almost ever known) without fire (for that was raked up), and I would not disturb her. After we had then sat silent a while, she with sovereign authority said, "I command you to go and lie up-chamber." At which I laughed and replied that she had expressly inverted the sacred text now and read it (as the woman did to her blind husband), "Husbands obey your wives." After profound silence again for a while, I at last very lovingly said, "My dear, if you will make up so far as to admit me to bed with you tonight, then if we can't make up matters between ourselves, and you think it worth-while, we'll refer the case between us to any one indifferent person whom you please on the morrow," to which she faintly consented. Then I raked up the fire and went to bed. She was muggy a while and said she meant I should go to bed up-chamber. [She] advised me to turn my back and not my face to her, but at last partially made up the matter, and we lay peaceably till the morning when we wholly finished the matter and got pretty well reconciled. (Though she had before said she never would be reconciled again, but

86

[would] expose me to the whole parish and go home, and after [being] abed got up twice in her smock to look after me, going into the closet and into the kitchen.) And so the controversy ended for that time.

Dissolving a Marriage
↦↤

Petitions for and decrees of divorce from Connecticut, New Netherland, and Massachusetts, in J. Hammond Trumbell, ed., *The Public Records of the Colony of Connecticut* (Hartford, 1850–1859), vol. 1, pp. 301, 362; *The Register of Salmon Lachaire, Notary Public of New Amsterdam, 1661–1662*, ed. Kenneth Scott and Kenn Stryker-Rodda, New York Historical Transcripts: Dutch (Baltimore: Genealogical Publishing Company, 1978), p. 96; and *Records and Files of the Quarterly Courts of Essex County, Massachusetts, Vol. 7, 1678–1680* (Salem, Mass.: Essex Institute, 1919), p. 418.

The examples that follow reflect the most common justifications for divorce in colonial America: desertion, physical abuse, adultery, and a raucous incompatibility that disturbed the community.

↜↝

[Connecticut, 1655] This Courte considering the sad complaint of Goody Beckwith, of Fairefield, in reference to her husbands deserting of her, doe declare yt by wtt evidences hath beene prsented to them of ye manner of her husbands departure and discontinnuance they judge that if the said Goody Beckwith, wife of Thomas shall uppon her oath testfie to the Magistrates that are shortly to keepe Courte at Strattford, that her husbands departure was as others have testified it to bee; and yt shee hath not heard from him nor of him any wayes since hee deserted her, the said Magistrates may give her a bill of Divorce & sett her free from her said husband.

[Connecticut, 1657] This court duely & seriously considering what evidence hath bene prsented to them by Robert Wade, of Seabrooke, in reference to his wives unworthy, sinfull, yea, unnaturall cariage towards him the said Robert, her husband, notwthstanding his constant & comendable care & indeavors to gaine fellowship wth her in the bond of marriage, and that either where [were] shee is in England, or for her to live wth him here in New England; all wch being slighted & rejected by her, disowning him & fellowship wth him in that sollemne covenant of God betwene them, & all this for neare fifteene yeares; They doe hereby declare that Robert Wade is from this time free from Joane Wade, his late wife & that former Covenant of marriage betweene them.

[NEW NETHERLAND, 1662] The Humble Petition of Nora Houlderen of Flushing To the Right Honorable the General of New Netherland.

Your poor petitioner humbly showeth her miserable condition and situation caused by her husband Denis Houlderen's immoderate drunkenness and most unseemly life, tending not only to the utter ruin, yea to the beggary of me and my children, but I run in daily danger of my life, [he] constantly inflicting on me intolerable blows, calling me all the bad names he can think of, and this is his daily work, besides his adulterous defiling of the marriage bed, the just cause of separation. Therefore, to prevent further evil which threatened me and my children, I humbly pray Your Honors that Your Honors will please to grant me a bill of divorce; so doing praying for you and yours I remain your Honors to command.

[MASSACHUSETTS, CA. 1680] Thomas Brockett's petition to the Salem court: that "under ye greate affliction that he groanes under, by reason of his wifes cruell carriage towards him, is compelled to make his address to yor honors, to declare unto you his pittifull case wch he is brought into by reason of his wifes cunning & fraudulent dealing with him. . . . being a poore simple man as that he was ouercome to yeild to sett his hand to a writing: made to Mr. Crumwell; whereby is alienated & made away from yor poore petitioner howse and Land & all that he hath; so that he hath not now so much as an howse at his command to cover his head under; nor any other thing for his relief more then what ye Lord helps his poore old hands to worke for, besides her unchristian & inhumane carriage to me when at any Tyme I am in ye howse with her; wch christian modesty forbids me to speake of; although it be not hid from my neighbors; who are able to give full evidence for me."

GIVING PUBLIC NOTICE

↦↤

Advertisements in *New York Weekly Journal,* May 26, 1735; *Pennsylvania Chronicle,* August 10–17, 17–24, 1767; *Pennsylvania Gazette,* June 6, 1781; and *Pennsylvania Packet,* April 15, 1783.

As the following selection of public notices demonstrates, white colonists frequently felt it necessary to make their marital problems public. Most of the newspaper notices were repudiations of debt responsibilities. But some, like Mary Dodd's warning about Jesse

Dougherty, appear to be motivated by concern for the welfare of other, unsuspecting women. As the final example indicates, however, not all the unscrupulous characters were men.

✦

[MAY 26, 1735] We hear that the wife of a certain Merchant of this city, while her husband was in the country, broke open his scrutore [escritoire], and took out his will, of which she was exectrix; and went in widow's weeds to Doctor's Sommons, under a pretence that he was dead, and prov'd the same; by virtue whereof she receiv'd all his money in the stocks, and is gone over sea.

[AUGUST 10–17, 1767] Whereas Elizabeth Perkins, Wife to me the Subscriber, of the Township of Willingburg and County of Burlington hath not only eloped from my Bed and Board, but otherwise behaves in a very unbecoming manner toward me; and as I am apprehensive from what I have already experienced, she may endeavor to run me in Debt, I am obliged to take this public Method to forewarn all Persons from trusting her on my Account, as I am determined I will not pay a single Farthing of her contracting from the Date hereof. And I hope no Person will encourage her on such Occasions, as it may be a Prejudice to me, and will render them liable to Prosecution. Joseph Perkins

[AUGUST 17–24, 1767] Joseph Perkins, of the township of Willingborough, and county of Burlington, my graceless husband, having maliciously advertised to the world, that I have eloped from his bed and board, run him in debt, and otherwise behaved in an unbecoming manner towards him, I am obliged to take this method solemnly to declare, that those charges against me have not the least foundation in truth, which can be easily made to appear; and were entirely occasioned by my refusing to assign over to him the little interest I have, that he might squander it away in disorderly company, as he hath done the greatest part of his own, and my declining to entertain and encourage the infamous guests he frequently brought to his house, where, amidst the most notorious scenes and disorder, I often met with treatment, which would have shocked a savage of the Ohio, which at last obliged me to fly to my mother's house in this city, which I unfortunately left, as the only sanctuary I could expect to find from his persecutions. There being a greater probability of his running me in debt, than my injuring him in that manner, I desire that no person may trust him from an expectation that I will

pay his debts for I have determined never to pay a farthing of his contracting
from the date hereof.

[JUNE 6, 1781]
Whereas Jane, my wife,
without quarrel or strife,
hath eloped from my bed and boarding.
This caution I give,
It's as true as I live,
For her I will not pay one farthing,
or debts she may make,
After this date,
in my policy I hope there's no evil;
Now I have set forth the same,
I here sign my Name,
which is Marmaduke Hivel.

[APRIL 15, 1783] Whereas a certain Mary Carson, of this city, has at different times declared herself my wife, and alledges that she is lawfully married
to me, in order to obtain credit with the world, and to enable her to procure
those necessaries at my expence, which neither her own character nor fortune otherwise have done: In order therefore to guard myself against further
injuries, from a woman whose looseness of conduct has already been the cause
of almost compleating my ruin, I think it proper to declare, that I never was
nor ever harboured an idea of being married to her; that she was married to
another man at the time when she alledges her marriage with me to have
been made: And I hereby forwarn all persons from trusting her on my account, as I will pay no debts of her contracting.

John Carson

OFFENDING WOMEN
↔↩

The sentencing of Elizabeth Tooker, 1641; Awk-Whew, 1674; and Mary
Gridley, Mary Punnell, Mary Wharton, and Mary Gibb, 1765–1776. Lower
Norfolk County Order Book, 1637–1646 (transcript), excerpted in Warren M.
Billings, *The Old Dominion in the Seventeenth Century* (Chapel Hill: University
of North Carolina Press, 1975), p. 102; *Publications of the Colonial Society of
Massachusetts* 29 (1933), p. 485; *Records of the Suffolk County Court*, vol. 30
(Boston: Colonial Society of Massachusetts, 1933), pp. 914, 605, 677.

Despite all exhortations of ministers, lawmakers, and community leaders, many colonial women did not confine their sexual activity to marriage. It was common throughout the colonial period for couples to engage in premarital sex, and a significant percentage of seventeenth- and eighteenth-century brides were pregnant on their wedding day. Laws punishing bastardy and procedures for determining the man responsible for the birth of an illegitimate child were in place in every colony. In the following examples, however, we focus on exceptional cases in which women's flagrant disregard for social norms and accepted moral values disturbed authorities greatly. From the unrepentent Elizabeth Tooker to the repeat offender Mary Gridley Wharton, these women were seen as confirming the notion that women were weaker "moral vessels" than men—and that neither marriage nor punishment could control them all.

⁺∿⁺

Whereas Elizabeth Tooker (Elizabeth Hauntine) was ordered by a court holden the 12th of April 1641, for the foul crime of fornication committed by her, to do penance in their chapel of ease, situated in Elizabeth River according to the full intent and meaning of the said order, and she, the said Elizabeth, being brought to the said Chapel of Ease to perform the said penance, in which time of performance and exhortation delivered unto her by the minister admonishing hir to be sorry for hir foul crime committed, but she the said Elizabeth not regarding the good admonition of the said minister, not obeying the tenor of the said order did, like a most obstinate and graceless person, cut and mangle the sheet wherein she did penance, It is Therefore ordered that the said Elizabeth shall receive at present, 20 lashes on the bare back and, on the Sunday come fort night, do penance in the aforesaid Chapel of Ease according to the tenor of the said spiritual laws and forms of the Church of England in that case provided.

Awk-Whew Indian Squaw Sentenc[ed]
Awk-whew Indian Squaw, standing committed to prison to answer at this Court for her keeping company with Joseph Indian as his wife when hee hath another wife that is Living; which Shee Owned in Court: The Court Sentenc[ed] her to bee whipt with Fifteen Stripes & to pay fees of Court & prison standing committed until the Sentence bee performed.

Mary Wharton Sentencd the Wife of Phillip Wharton
Mary Wharton being complained of & imprisoned for unclean carriages with Ezekiel Gardiner The Court having heard & considered of what was proved agt [against] her & what Shee herselfe confessed do Sentence her to

91

bee whip't severely with thirty Stripes at a carts tayle from her own house to the prison & then to bee committed to the house of correction there to bee kept according to the order of the house untill the next Court of this County & to pay Fees of Court standing committd &a.

WHARTON & GRIDLEY bound to ye good behavior

Phillip Wharton and Mary Gridley formerly his wife being bound over to this Court to answer for theire disorderly and offensive cohabiting together having Sued out a divorce, they ownd they did live together: Sentenced to give in bond with Sureties of twenty pounds apeice for theire good abbearance untill the next Court of this County, especially to refrain the Company of each other and to pay fees of Court standing comittd &c.

Punnell Sentencd

Mary Punnell being imprisoned for her committing of Fornication & called before the Court to answer for the same, Shee appeared & confessed the Fact & brought her Childe into the Court with her chargeing one James Jarret to bee the Father thereof. The Court having considered of her offence doe Sentence her to bee whip't with Fifteen stripes & to pay Fees of Court & prison And doe Order that Shee bee returned to Milton from whence Shee came & if Shee bee not able to pay her charges nor can procure any Friend to doe it, that then the Town of Milton pay the same & entertain her according to law.

Gibbs Sentencd

Mary Gibbs being presentd for lascivious carriages & suspition of adultery. The Court having heard & considered of what was alleaged & proved agt her Sentencd her to bee whip't at the cart's tayle with twenty Stripes in compa [company] wth Mary Wharton from her house to the prison & to pay fees of Court standing committd &a.

CHAPTER THREE

Women's Work

PRODUCTIVE ACTIVITY that was defined as "women's work" existed in the European, African, and Indian societies of early America, but the gendered division of labor in these cultures was far from the same. Among the agricultural Indian tribes of the eastern woodlands region, women were the cultivators and distributors of food and other vital supplies. Among the white colonists, farming was designated a male task, and although women tended kitchen gardens and orchards, their primary work responsibilities—the processing and preparation of food and the home manufacture of clothing, candles, and other domestic items—were household-based. In many African societies, as in Indian ones, women were the agriculturalists. (When these women were brought to the colonies as slaves, their work continued to be in agriculture, but this role designation was not a sign of respect for African traditions on the part of white slave masters.) Europeans, Indians, and Africans all assumed that the gendered division of labor conformed to basic, "natural" differences between men and women in character, temperament, and physical abilities.

Although hunting remained central to the economies of some Canadian and northern tribes, most of the Indian cultures that encountered English colonists relied on agriculture for their food supplies. Farming supplied almost 90 percent of the food in Iroquois communities, for example. The gendered division of labor among the Iroquois, Cherokee, Choctaw, and Creek, as well as other eastern tribes, established women as the primary cultivators, responsible for planting corn, squash, and beans, and men as the hunters, responsible for the extra protein in the Indian diet. These domains did overlap. Men assisted in the clearing of land for planting; women set up and took down the hunting camps, tanned the hides and pelts, and, as trade developed with white colonists, served as contacts between Indian hunters and white traders.

It is well known that European observers of Indian culture were either bewildered or appalled—or both—by the Indians' disregard for what the Europeans considered proper work roles. White missionaries and traders have left numerous accounts of their negative reactions to the sight of Indian women tilling fields and harvesting crops while Indian men appeared to sit idly in the villages or engaged in frivolous activities such as playing ball or doing handicraft work. That Indian males hunted did little to redeem them as "masculine" in the sight of English commentators in particular, for in England hunting was not a vital economic contribution to the family or society but a sport enjoyed by aristocrats. These Eurocentric observers were quick to conclude that Indian women had been reduced to slavery and Indian men to effeminacy by their deviant division of labor. Not every white colonist agreed, of course. White women taken captive by Indians frequently chose to remain with their captors rather than be ransomed. Favorable work conditions were one reason given for the reluctance of these women to return to white society. For example, Mary Jemison, who made her life among the Seneca, insisted that Seneca women's work was no more severe or repetitious than the work of English women and girls. As a Seneca Jemison did not have to spend tiresome hours and days at the spinning wheel or washing and mending clothes, and her daily tasks were not performed in the isolation of the individual farmhouse. Instead, Seneca women worked collectively, moving together from field to field as they planted, hoed, or weeded.

Indian women in farming societies were not simply the agricultural labor force. In their role as cultivators they enjoyed considerable authority and power, for they controlled both the land and the harvest and determined the use and distribution of surplus crops. They were neither economically dependent on men nor constrained by laws or customs such as those of the European settlers, which focused on the preservation of private property and privileged men above women.

In English society, women's work was centered in the processing, preservation, and production of essential family supplies. On the whole, theirs were skilled tasks, requiring training and the long apprenticeship daughters and servant girls served with the mistress of the household. The repertoire of craft activities that formed the core of women's work, known as "housewifery," included spinning, sewing, butter churning, candle making, beekeeping, preservation of fruits and vegetables, slaughtering of farm animals, and preservation of meat products. In seventeenth-century colonial society, few homes contained the necessary equipment for all forms of household production; in the eighteenth century, growing colonial affluence, the rise of specialty shops, and especially the availability of cheap English-manufactured cloth made household production of several vital goods unnecessary. Thus, necessity or opportunity ensured that few colonial households actually were self-sufficient and that few colonial housewives in fact were responsible for the full spectrum of household manufactures. However, women were also responsible for the maintenance of the household, including cleaning and the preparation of daily meals, and their domain extended from the kitchen or hearth to the garden and the orchard.

Under ideal circumstances women did not work in the fields. But colonial circumstances were rarely ideal. In new settlement areas and among poor farm families in older colonial communities, wives and daughters helped with planting and harvesting. Throughout the colonial period, poorer women—especially the wives and daughters of tenant farmers—worked in agriculture, not only on their own family farms but in the landlord's fields. Records of poor rural women's receiving wages for field work and domestic work suggest that social class was critical in determining white women's work roles.

English law restricted the participation of women, especially married women, in the labor market, in trade, and in the crafts and professions. A married woman had no legal identity independent of her husband, and thus, technically, she could not buy or sell property or goods, incur debts, sue or be sued, or sign contracts. However, historians continue to discover evidence that these laws of *feme covert* were not strictly applied. In the eighteenth-century Pennsylvania backcountry, for example, women participated in a bustling trade economy by selling farm and household produce. Wives worked with their husbands as shopkeepers and operators of small businesses, and on their own as midwives, seasonal laborers, and, in urban areas, purveyors of goods and special services. When they became widows, colonial white women often served as executors of estates; despite many restrictions on their control of property, some of these women managed to increase the estates left in their care by their husbands through their own labors and through judicious business investments. Single women, or *femes sole*, did have full economic (though not political) identities in colonial society. And married women who were deserted by their husbands, or whose husbands' occupations carried them away for long periods of time (sailors, in particular), could petition for *feme sole* status. Some colonies passed *feme sole* trader acts providing the needed legal rights to all who met specific qualifications. On the whole, colonial governments preferred to enable women to support themselves rather than provide them with poor relief. Thus, single and married women entered the marketplace as greengrocers, domestic servants, wet nurses, tavern- and innkeepers, midwives, seamstresses, and operators of boardinghouses. Widows ran the businesses left to their care by husbands, including newspapers, iron mills, and plantations.

Many of the African women and men who were brought to the colonies came with well-developed skills in agriculture, including rice cultivation. However, the work roles assigned to enslaved women—and men—did not necessarily conform to their traditions. White masters set aside their assumptions about women's proper work domain by sending slave women and girls into the fields to do hard labor with the hoe. But as farm equipment improved and as masters shifted some slaves into craft work such as brick making, coopering, and blacksmithing, women's position in the work hierarchy suffered. Black men were assigned to the plow or the craft work while women continued to perform the more menial tasks of weeding, hoeing, worming the tobacco, and clearing swamps. Few colonial slave women on tobacco or rice plantations were put into domestic service, although in the prerevolutionary years, when English cloth was boycotted, slave women were recruited for spinning. Individual slave women, rented out by widows or by their masters, were more likely to be employed as domestic help. A gendered division of labor also emerged in the slave quarters, where women were responsible for domestic duties such as cooking and cleaning and men were expected to hunt and fish when the opportunity arose. Employment opportunities for free black women in the colonies were narrow: farm labor, washing, basic sewing, and prostitution were the most common work. Wealthy urban women in cities like Philadelphia and Boston did employ black domestic servants when white ones were scarce, and the diaries of these elite colonists suggest that black women were employed as cooks in some households.

In the eighteenth century, as the impact of the consumer revolution increased and as class distinctions became more salient, the gendered division of labor was crosscut by class and race and degree of urbanization. The household remained the site of productive activity for wealthy white women as much as for their poorer counterparts, but the composition of "housewifery" changed. Daughters of the elite learned fancy sewing while poor girls relied on plain stitching as a source of income for their families. The preparation and presentation of meals among the wealthy no longer involved the processing of raw materials into usable products for the table, since elite urban women shopped for food rather than manufacturing it. The labor of black women, free and enslaved, and of the urban poor sustained the genteel lifestyle of these prosperous housewives.

PRESCRIPTIVE DOCUMENTS

SPIRITUAL SPINNERS

Edward Taylor, "Huswifery," in Thomas H. Johnson, "Edward Taylor:
Puritan 'Sacred Poet,' " *New England Quarterly* 10, no. 2 (June 1937),
pp. 291–292.

The close identification of women and the spinning wheel pervaded English colonial society, where the female members of a family were commonly referred to as "the distaff side." Mothers, weary of the tedium of spinning, eagerly passed this chore along to their daughters. A woman who did not marry might have to continue to sit long hours before the wheel in order to earn her keep in a brother's or sister's home; thus, unmarried women were referred to as "spinsters." It is likely, however, that many women escaped the task altogether. Most seventeenth-century colonists could not afford the necessary equipment, and by the eighteenth century, cheap imported English cloth could be purchased. When patriotic women rallied to the boycott of English cloth in the 1760s and 1770s, many who volunteered for "spinning bees" had to be instructed in the craft. Nevertheless, the imagery remained strong enough for the Puritan minister Edward Taylor to use it in the following poem to describe women's relationship with their God.

+∼+

> Make me, O Lord, thy spinning wheel complete.
>   Thy holy word my distaff make for me.
> Make mine affections thy swift flyers neat.
>   And make my soul thy holy spool to be.
>   My conversation make to be thy reel
>   And reel the yarn thereon spun of thy wheel.
> Make me thy loom then; knit therein this twine;
>   And make thy holy spirit, Lord, wind quills.
> Then weave the web thyself. The yarn is fine.
>   Thine ordinances make my fulling mills.
>   Then dye the same in heavenly colors choice,
>   All pinked with varnished flowers of paradise.
> Then clothe therewith mine understanding, will,
>   Affections, judgment, conscience, memory,
> My words, and actions, that their shine may fill
>   My ways with glory and thee glorify.
>   Then mine apparel shall display before ye
>   That I am clothed in holy robes for glory.

GETTING A COMPETENT MAINTENANCE

↦↤

"An Act Concerning Feme-Sole Traders," 1718, *Laws of the Commonwealth of Pennsylvania* (Philadelphia: John Bioren, 1810), vol. 1, pp. 99–100.

By passing the feme sole *trader acts, which permitted married women to function under certain circumstances as if they were* femes sole, *colonial governments served the interests of several parties in addition to women who needed to earn a livelihood. First, the governments protected themselves from the burden of supporting indigent females and their families. Second, they assisted men whose livelihood required them to be absent; otherwise, sailors and sea captains would return home to heavy debts. Finally, they benefited local creditors who wished to collect outstanding debts from a family; the acts made women responsible for the debts incurred if their business faltered.*

✦

WHEREAS it often happens that mariners and others, whose circumstances as well as vocations oblige them to go to sea, leave their wives in a way of shopkeeping: and such of them as are industrious, and take due care to pay the merchants they gain so much credit with, as to be well supplied with shop-goods from time to time, whereby they get a competent maintenance for themselves and children, and have been enabled to discharge considerable debts, left unpaid by their husbands at their going away; but some of those husbands, having so far lost sight of their duty to their wives and tender children, that their affections are turned to those, who, in all probability, will put them upon measures, not only to waste what they may get abroad, but misapply such effects as they leave in this province: For preventing whereof, and to the end that the estates belonging to such absent husbands may be secured for the maintenance of their wives and children, and that the goods and effects which such wives acquire, or are entrusted to sell in their husband's absence, may be preserved for satisfying of those who so entrust them, *Be it enacted,* That where any mariners or others are gone, or hereafter shall go, to sea, leaving their wives at shop-keeping, or to work for their livelihood at any other trade in this province all such wives shall be deemed, adjudged and taken, and are hereby declared to be, as feme-sole traders, and shall have ability and are by this act enabled, to sue and be sued, plead and be impleaded at law, in any court or courts of this province, during their husbands' natural lives, without naming their husbands in such suits, pleas or actions: And when judgments are given against such wives for any debts contracted, or sums of money due from them, since their husbands left them, executions shall be awarded against the goods and chattels in the possession of such wives, or in the hands or possession of others in trust for them, and not against the goods and chattels of their husbands; unless it may appear to the court where those executions are returnable, that such wives have, out of their separate stock or profit of their trade, paid debts which were contracted by their husbands, or laid out money for the necessary support and maintenance of themselves and children; then, and in such case, executions shall be levied upon the estate, real and personal, of such husbands, to the value so paid or laid out, and no more.

II. *And be it further enacted*, That if any of the said absent husbands, being owners of lands, tenements, or other estate in this province, have alien[at]ed, or hereafter shall give, grant, mortgage or alienate, from his wife and children, any of his said lands, tenements or estate, without making an equivalent provision for their maintenance, in lieu thereof, every such gift, grant, mortgage or alienation, shall be deemed, adjudged and taken to be null and void.

III. *Provided nevertheless*, That if such absent husband shall happen to suffer shipwreck, or be by sickness or other casualty disabled to maintain himself, then, and in such case, and not otherwise, it shall be lawful for such distressed husband to sell or mortgage so much of his said estate, as shall be necessary to relieve him, and bring him home again to his family, any thing herein contained to the contrary notwithstanding.

IV. But if such absent husband, having his health and liberty, stays away so long from his wife and children, without making such provision for their maintenance before or after his going away, till they are like to become chargeable to the town or place where they inhabit; or in case such husband doth live or shall live in adultery, or cohabit unlawfully with another woman, and refuses or neglects, within seven years next after his going to sea, or departing his province, to return to his wife, and cohabit with her again; then, and in every such case, the lands, tenements and estate, belonging to such husbands, shall be and are hereby made liable and subject to be seized and taken in execution, to satisfy any sum or sums of money, which the wives of such husbands, or guardians of their children, shall necessarily expend or lay out for their support and maintenance; which execution shall be founded upon process of attachment against such estate, wherein the absent husband shall be made defendant; any law or usage to the contrary in any wise notwithstanding.

A SERVANT'S EDEN

↔ ↔

Advertisement for servants, 1656, from John Hammond, "Leah and Rachel, or, The Two Fruitful Sisters, Virginia and Maryland: Their Present Condition, Impartially Stated and Related," in Peter Force, *Traces and Other Papers Relating Principally to the Origin, Settlement, and Progress of the Colonies in North America* (Washington, D.C.: M. St. Claire Clarke and Peter Force, 1844), pp. 12–15.

In recruiting a labor force for the early Chesapeake tobacco plantations, advertisers took pains to dispel rumors that life there was brutish and primitive. In the advertisement below, the author assured prospective indentured servants that the customary holidays would be observed, the working day would be reasonable, and masters would honor the gendered division of labor that kept women out of the fields—as long as a woman was not a "nasty wench." Although women's interests are addressed, the advertisement focuses on men since planters' greatest need was for a steady supply of able-bodied field workers. The demand for young males skewed the sex ratio dramatically in both Virginia and Maryland, where male-to-female ratios of 3 to 1, sometimes as high as 6 to 1, were common throughout the seventeenth century. Assuming that all young women hoped to marry, one Marylander quipped that this sex imbalance made his colony "a paradise for women."

꒰꒱

The labor servants are put to is not so hard nor of such continuance as husbandmen nor handcraftmen are kept at in England. I said little or nothing is done in winter time. None ever work before sun rising nor after sunset. In the summer they rest, sleep, or exercise themselves five hours in the heat of the day. Saturday afternoon is always their own. The old holidays are observed and the Sabbath spent in good exercises.

The women are not (as is reported) put into the ground to work, but occupy such domestic employments as housewifery as in England, that is, dressing victuals, righting up the house, milking, employed about dairies, washing, sewing, etc., and both men and women have times of recreation, as much or more than in any part of the world besides. Yet some wenches that are nasty, beastly, and not fit to be so employed are put into the ground, for reason tells us, they must not at charge be transported and then maintained for nothing, but those that prove so awkward are rather burdensome than servants desirable or useful.

Those servants that will be industrious may in their time of service gain a competent estate before their freedoms, which is usually done by many, and they gain esteem and assistance that appear so industrious. There is no master almost but will allow his servant a parcel of clear ground to plant some tobacco in for himself, which he may husband at those many idle times he had allowed him and not prejudice, but rejoice his master to see it, which in time of shipping he may lay out for commodities, and in summer sell them again with advantage.

I think it better for any that goes over free, and but in a mean condition, to hire himself for reasonable wages of tobacco and provision, the first year, provided he happen in an honest house, and where the mistress is noted for a good housewife, of which they are very many (notwithstanding the cry to the contrary) for by that means he will live free of disbursement, have something to help him the next year, and be carefully looked to in his sickness (if he chance to fall sick) and let him so covenant that exceptions may be made, that he work not much in the hot weather, a course we always take with our new hands (as they call them) the first year they come in.

If they are women that go after this manner, that is paying their own passage, I advise them to sojourn in a house of honest repute, but by their good carriage, they may advance themselves in marriage, by their ill, overthrow their fortunes. And although loose persons seldom live long unmarried if free, yet they match with as dissolute as themselves and never live handsomely or are ever respected.

''HUSWIFERY'' AIDS

↔ ↔

Elizabeth Smith, *The Complete Housewife, or Accomplished Gentelwoman's Companion*, 5th ed. (Williamsburg, Va.: William Parks, 1742), pp. 7, 8, 191.

As the consumer revolution spread throughout eighteenth-century America, a genteel lifestyle became an essential marker of social status. A wealthy woman's "huswifery" duties changed dramatically as eating became dining and elaborate rituals of visiting and socializing replaced simpler gatherings. Homes had to be equipped with furniture suitable to specialized rooms such as parlors and bedrooms. Trenchers and communal cups were replaced by individual place settings cleaned for each meal; sugar tongs and teapots had to be polished; menus had to be planned and ingredients purchased from greengrocers, butchers, and confectioners. Books appeared, like the one excerpted below, offering expert advice on cooking, decorating, health, and manners.

↜↝

A PIGEON PYE.

Truss and season your Pigeons with savoury Spice, lard them with Bacon, and stuff them with Forc'd meat, and lay them in the Pye with the ingredients for savoury Pyes, with Butter, and close the Pye. A Lear, a Chicken, or Capon Pye, is made the same way.

TO COLLAR EELS.

Take your Eel and cut it open; take out the Bones, and cut off the Head and Tail, and lay the Eel flat on a Dresser, and shred Sage as fine as possible, and in it with black Pepper beat, Nutmeg grated, and Salt, and lay it all over the Eel, and roll it up hard in little Cloths, and tie it up tight . . . set over some water with Pepper and Salt, five or six Cloves, three or four Blades of Mace, and a Bay-leaf or two; boil it and the Bones and Head and Tail well together; then take out the Head and Tail, and put it away, and put in your Eels, and let them boil till they are tender; then take them out of the Liquor, and boil the Liquor longer; then take it off, and when 'tis cold, put it to your Eels, but do not take off the little Cloths till you use them.

To prevent Miscarrying.

Take of Dragon's blod the Weight of a silver Two-pence, and a Drachm of red Coral, the Weight of two Barley corns of Ambergrease, the Weight of three and mix them well together, and keep them close in a Box; and if you are frighted or need it, take as much at a Time as will lie on a Penny, and keep very still and quiet. Take it in a Caudle made with muscadine or Tent, and the Shucks of Almonds dried and beaten to Powder, and thicken it with Yolks of Eggs. Take it in a Morning fasting, and at Night going to Bed; this do 'til you are out of Danger, and lay the following plaister to the Back; Take Venic Turpentine, and mix with it Bole Armoniac, and spread it on black brown paper the Length and Breadth of a Hand, and lay it to the small of the back, keeping bed.

DESCRIPTIVE DOCUMENTS

THE HARSH REALITIES OF SERVITUDE

"The Trapanned Maiden," *Virginia Magazine of History and Biography* 4 (July 1896), pp. 218–220.

The anonymous author of this verse describes the harsh fate of a trapanned, or kidnapped, female servant in seventeenth-century Virginia. Forced to work long hours each day in the field and in the mill, serving as maid and baby-minder for a cruel mistress, poorly fed and clothed, this unwilling immigrant refutes every claim made by the recruiter in the advertisement above.

The Girl was cunningly trapan'd
Sent to Virginny from England;
Where she doth Hardship undergo,
There is no cure, it must be so;
But if she lives to cross the main,
She vows she'll ne'er go there again.

Give ear unto a Maid
That lately was betray'd,
And sent into Virginny, O:
In brief I shall declare,
What I have suffered there,
When that I was weary, O.

When that first I came
To this land of Fame,
Which is called Virginny, O:
The Axe and the Hoe
Have wrought my overthrow,
When that I was weary, O.

Five years served I
Under Master Guy,
In the land of Virginny, O:
Which made me for to know
Sorrow, Grief, and Woe,
When that I was weary, O.

When my Dame says, Go,
Then must I do so,
In the land of Virginny, O:
When she sits at meat
Then I have none to eat,
When that I was weary, O.

The cloathes that I brought in,
They are worn very thin,
In the land of Virginny, O:
Which makes me for to say
Alas! and well-a-day,
When that I was weary, O.

Instead of Beds of Ease,
To lye down when I please,

In the land of Virginny, O:
Upon a bed of straw,
I lay down full of woe,
When that I was weary, O.

Then the Spider, she
Daily waits on me,
In the land of Virginny, O:
Round about my bed
She spins her tender web,
When that I was weary, O.

So soon as it is day,
To work I must away,
In the land of Virginny, O:
Then my Dame she knocks
With her tinder box,
When that I was weary, O.

I have played my part
Both at Plow and Cart,
In the land of Virginny, O:
Billats from the Wood,
Upon my back they load,
When that I was weary, O.

Instead of drinking Beer,
I drink the waters clear,
In the land of Virginny, O:
Which makes me pale and wan,
Do all that e'er I can,
When that I was weary, O.

If my Dame says, Go,
I dare not say no,
In the land of Virginny, O:
The water from the spring
Upon my head I bring,
When that I was weary, O.

When the Mill doth stand,
I'm ready at command,
In the land of Virginny, O:

The Mortar for to make,
Which made my heart to ake,
When that I was weary, O.

When the child doth cry,
I must sing, By-a-by,
In the land of Virginny, O:
No rest that I can have
Whilst I am here a slave,
When that I was weary, O.

A thousand Woes beside,
That I do here abide,
In the land of Virginny, O:
In misery I spend
My time that hath no end,
When that I was weary, O.

Then let Maids beware,
All by my ill-fare,
In the land of Virginny, O:
Be sure thou stay at home,
For if you do here come,
You will all be weary, O.

But if it be my chance,
Homeward to advance,
From the land of Virginny, O:
If that I once more
Land on English shore,
I'll no more be weary, O.

An Eighteenth-Century Daughter Begs for Assistance

↦ ↤

Elizabeth Sprigs to John Sprigs, September 22, 1756, in Isabel Calder, ed.,
Colonial Captivities, Marches, and Journeys (New York: Macmillan, 1935),
pp. 151–152.

*Like the trapanned maiden of the seventeenth century, this indentured servant in
Maryland described a life of physical hardship, deprivation, and abuse. By midcen-
tury, an English bound servant in the Chesapeake was likely to find herself in the*

minority since slavery had become the primary labor source in the region. Thus Elizabeth Sprigs punctuated her account of her difficulties by reporting that many African Americans were better treated than she.

᜶

Honred Father

My being for ever banished from your sight, will I hope pardon the Boldness I now take of troubling you with these, my long silence has been purely owing to my undutifullness to you, and well knowing I had offended in the highest Degree, put a tie to my tongue and pen, for fear I should be extinct from your good Graces and add a further Trouble to you, but too well knowing your care and tenderness for me so long as I retaind my Duty to you, induced me once again to endeavour if possible, to kindle up that flame again. O Dear Father, belive what I am going to relate the words of truth and sincerity, and Ballance my former bad Conduct [to] my sufferings here, and then I am sure you'll pitty your Destress[ed] Daughter, What we unfortunat English People suffer here is beyond the probibility of you in England to Conceive, let it suffice that I one of the unhappy Number, am toiling almost Day and Night, and very often in the Horses druggery, with only this comfort that you Bitch you do not halfe enough, and then tied up and whipp'd to that Degree that you'd not serve an Annimal, scarce any thing but Indian Corn and Salt to eat and that even begrudged nay many Negroes are better used, almost naked no shoes nor stockings to wear, and the comfort after slaving dureing Masters pleasure, what rest we can get is to rap ourselves up in a Blanket and ly upon the Ground, this is the deplorable Condition your poor Betty endures, and now I beg if you have any Bowels of Compassion left show it by sending me some Relief, C[l]othing is the principal thing wanting, which if you should condiscend to, may easely send them to me by any of the ships bound to Baltimore Town Patapsco River Maryland, and give me leave to conclude in Duty to you and Uncles and Aunts, and Respect to all Friends

Honred Father
Your undutifull and Disobedient Child
Elizabeth Sprigs

An Apprentice in the New Republic

⇥⇤

Indenture of Eunice Allis to Joseph Bennett, January 10, 1789 (Courtesy of the Case Western Reserve Historical Society, Cleveland, Ohio).

Unlike Elizabeth Sprigs and the trapanned maiden, Eunice Allis entered servitude with a contract overseen by her parents and by local authorities. The document does not reveal what trade or set of skills the ten-year-old girl would learn from her new master, but it does stipulate a code of behavior for her and a set of responsibilities for him. Allis's parents and her new master were neighbors in a small, settled community, making physical abuse less likely than in the Chesapeake and the remedy for it more easily achieved.

֍

This indenture witnesseth that Eunice Allis Daughter of Benjamin Allis all of Lebanon in Columbia County and State of New York hat put herself, by and with the consent of her Parents and by those present doth put herself Apprentice to Joseph Bennett of Lebanon aforesaid yeoman to be taught by him from the Day of this Date for and during the term of Seven years, six months and twenty one days next issuing of these presents, which renders her the age of eighteen years. During all which time she the said Apprentice her said master shall faithfully serve, his secrets keep, his lawful commands obey. She shall do him no damage, nor see it done by others without telling him or giving him notice of the same, she shall not waste his goods, nor lend them unlawfully to others, she shall not commit fornication, nor contract Matrimony during said time, nor haunt bad houses, but in all things behave herself as a faithful apprentice ought to do during said time. And the said Joseph Bennett shall in the utmost of his [indeavor] to teach her as aforesaid and honoure or cause to be procured for the said apprentice sufficient meat, drink, apperal, washing and lodging fitting for an apprentice during said term and give her suitable learning. And at the expiration of said term will decently cloth her after the Manner of the Church to which she belongs. And for the true performance of all and every of the said covenants and agreements each of the said parties bind themselves to the other by those present. In witness thereof they have hereunto interchanged their hands and seals this tenth day of January in the year of our Lord one thousand seven hundred and eighty nine.

In the presence of Amos Hammon [and] Isaac Crouch

> Benjamin Allis [signature]
> Mary Allis   her mark
> Joseph Bennett [signature]
> Eunice Allis   her mark

A BLACK WOMAN MUST PROVE SHE IS FREE

֍

Grace [Jackson] to————, February 8, 1797; and William Poole to Robert Smith, Jr., January 15, 1798, in M. M. Pernot, ed., *After Freedom* (Burlington, N.J.: Burlington County Historical Society, 1987), pp. 1–2; 2–3.

Unlike Eunice Allis, Grace Jackson was not a recognized member of the community in which she labored as an indentured servant. As a stranger in the town of New Castle and as an African American, she was immediately suspect. Indeed, the first response of the authorities was to imprison her as a possible runaway slave. The burden of proof fell on her, and before William Poole produced the necessary evidence, Grace Jackson was sold into servitude and incurred debts that threatened to keep her a bound laborer for a long time. Poole's letter offers a glimpse of the cycle of poverty in which workers like Grace Jackson were caught.

✛

FEBRUARY 8TH NEW CASTLE

Sir This is to inForm you of my setuision in this ples I was tecken up for a Ronawe and put in Jeal and sold out a servent for fiftenn months if Mr Joseph Cinsey wood be Plesed to send my pass with the berer this Negro man you will obledg youer wellwisher Mr. John Cox is greas. . . . My pass is in youer ofess.

[JANUARY 15, 1798]

Esteemd Friend

I went this day to New Castle & upon enquiry of Joseph Tatlow the Magistrate of that place & who committed Grace Jackson to the Jail there, I found she had been free since the 7th month last, and at present is employd by a person named Calhoon of New Castle at 3s p(er) week—I went to Calhoons saw Grace told her my errand to New Castle, and enquired if it was her wish to go to Burlington—she shew'd no anxiety to leave the place at present—but said she should return to her old home in the Spring—at any time she chooses to leave there Tatlow has promised to give her a generall pass, & I have informed her that I hold in my hand evidence of her freedom & should she fall into any difficulty to apply to me—the charges against her has amounted to a considerable sum—within a few weeks after her Commitment she was taken Sick—Tatlow then took her to his house where she lay very ill some time—upon her recovery it was discovrd she was pregnant—after boarding some time at a Certain Davis's in that place, she was sent to the Poor House of the County where she was deliver'd and incur'd a debt of about 8 [?] which stands against her on the Books of the house but which will I expect never be paid by her.

I enclose a Bill of the Charges upon which she was sold or rather to pay which she agreed to serve 15 months—besides those Tatlow has a charge against her for £2.10g for Board Medcine & attendance during the time she was ill at his house—this Bill he is of the opinion the Trustees of the Poor ought to pay—but they have refused & he means to collect it of Grace—this I think will be very difficult as her wages are verry small & she is bare of Cloathing—I shall endeavor to prevail upon the Trustees of the Poor to allow the bill, but it is hardly probable I shall succeed—it will perhaps be proper to inform that Grace's child died young, so that she has at present no incumbrance unless it be some black suitor which it was suggested she had, & perhaps this will account for her not wishing to leave a place where she has suffered so heavily. . . . Farewell, Wm Poole.

A Glimpse of Poverty

↦↤

Judith Stevens to John Murray, Gloucester, October 1, 1775, Judith Sargent Murray Papers, Mississippi Department of Archives and History, Jackson, Miss.

Although Grace Jackson spent time in the poorhouse while she was pregnant, she returned to the workforce soon after the baby was delivered. Other women, however, were unable to find work or too infirm or elderly to seek it. These women had little recourse but long-term reliance on the charity of the state. When Judith Stevens went to the almshouse to hire a domestic servant for her mother, she entered a hidden world of misery and poverty that shocked her. For hundreds of women—former servants, single mothers, elderly widows—that misery was an all-too-familiar way of life.

↜↝

Take now, my dear Sir, an account which will, I have no doubt interest your humanity. My Mother being in want of a domestic, conceived it would be beneficial to the Community, were she to receive a female from the home which stands among us, a shelter for indigent and unfortunate people and for the purpose of selecting a proper person she commissioned me to pay a visit to this temporary prison.

Our Alms house is occupied by unsucessful industry, destitute vice, miserable Old Age; and helpless infancy. This miscellaneous receptacle of suffering is romantically situated at the foot of a steep. Huge rocks form a semicircle, inclosing every part of the house except the front which is washed by a river. Its appearance was in no sort discriptive of the . . . sheltered. . . . Here deformed childhood, and those decrepid years . . . I passed through many divisions of this abode of wretchedness, in pursuit of an [ancient] Woman, from whom I received the rudiments of reading and who I had lately learned had fled to this last resort of wretchedness. I sought and at length found her. As I was formaly a favourite she rejoiced to see me. . . . How unconcerned are the children of opulence. How meager is the provision made for the suffereing part of our species. Benevolence, it should seem is fled from our globe, and compassion no more inhabits the breast of men. . . .

DEHGEWANUS DESCRIBES HER WORK

↔↔

James E. Seaver, *A Narrative of the Life of Mrs. Mary Jemison* (Canandaigua, N.Y., 1824), pp. 46–47.

In 1758 the Jemison family of Pennsylvania was captured by French-allied Indians, who killed everyone in the family except fifteen-year-old Mary Jemison. She was adopted into the Seneca Iroquois tribe, took the name Dehgewanus, and, after marrying a Delaware warrior, started a family of her own. When offered the opportunity to return to white society, Dehgewanus declined. Like hundreds of other captives, she remained with her adopted culture until her death. Shortly before she died, she recounted her personal history to the Reverend James Seaver, who published the account in 1824. In the excerpt below, Dehgewanus describes "women's work" among the Seneca.

~+

Our labor was not severe; and that of one year was exactly similar, in almost every respect, to that of the others, without that endless variety that is to be observed in the common labor of the white people. Notwithstanding the Indian women have all the fuel and bread to procure, and the cooking to perform, their task is probably not harder than that of white women, who have those articles provided for them; and their cares certainly are not half as numerous, nor as great. In the summer season, we planted, tended and harvested our corn, and generally had all our children with us; but had no master to oversee or drive us, so that we could work as leisurely as we pleased. We had no ploughs on the Ohio; but performed the whole process of planting and hoeing with a small tool that resembled, in some respects, a hoe with a very short handle.

Our cooking consisted in pounding our corn into samp or hommany, boiling the hommany, making now and then a cake and baking it in the ashes, and in boiling or roasting our venison. As our cooking and eating utensils consisted of a hommany block and pestle, a small kettle, a knife or two, and a few vessels of bark or wood, it required but little time to keep them in order for use.

Spinning, weaving, sewing, stocking knitting, and the like, are arts which have never been practised in the Indian tribes generally. After the revolutionary war, I learned to sew, so that I could make my own clothing after a poor fashion; but the other domestic arts I have been wholly ignorant of the application of, since my captivity. In the season of hunting, it was our business, in addition to our cooking, to bring home the game that was taken by the Indians, dress it, and carefully preserve the eatable meat, and prepare or dress the skins.

A Rural Woman's Lament

↦↤

"Ruth Belknap's Reply to Edward Taylor," 1782, Massachusetts Historical Society *Collections*, 6th ser., 4, pp. 228–229n.

The Reverend Edward Taylor exalted women's household tasks, but a housewife from Dover, New Hampshire, set to verse a more realistic view of the repetitive, physically exhausting chores that faced an eighteenth-century rural white woman every day.

↜↝

Up in the morning I must rise
Before I've time to rub my eyes.
With half-pin'd gown, unbuckled shoe,
I haste to milk my lowing cow.
But, Oh! it makes my heart to ake,
I have no bread till I can bake,
And then, alas! it makes me sputter,
For I must churn or have no butter.
The hogs with swill too I must serve;
For hogs must eat or men will starve.
Besides, my spouse can get no cloaths
Unless I much offend my nose.
For all that try it know it's true
There is no smell like colouring blue.
Then round the parish I must ride
And make enquiry far and wide
To find some girl that is a spinner,
Then hurry home to get my dinner.

All summer long I toil & sweat,
Blister my hands, and scold & fret.
And when the summer's work is o'er,
New toils arise from Autumn's store.
Corn must be husk'd, and pork be kill'd,
The house with all confusion fill'd.
O could you see the grand display
Upon our annual butchering day,—
See me look like ten thousand sluts,
My kitchen spread with grease & guts,—
You'd lift your hands surpris'd, & swear
That Mother Trisket's self were there.

Ye starch'd up folks that live in town,
That lounge upon your beds till noon,
That never tire yourselves with work,
Unless with handling knife & fork,
Come, see the sweets of country life,
Display'd in Parson B[elknap's] wife.

A RURAL GIRL KEEPS BUSY

↔ ↤

Diary of Abigail Foote, 1775, excerpted in Alice Morse Earle, *Home Life in Colonial Days* (New York: Macmillan, 1898), p. 253.

Busy farm women throughout the colonies jotted down the chores they needed to do and those they had accomplished in daybooks. These books were not really diaries, and only occasionally did women or girls take the time to reflect on their emotional state. When they did, most spoke of boredom, exhaustion, and a longing for a moment of time to themselves. Unlike the elite young women of urban society, this Connecticut girl had little time for socializing or self-improvement in her busy day.

↜

Fix'd gown for Prude,—Mend Mother's Riding-hood,—Spun short thread,—Fix'd two gowns for Welsh's girls,—Carded tow,—Spun linen,— Worked on Cheesebasket,—Hatchel'd flax with Hannah, we did 51 lbs. apiece,—Pleated and ironed,—Read a Sermon of Doddridge's,—Spooled a piece,—Milked the cows,—Spun linen, did 50 knots,—Made a Broom of Guinea wheat straw,—Spun thread to whiten,—Set a Red dye,—Had two

Scholars from Mrs. Taylor's,—I carded two pounds of whole wool and felt Nationly,—Spun harness twine,—Scoured the pewter.

A Planter's Schedule

↦ ↤

Eliza Lucas to Miss B[artlett], March–April 1740, in *The Letter Book of Eliza Lucas Pinckney*, ed. Elise Pinckney and Marvin R. Zahniser (Chapel Hill: University of North Carolina Press, 1972), pp. 34–35.

The life of this elite young woman was as busy as Abigail Foote's, but more intellectually challenging. Eliza Lucas (later Pinckney) was the daughter of a naval officer with plantations in South Carolina and the Caribbean. She was exceptionally well educated by her father, who left her in charge of his three Carolina plantations when he returned to active naval duties in 1740. Lucas proved to be a shrewd businesswoman and an innovative agriculturalist whose successful experiments with indigo plants resulted in a new export item for her colony. She was a strong advocate of John Locke's educational theories, which may have influenced her decision to educate slave children on her plantation. This letter to a close friend suggests the range of activities and interests available to an elite eighteenth-century colonial woman.

↜↝

Dr. Miss B

. . . Why, my dear Miss B, will you so often repeat your desire to know how I triffle away my time in our retirement in my fathers absence. Could it afford you advantages or pleasure I should not have hesitated, but as you can expect neither from it I would have been excused; however, to show you my readiness in obeying your commands, here it is.

In general then I rise at five o'Clock in the morning, read till Seven, then take a walk in the garden or field, see that the Servants are at their respective business, then to breakfast. The first hour after breakfast is spent at my musick, the next is constantly employed in recolecting something I have learned least for want of practise it should be quite lost, such as French and short hand. After that I devote the rest of the time till I dress for dinner to our little Polly and the two black girls who I teach to read, and if I have my papa's approbation (my Mamas I have got) I intend [them] for school mistres's for the rest of the Negroe children—another scheme you see. But to proceed, the first hour after dinner as the first after breakfast at musick, the rest of the afternoon in Needle work till candle light, and from that time to bed time read or write. 'Tis the fashion here to carry our work abroad with us so that having company, without they are great strangers, is no interruption to that affair; but I have particular matters for particular days, which is an interruption to mine. Mondays my musick Master is here. Tuesdays my friend Mrs. Chardon (about 3 mile distant) and I are constantly engaged to each other, she at our house one Tuesday—I at heres the next and this is one of the happiest days I spend at Woppoe [one of the Lucases' plantations]. Thursday the whole day except what the necessary affairs of the family take up is spent in writing, either on the business of the plantations, or letters to my friends. Every other Fryday, if no company, we go a vizeting so that I go abroad once a week and no oftener. . . . O! I had like to forgot the last thing I have done a great while. I have planted a large figg orchard with designs to dry and export them. I have reckoned my expence and the prophets to arise from these figgs. . . .

ENSLAVED WOMEN IMPROVE THEIR MASTER'S LAND
↔ ↔

Diaries of George Washington, 1748–1799, ed. John C. Fitzpatrick (Boston: Houghton Mifflin, 1925), pp. 293–295.

While genteel plantation mistresses and urban merchants' wives pored over cookbooks and illustrations of the latest London fashions, the majority of African American women continued to labor in the tobacco fields and rice paddies of the south. The women owned by George Washington performed a variety of agricultural tasks, from hoeing, fence building, and threshing to grubbing and clearing swamps. Men and women appear to have performed some of the same tasks, but always in sex-segregated work groups.

〜

JANUARY 1788   THURSDAY, 3D
Visited the plantations at the Ferry, Dogue Run, and Muddy Hole.

At the first the women were taking up and thinning the trees in the swamp which they had before grubbed. The men were getting stakes and trunnels for fencing and making racks to feed the creatures in. Began yesterday and would about finish today sowing the New Meadow at this (which was too thin of timothy) with a quart of timothy seed to the acre.

At French's they were putting up racks to feed the cattle in. One man was getting stakes for fencing.

At Dogue Run, the women began to hoe the swamp they had grubbed in order to prepare it for sowing in the spring with grain and grass seeds. The men were cutting the tops of the trees which had been fallen for rails into coal-wood.

At Muddy Hole, the women after having threshed out the peas, went about the fencing, two men getting stakes, etc., for it.

FRIDAY, 4TH

Ride to all the plantations.

In the Neck the men were getting posts and rails; the women were threshing oats.

At Muddy Hole, the men were getting rails and the women making fences.

At Dogue Run, the men were cutting coal-wood and the women hoeing swamp as yesterday.

At French's the men were cutting and mauling fence stakes and the women levelling old ditches and grubbing.

At the Ferry, the men were getting stakes, making racks, etc., and the women thinning trees in the swamp.

MONDAY, 7TH

Visited the plantations at Dogue Run and French's. At the first the women (though the ground was too hard to hoe) were grubbing and otherwise preparing the swamp for meadow. The men were cutting as usual.

At French's (except Abram who was cutting stakes) the rest were threshing out peas.

Set the women belonging to the Ferry and to Muddy Hole to grubbing the woods in front of the house, adjoining the last year's corn.

A YOUNG SLAVE WOMAN'S MARKETABLE SKILLS

↦ ↤

Advertisement in *New York Weekly Journal*, September 30, 1734.

In the middle and New England colonies, slave women were employed in the wheat fields and on family farms. But in the urban centers, prosperous families sometimes purchased an African American woman to serve as cook, maid, or housekeeper. Thus, in the eighteenth century the "mammy" was more likely to be a Philadelphia slave than a resident on a Chesapeake plantation. This advertisement suggests the skills and character traits that made a slave woman marketable in colonial urban households.

↜↝

To be sold, a young negro woman about 20 years old; she does all sortes of household work, she can brew, Bake, Boil Sope, Wash, Iron and starch; and is a good dairy woman, she can card and spins at the great wheel. Cotton Tow and Wooll, and she has another good property she neither drinks Rum, nor smokes tobacco, nor no strong liquer, and she is a strong hale healthy well sett wench, she can cook pretty well for Roast and Boil'd. She is very mild and quiet, I believe she has had the small pox when a child, she is pretty well cloath'd both with linnen and woollen. Enquire of John McLennan at the Upper End of Beaver Street, near the Royal Bowling Green, and know farther.

WAGE-EARNING WOMEN

↦ ↤

Work record of John Rock and His Wife, 1792–1793, George Brinton Account Book, Chester County Historical Society, West Chester, Pa.

The wives and daughters of tenant farmers and poorer landowners did both household and field work for wages in colonies, and later states, such as Pennsylvania and Massachusetts. The account book below provides information on the hours, wages, and tasks performed by a married couple at the end of the eighteenth century. Mrs. Rock worked in the Brinton home, but she also put in a few hours harvesting potatoes and reaping and binding wheat.

| | | | RATE | |
| | | DAYS | PER DAY | |
MONTH	TASK	WORKED	*Shilling*	*Pence*
Mar.	Loading dung	6	2	
Apr.	Plowing, spreading dung, harrowing	17	2	
May	At corn, washing sheep, trimming meadow, weeding wheat	9.5	2	
June	At hay	8.37	3	
	At hay (Rock's Wife)	1.75	1	6
	In house (Rock's Wife)	1		7
	At corn	2	2	
	Total	13.12		

July	Cradling	6.25	5	
	Raking and binding wheat	3	3	
	Reaping and binding wheat (Rock's wife)	1.75	1	6
	In house (Rock's Wife)	9		7
	At potatoes, trimming	3	2	
	Tending masonry, reaping, fencing	5.25	2	6
	Total	28.25		
Aug.	Mowing hay	11	3	
	In house (Rock's Wife)	10.5		7
	Plowing, drawing wood for cider mill, beating flax, at potatoes	10	2	
	Total	31.5		
Sept.	At hay (no mowing), loading dirt, plowing, other work	21.25	2	
	Threshing 25 bus. wheat for seed			5 (per bu.)
Oct.	Plowing, at buckwheat, potatoes, apples and cider	20	2	
	At potatoes (Rock's Wife)	1	1	6
	Total	21		
Nov.	At cider, corn, cutting wood, fencing, killing bull, plowing orchard	14	2	
Dec.	Drawing logs, thrashing clover seeds, killing pigs	5.75	2	
	Cleaning 18.5 bus. wheat			6 (per bu.)
Jan.	Drawing logs, sawing	2.5	2	
Feb.	Thrashing 33.5 bus. wheat			6 (per bu.)

EARNING A LIVING

→←

Advertisements in *Independent Gazetteer*, April 15 and 22, 1786; and *Pennsylvania Packet*, September 23, 1780.

Women's Work

The eighteenth-century equivalent of want ads in urban newspapers offer a glimpse of the skills and work experience women acquired and employers sought. These samples are representative if not exhaustive.

৵

[APRIL 15, 1786]
Wants a Place,
As a Wet Nurse,
A Woman with a good Breast of Milk,
That can be well recommended
Inquire of the Printer

[APRIL 22, 1786]

A Middle aged woman who can procure good recommendations, would be glad of a place as a housekeeper in a respectable family, either in the town or country. Inquire at Mr. Robinson's Bricklayer, second street near Chestnut Street.

[SEPT 23, 1780]

Wanted at a Seat about half a day's journey from Philadelphia, on which are good improvements and domestics, A single Woman of unsullied Reputation, an affable, cheerful, active and amiable Disposition; cleanly, industrious, perfectly qualified to direct and manage the female Concerns of country business, as raising small stock, dairying, marketing, combing, carding, spinning, knitting, sewing, pickling, preserving, etc., and occasionally to instruct two young Ladies in those Branches of Oeconomy, who, with their father, compose the Family. Such a person will be treated with respect and esteem, and meet with every encouragement due to such a character.

A NURSE SEEKS A PAY RAISE

↔↩

Petition of Alice Redman, *Maryland Historical Magazine* 17 (1922), p. 379.

The American Revolution is rarely thought of as a war that provided job opportunities for women. Volunteer associations participated in the mobilization for war, collected funds, sewed uniforms, and knitted socks for soldiers, while camp followers served as nurses and cooks for the army. This petition, however, suggests that some women earned wages by turning civilian workforce skills to wartime service. Nursing,

Alice Redman's occupation, emerged as a major female profession a century later during the Civil War.

To the honourable the Governor and council
The Humble Petition of Alice Redman one of the nurses at the hospital.

Humbly Sheweth, that your petitioner has been a nurse at the hospital for about a year she has been deligent and carefull in her office, which she your petitioner humbly beg for an augmentation to her pay as she only is allowed two dollars a month she has at this present time sixteen men for to cook and take care off she your petitioner as since she has been a nurse had a great deal of trouble she is oblige to be up day and night with some of the patients and never has been allowed so much as a little Tea, or Coffee which she your petitioner hopes your honors will take this petition into your consideration and your Petitioner in duty Bound will Ever Pray.

Alice Redman.

P.S. She your petitioner out of that two dollars p[er] month is oblige to buy brooms and the soap we wash with if your honors will please to relieve your petitioner your petitioner will ever be bound to pray.

A. Redman.

A FEMALE PHYSICIAN

↦↤

Advertisement in *Pennsylvania Packet*, December 11, 1784.

The professionalization of medicine, like law, diminished the opportunities for participation by women. Yet in the eighteenth century there was still little to prevent a person from claiming expertise in anything from pharmaceuticals to surgery. In the announcement printed below, Mrs. Kayser advertises skills ranging from the treatment of mild infections to dental hygiene to the cure of ulcers, and declares she has certificates earned outside Pennsylvania to support those claims.

↜↝

Mrs. Kayser begs to inform the Public That she has a safe and peculiar method for the cure of the fever and Ague, and will undertake to perfect the cure in five days. She likewise cures the scurvy in the gums, and makes the teeth most beautifully white in a few minutes; also cures the rheumatism, chin cough, fore eyes, the flux, all sorts of ulcers, and many other diseases toe tedious to mention.

She has had the pleasure to practice in the general way of Physic and

Surgery with very great success, both in Baltimore and different parts of Virginia, from which, if it was desired, she could produce good certificates.

Mrs. Kayser is to be consulted with from Ten to Twelve in the forenoon, and from Three to Eight in the afternoon, next door but one to the Three Tons, in Third Street, between South and Shippen streets.

An Innkeeper Sues

↔ ↔

Elizabeth Jourdain v. Henry Campbell, 1720, Mayors Court Papers, Box 6, folder 3, Division of Old Records, New York City County Court.

Not all women earned their livings as skilled or unskilled laborers. Women with some capital might operate a variety of businesses, including inns and taverns, small dry goods shops, greengroceries, schools, and print shops. Elizabeth Jourdain, a New York widow, may have run an inn or tavern, but as this suit for debt makes clear, she had taken in at least one boarder. When Henry Campbell refused to pay his bill, Jourdain sued for payment and damages.

↔↔

Mayors Court anno Septimo George Y Regis
City of New York
Elizabeth Jourdain widdow doth complaine against Henry Campbell in custody for that whereas the said Henry the second day of January in the seventh year of the reign of our sovereign lord George of Great Britain King at the city of new York to wit at the Dock Ward of the same city and within the jurisdiction of this court was indebted unto her the said Elizabeth in five pounds seven shillings and eight pence half penny current money of New York as well for the diet of him the said Henry as for liquor by her the said Elizabeth unto him the said Henry and that his special instance and request before that time found and provided and sold and delivered and being thereof indebted said Henry in consideration thereof afterwards [to wit] the same day year and place aforesaid and within the jurisdiction aforesaid assumed upon himself and to her the said Elizabeth then and there faithfully promised that he the said Henry the aforesaid sum of five pounds seven shillings and eight pence half penny unto her the said Elizabeth when he should be there unto afterwards required would well and faithfully pay and content nevertheless the said Henry his promise and assumpcion aforesaid in form aforesaid made not regarding but imagining and fraudulently intending her the said Elizabeth in this behalfe craftily and subtlely to deceive and

defraud the aforesaid sum of five pounds seven shilling and eight pence unto her the said Elizabeth although to do the same the said Henry afterward [to wit] the same day year and place aforesaid and within the jurisdiction aforesaid her the said Elizabeth was thereunto required hath not paid but the same to her [as yett] to pay hath altogether refused and still doth refuse to the damage of the said Elizabeth tenn pounds and of this she brings her suite.

EDUCATORS ADVERTISE

↔↔

Advertisements in *Virginia Gazette*, February 27, 1772, and December 27, 1776.

Schoolteaching became a major female occupation in the nineteenth century, but women operated schools throughout the colonial period and in the early republican era as well. The advertisements excerpted below list the course offerings considered appropriate for young ladies in the 1770s. After the Revolution, young ladies' academies sprang up, offering more rigorous academic curricula.

↔↔

E. Armston (or perhaps better known by the name of Gardner) continues the Schools at Point Pleasant, Norfolk Borough, where [there] is a large and convenient House proper to accommodate young Ladies as Boarders; at which School is taught Petit Point in Flowers, Fruit, Landscapes, and Sculpture, Nuns Work, Embroidery in Silk, Gold, Silver, Pearls, or embossed, Shading of all Kinds, in the various Works in Vogue, Dresden Point Work, Lace, Catgut in different Modes, Muslin after the Newest Taste, and most elegant Pattern, Waxwork in Figure, Fruit, or Flowers, Shell ditto, or grotesque, Painting in Water Colours and Mezzotints. . . . Specimens of the Subscriber's Work may be seen at her House, as also of her Scholars; having taught several Years in Norfolk, and elsewhere to general Satisfaction. She flatters herself that those Gentlemen and Ladies who have hitherto employed her will grant her their further indulgence, as no endeavors shall be wanted to complete what is above mentioned, with a strict attention to the Behavior of those Ladies entrusted to her Care.

Reading will be her peculiar Care; Writing and Arithmetick will be taught by a Master properly qualified; and, if desired, will engage Proficients in Musick and Dancing.

Mrs. Neill (who for a considerable Time past, has lived in Colonel Lewis's Family, Gloucester County) purposes to open a Boarding School in Williamsburg for the Reception of young Ladies, on the Same Plan of the English Schools, provided a sufficient Number of Scholars engage, to enable her for such an Undertaking. She will instruct them in Reading, Tambour, and other Kinds of Needle Work, find them Board and Lodging, Washing &c. for one Guinea Entrance and thirty pounds a Year. The best Masters will attend to teach Dancing and Writing. She will also teach the Guittar. Those who choose to learn any of those Accomplishments [are expected] to pay for each separately. . . . As Nothing tends more to the Improvement of a Country than proper Schools for Education of both Sexes, she humbly hopes her Scheme will meet with Encouragement, and the Approbation of the Ladies and gentlemen of this State; and that those who choose to lend their Children will please to let her know as soon as possible, that she may provide accordingly for their Reception. . . . Direct for her at Col. Lewis's, Senior, in Gloucester, or at Mess. Dixon & Hunter in Williamsburg.

Mrs. Neill will take Day Scholars at one Guinea Entrance, and four Guineas per year.

INVESTORS AND DIVESTORS

++ ++

Joanna Markham v. Jacob Swan, 1717, Mayors Court Papers, Division of Old Records, New York County Court, Box 4, folders 35, 36; and advertisement in *Georgia Gazette,* October 21, 1767.

Widows with capital or real estate could earn income by becoming investors in business enterprises or by disposing of property wisely. Although widows rarely controlled large sums, it is likely that their capital played a critical role in the development of American businesses in the eighteenth century. In the examples quoted below, Joanna Markham sues for default on a loan made to the owner of a small business, and Elizabeth Anderson offers two tracts of land to prospective buyers.

+~+

Mayor's Court, February anno tertio georg y Regis

Joanna Markham widdow complaines of Jacob Swan otherwise called Jacob Swan of the City of New York Hatter of a plea that he Render unto her Twenty pounds current money of New York which to her he oweth and unjustly detaineth for that whereas the said Jacob the thirty-first day of May in the year of our Lord aforesaid seven[teen] hundred and fourteene at the city of New York to wit at the Dock Ward of the said city and within the jurisdiction of this court by his Certaine Writeing Obligatory Sealed with the seale of him the said Jacob and for the court aforesaid the king now here shown and Jacob acknowledged himself to be held and firmly bound unto the said Joanna in the aforesaid twenty pounds to be paid to the said Joanna [when he should be thereof required] nevertheless the said Jacob [altho often required] the aforesaid twenty pounds unto her the said Joanna hath not paid but the same to her as . . . hath hitherto altogether refused and still doth refuse to the damage of her the said Joanna five pounds and thereof she brings her suit.

TO BE SOLD

A tract containing 150 acres of good pine and red oak land, in the parish of St. George, bounded north-east by land of Henry OverStreet, northerly by land of Elizabeth Anderson, and on all other sides by vacant lands. Another tract, containing 150 acres of good oak and pine land in said parish, bounded Northeast by land of Henry Overstreet, southerly by land of Elizabeth Anderson, and on all other sides by vacant lands.—Any person inclinably to purchase both or either of the above tracts of land may apply in Savannah to Elizabeth Anderson.

CHAPTER FOUR

Religion

O NE OF THE MAJOR THREADS running through the lives of colonial white women was the importance of Christian, and primarily Protestant, theology in molding their personal and social identity. The influence was both profound and contradictory, for the majority of denominations categorized women collectively yet also acknowledged their individual souls.

As a sex, women were assumed to share particular moral weaknesses and divinely prescribed social burdens. The descendants of Eve, it was believed, had inherited a propensity to temptation that required their subordination to man's superior moral judgment and greater rationality. The prescriptive literature of the church—which included the sermons and religious tracts that interpreted the Scriptures—was frequently used to legitimate women's subordination to fathers and husbands in the family as well as to circumscribe their participation within the church. Only the Quakers, the most radical of the dissenting sects in the colonies, abandoned the notion that Eve's temptation placed a special burden on the souls of women. The Quakers argued that the coming of Christ had erased all punishments for Eve's sins and set men and women on an equal footing in their capacity for moral awareness and individual moral responsibility.

As institutions, most Protestant churches were influenced by the belief in women's collective moral weakness. They excluded women from the ranks of the clergy, restricted their formal role in institutional decision making, and regulated their participation in the worship service. St. Paul's injunction that women keep their silence in the church justified the exclusion of women from active roles in all three areas. While it is true that the colonial evangelical sects that emerged in the eighteenth century sometimes allowed women preachers, this practice diminished, or in some cases was entirely eliminated, as the sects gained respectability and a firm foothold in the community. Again, the Quakers were a noticeable exception to the rule of an all-male ministry. The question was partly moot, of course, since no minister of either sex officiated at a Quaker meeting. But the Quakers allowed women to proselytize, and Quaker women played an active role in church administration and governance through their own autonomous monthly meetings.

Yet if women lacked formal power in most Protestant churches, they did not lack influence. New England's Puritan women led campaigns for the creation of new churches when the distances between their farms and the existing church were too great. By making their opinions known, women influenced the tenure of Puritan ministers and the promotion of clergy within the church. Later, in the widespread reaffirmation of faith called the Great Awakening, women often initiated a family's search for spiritual rejuvenation. Finally, at the end of the eighteenth century, a new evaluation of the relative spiritual capacities of men and women began to emerge. By the close of the colonial era, a reversal was under way in the established view of the relative moral capacities and propensities of men and women: women were lauded as the sex more open to religious sensibility and more sensitive to moral nuances. This new vision of women was fully elaborated in the middle-class world of the nineteenth century.

Although Christianity encouraged or allowed assumptions about women's collective character and place within the church, most Protestant sects also insisted that salvation was an individual quest every woman could pursue. Thus, they encouraged a woman to attend to, develop, and realize fully her individual spirituality. The evidence suggests that many women chose to do so. Like women's personal writings on any subject, letters or diaries detailing the search for personal salvation in seventeenth-century colonial society are rare. However, we do have other forms of documentation. For example, the institutional records of New England's Puritan churches offer proof of many women's quest for "saving grace," and Quaker and Anglican eulogies, sermons, and deathbed statements demonstrate women's concern to honor Christian precepts in their lives and to examine the readiness of their souls at the moment of their death.

The regular cycle of pregnancy and childbirth gave an immediacy to women's consideration of their personal salvation. Eighteenth-century letters and diaries stress the attention expectant mothers paid to the condition of their souls as they faced what they called their "travail." Religion provided an explanation and consolation for events in women's daily lives such as the death of infants and children and violent conflicts with Indians. It also provided an identity that, for most Anglo-European colonists, set them apart from—and above—both native Americans and Africans. Whether they were active churchgoers or not, colonial white women lived in a culture shaped by Christian cosmology and precepts, which created the context for their social and personal relationships. Thus, Puritan wives reminded themselves that love of Christ must stand above the love of a mortal man. Few women challenged the religious prescription that a wife obey her husband, even if many honored it only in the breach. The religious culture of the seventeenth and eighteenth centuries reinforced and legitimated women's social and legal subordination, yet it also sanctioned a woman's identity as an individual moral being and often encouraged her to examine her own spirituality.

Unfortunately, most of what historians know about Indian religious beliefs and practices during the colonial period comes from observations by Catholic and Protestant missionaries and traders. Some of these observers intended their accounts of Indian society to serve as morality lessons for their European readers, proving the superiority of Christianity and the dangers of degeneracy in pagan societies. Others tried to be impartial but, not understanding the context or meaning of much of what they saw, filled in critical information gaps with interpretations drawn from their own English or European cultures. Their official reports, travel journals, and diaries tell us more about the European mindset than about the Indian societies they described. Because Indian societies relied on oral rather than written traditions, we know very little about the role of religion in the lives of Indian women as they themselves or their male counterparts might have explained it.

On the whole, Indian faiths were not constructed around an absolute monotheism, nor did they generate separate institutions to contain and direct worship. Indian cultures, like most African cultures, distinguished between the sacred and the profane but saw the two as interconnected and interdependent. Indian creation stories, unlike the Biblical one, did not set up social, familial, or political systems that privileged men. Most of the Indian stories revolved around the origins of the physical world rather than of human society. In the agricultural tribes encountered by the English colonists, female figures played as central a role in the creation process as males. For example, the Iroquois spoke of a woman who falls from the Sky World and creates the earth. On earth she gives birth to a daughter, and from the breasts of this daughter spring the "three sisters" who make human life possible: corn, beans, and squash. In most Eastern Woodland tribes, women participated in key ceremonies and rituals, especially those that celebrated women's agricultural activities and their role as childbearers. Among the Seneca, the Woman's Dance, a ritual honoring the cultivation of corn, called for men to chant while women performed the steps of the dance. In the fall season women dominated the Thanks-to-the-Maple Ceremony because they were responsible for tapping the maple trees for syrup. Women were also recognized as spiritual leaders, along with men, in most of the agricultural tribes. In the Iroquois communities women were included among the "keepers of the faith," leaders whose position had no analogy in Christian communities that adhered to Pauline doctrine regarding women. The Seneca's Chanters of the Dead, who helped both men and women understand their dreams of dead relatives and friends, were traditionally led by a woman. Among the tribes whose

economic and social systems were based on hunting, religious authority usually rested with males. Thus, the shamans, or priests, of most
Canadian Indian societies were men.

African women brought a variety of religious traditions with them
in their forced immigration to English America. Slavery, however,
rarely allowed for the full recreation of these traditions, and the ethnic
mix on the plantations rarely allowed any single tradition to dominate.
Yet when members of the African plantation communities adopted
Christianity, they often blended it with African religious beliefs and
practices that were common to most of the ethnic groups represented.
Historians have traced practices such as ecstatic trances and spirit possession (both of which might strike a familiar chord for survivors of
the Salem witch-hunts) that survived in the transition to Christianity.
Other African traditions, such as conjuration and sorcery, persisted as
independent alternatives to Christianity. Black women as well as men
could be conjurers, and could be blessed—or cursed—with the gift of
second sight, allowing them a window into the supernatural world.
Women could also join the ranks of witches, wielding magical powers
within their communities. As healers, interpreters of signs, or agents
of evil, these women enjoyed a particular authority in the community.

During the colonial period slave masters showed little interest in
converting their forced laborers to Christianity. Some feared that the
legality of slavery would be called into question if African workers
could not be labeled as heathens or pagans. Most, however, were simply uninterested in diminishing the differences between themselves
and their African laborers. In the late seventeenth century, under the
prodding of the Anglican church, plantation owners did take steps to
convert slaves to Christianity. The religious instruction they favored
stressed the virtues of obedience and patience. The degree of accep-
tance or resistance to the religion of the dominant culture varied from
plantation to plantation, from rice-growing regions to tobacco areas,
and from south to north. The greatest shift in religious loyalties occurred during the Great Awakening, when southern blacks as well as
poor whites became enthusiastic converts to the evangelical sects that
held out the promise of equality and critiqued the excesses and degeneracy of the planter elite. In Virginia and Maryland, as in New

England, women provided significant support for evangelical faiths such as the Methodists and Baptists. But both of these sects adopted more conservative positions regarding race and gender as the century ended. In northern cities, particularly after the American Revolution, free blacks established churches that became centers of African American community life—and thus of women's lives. Probably few Africans shared the view of the black Boston poet Phillis Wheatley that an introduction to Christianity made slavery tolerable, but many northern black women, slave and free, did construct a religious identity around Protestantism.

PRESCRIPTIVE DOCUMENTS

WHOSE GOD?

Roger Williams, *A Key into the Language of America*, London, 1643.

Although religion and religious institutions played an important role in the Christian world of the colonists, few showed any interest in recording or understanding Indian religious beliefs. When missionaries did comment on Indian religions, their reports were rarely unbiased. Puritan dissenter Roger Williams, however, made an attempt to understand the religious beliefs of the Narragansets. In the excerpt below, Williams noted that both men and women participated in worship rituals and that the Narragansets believed both women and men have souls.

Obs[ervation]. He that questions whether God made the World, the Indians will teach him. I must acknowledge I have received in my converse with them many Confirmations of those two great points, Heb. 11. 6. viz:

1. That God is.
2. That hee is a rewarder of all them that diligently seek him.

They will generally confesse that God made all: but them in special, although they deny not that English-mans God made English Men, and the Heavens and Earth there! yet their Gods made them, and the Heaven and Earth where they dwell. . . .

Obs. These doe begin and order their service, and Invocation of their

Gods, and all the people follow, and joyne interchangeably in a laborious bodily service, unto sweating, especially of the Priest, who spends himselfe in strange Antick Gestures, and Actions even unto fainting. . . .

Obs. They believe that the soules of Men and Women goe to the Souwest, their great and good men and Women to *Cautàntoouwit* his House, where they have hopes (as the Turkes have) of carnall Joyes: Murtherers thieves and Lyers, their Soules (say they) wander restlesse abroad.

Eve's Legacy

↔ ↔

Cotton Mather, *The Angel of Bethesda* (1724), ed. Gordon W. Jones (Worcester, Mass.: American Antiquarian Society and Barre Publishers, 1972), pp. 233–236.

In this excerpt the influential Puritan minister Cotton Mather ponders why women endure greater physical suffering than men. His answer is orthodox: women's travail results from Eve's transgression in paradise. But Mather consoles women with the thought that the pains and perils of childbirth lead them to piety and set them on the path to salvation, perhaps sooner than the men of their family.

+~+

The Sex that is called, *The Weaker Vessel,* has not only a share with us, in the most of our Distempers, but also is liable to many that may be called, Its *Peculiar Weaknesses.* Many others besides *Varandaeus,* have written Large Treatises of *Womens Diseases.* I have readd . . . That Physicians have *Two Woman-Patients* to *One Man:* And it is only likely to be True. But inasmuch as both Sexes Dy in a more Equal Proportion, This is very much for the Honour of the Physicians, who cure them, or for the Dishonour of us Men, who Dy as much by our *Extravagancies* as *Women* do by thier *Infirmities.*

Poor Daughters of Eve, Languishing under your *Special Maladies,* Look back on your *Mother,* the *Woman,* who being *Deceived,* was first in the *Transgression,* that has brought in upon us, all our *Maladies.* Beholding your *Affliction* and your *Misery,* in the midst of your *Lamentations* under it, Remember that Wormwood and Gall of the Forbidden Fruit; Lett your Soul have them still in *Rememberance,* and be humbled in you. Under all your Ails, think, The Sin of my Mother, which is also my Sin, has brought all this upon me!

But then, Look up to your Saviour, who will one Day sett you free from all these Maladies: And in the mean time will make all things work together for good unto you.

And oh! That this Good may come out of these *Maladies*, That you Shall be distinguished by the *Blessings* of an *Healed Soul;* and that you shall be the more full of goodness; the more Exemplary for *Whatsoever Things are Lovely, and Whatsoever Things are of good Report!*

Lett your *Patience* also, bear a proportion to your Humbling and Grievous Exercises.

And the more obnoxious your Tender and Feeble Constitutions are unto a Variety of Distempers, the more lett you Temperence and Caution be, that you may not bring Distempers on yourself. . . .

Chap. Llll. Retired *Elizabeth.*
A Long, tho' no very *Hard, Chapter*
for, A WOMAN whose *Travail* approaches.
with Remedies to Abate the *Sorrows of Child-bearing.*

. . . Some Advice is now to be offered, unto a Daughter of Eve, [Lett her also give me Leave to call her, *An Handmaid of the Lord!*] who Expects anon the Arrival of a Time, when her *loins* will be *filled* with *Pain, Pangs will take hold on her, the Pangs of a Woman which travaileth.* Tis Now, Sure, if ever, a Time wherein it may be Expected, that she will hearken to the Counsils of God; This, if any, is the Time, wherein the Methods and Motions of Divine Grace, will *find her.* Certainly, she will be concerned, that a *Sudden Destruction,* and a fearful and endless One, may not come as *Travail upon a Woman with Child,* when the *Time of Travail* shall come upon her. The Truth is, That tho' the Hazards and Hardships undergone by *Travailing Women,* be a considerable Article of the Curse, which the *Transgression* whereinto our *Mother* was *Deceived* has brought upon a Miserable World, yett our Great REDEEMER has procured this *Grace* from God unto the *Daughters of Zion,* that the *Curse* is turned into a *Blessing.* The Approach of their *Travails,* putts them upon those Exercises of PIETY, which render them truly *Blessed* ones; *Blessed* because their *Transgression* is *forgiven; Blessed* because they are *Turned from their Iniquities.* And hence in Part it may come to pass, that tho' thro' the Evident Providence of God, watching over Humane Affairs, there is pretty near an Equal Number of Males and Females that are Born into the World, the Number of the Males who are apparently *Pious,* and partakers of a *New Birth,* is not so great as that of the *Females.* Be sure, t'wil argue a wonderful Stupidity of Soul, and Obstinacy in Sin, if the View of An *Approaching Travail,* do not make the poor Women Serious, and Cause them seriously to Consider their Condition, and bring them into a Considerate, Sollicitous, Effectual Preparation for Eternity.

DESCRIPTIVE DOCUMENTS
〜

COMPELLING WORSHIP
↦ ↤

The cases of Nicholas Moulder and Wife, and Eliphal Stretton and Martha Amee, 1675, *Publications of the Colonial Society of Massachusetts, Records of the Suffolk County Court*, part 2 (Boston: Colonial Society of Massachusetts, 1933), vol. 30, p. 599.

In New England, church and state were intricately intertwined. While no minister or magistrate argued that church attendance would ensure or even necessarily lead to salvation, these authorities insisted that attendance was required of all in a Christian community. The offending couples in the cases below were ordered to pay steep fines for the failure to attend services. The Massachusetts court records suggest that the mandatory attendance law was often broken.

〜

MOULDER

Nicholas Moulder & his wife present'd by the Grandjury for neglecting the publique worship of god in o'r publique meeting houses allowed by Law upon the Lords day; And being called to answer for the same, owned the presentm't. The Court Sentenc'd them to pay Forty Shillings in mony apeice as a fine to the County & fees of Court & order Execucion to issue out for the levying thereof in case they do not make paym't.

STRETTON & AMEE

Eliphal Stretton & Martha Amee present'd by the Grandjury for neglecting the publique worship of god in o'r publique meeting houses allowed by Law upon the Lords day, & being called they owned the presentm't The Court Sentenc'd them to pay Forty Shillings apeice in mony as a fine to the County & Fees of Court & order execution to issue out for the Levying of the same in case they do not make payment.

A DANGEROUS WOMAN
↦ ↤

"The Examination of Mrs. Anne Hutchinson at the Court of Newtown," November 1637, in Charles Francis Adams, ed., *Antinomianism in the Colony of Massachusetts Bay, 1637–1638* (Prince Society, 1894; reprint, New York: Burt Franklin, 1967, pp. 235–284.

Although Puritan theology prohibited women from preaching, women were not forbidden to express their religious fervor. Anne Hutchinson, learned, brilliant, and intensely religious, did just that, holding meetings at her home to discuss the minister's sermons. In these discussions Hutchinson supported the Reverend John Cotton's Antinomian views that the church could neither ensure grace and salvation nor declare with certainty whom among its members were saved. Hutchinson's growing popularity troubled authorities. Ultimately she was tried, found guilty of heresy, excommunicated, and exiled from the Bay Colony. In the exchange excerpted below, Hutchinson shows herself equal to the colonial governor himself in scriptural knowledge, intelligence, quick-wittedness, and self-confidence.

⚜

Mr. Winthrop, governor. Mrs. Hutchinson, you are called here as one of those that have troubled the peace of the commonwealth and the churches here; you are known to be a woman that hath had a great share in the promoting and divulging those opinions that are causes of this trouble, and to be nearly joined not only in affinity and affection with some of those the court had taken notice of and pased censure upon, but you have spoken divers things as we have been informed very prejudicial to the honour of the churches and ministers thereof, and you have maintained a meeting and an assembly in your house that hath been condemned by the general assembly as a thing not tolerable nor comely in the sight of God nor fitting your sex, and notwithstanding that was cried down you have continued the same, therefore we have thought good to send for you to understand how things are, that if you be in an erroneous way we may reduce you that so you may become a profitable member here among us, otherwise if you be obstinate in your course that then the court may take such course that you may trouble us no further, therefore I would intreat you to express whether you do not assent and hold in practice to those opinions and factions that have been handled in court already. . . .

Mrs. Hutchinson: I am called here to answer before you but I hear no things laid to my charge. . . . What have I said or done?

Gov.: Why for your doings, this you did harbour and countenance those that are parties in this faction that you have heard of.

Mrs. H.: That's matter of conscience, Sir.

Gov.: Your conscience you must keep or it must be kept for you.

Mrs. H.: Must not I then entertain the saints because I must keep my conscience? . . .

Mrs. H.: In entertaining those did I entertain them against any act (for there is the thing), or what God hath appointed?

Gov.: You knew that Mr. Wheelwright [an Antinomian minister] did preach this sermon and those that countenance him in this do break a law.

Mrs. H.: What law have I broken?

Gov.: Why the fifth commandment. . . .

Mrs. H.: I deny that for he saith in the Lord.

Gov.: You have joined with them in the faction.

Mrs. H.: In what faction have I joined with them?

Gov.: In presenting the petition.

Mrs. H.: Suppose I had set my hand to the petition what then?

Gov.: You saw that case tried before.

Mrs. H.: But I had not my hand to the petition.

Gov.: You have councelled them.

Mrs. H.: Wherein?

Gov.: Why in entertaining them.

Mrs. H.: What breach of law is that Sir?

Gov.: Why dishonouring of parents.

Mrs. H.: But put the case Sir that I do fear the Lord and my parents, may not I entertain them that fear the Lord because my parents will not give me leave?

Gov.: If they be the fathers of the commonwealth, and they of another religion, if you entertain them then you dishonour your parents and are justly punishable.

Mrs. H.: If I entertain them, as they have dishonoured their parents I do.

Gov.: No but you by countenancing them above others put honour upon them.

Mrs. H.: I may put honor upon them as the children of God and as they do honor the Lord.

Gov.: We do not mean to discourse with those of your sex but only this; you do adhere unto them and do endeavor to set forward this faction and so you do dishonour us.

Mrs. H.: I do acknowledge no such thing neither do I think that I ever put any dishonour upon you.

Gov.: Why do you keep such a meeting at your house as you do every week upon a set day?

Mrs. Hutchinson: It is lawful for me so to do, as it is all your practices, and can you find a warrant for yourself and condemn me for the same thing? The ground of my taking it up was, when I first came to this land because I did not go to such meetings as those were, it was presently reported that I did not allow of such meetings but held them unlawful and therefore in that regard they said I was proud and did despise all ordinances, upon that a friend came unto me and told me of it, and I to prevent such aspersions took it up, but it was in practice before I came. Therefore I was not the first.

Gov.: For this, that you appeal to our practice you need no confutation. If your meeting had answered to the former, it had not been offensive, but I will say that there was no meeting of women alone, but your meeting is of another sort, for there are sometimes men among you.

Mrs. H.: There was never any man with us.

Gov.: Well, admit there was no man at your meeting and that you was sorry for it, there is no warrant for your doings, and by what warrant do you continue such a course?

Mrs. H.: I conceive there lies a clear rule in Titus [Titus 2.3–51] that the elder women should instruct the younger and then I must have a time wherein I must do it.

Gov.: All this I grant you, I grant you a time for it, but what is this to the purpose that you, Mrs. Hutchinson, must call a company together from their callings to come to be taught of you?

Mrs. H.: Will it please you to answer me this and to give me a rule, for then I will willingly submit to any truth. If any come to my house to be instructed in the ways of God, what rule have I to put them away?

Gov.: But suppose that a hundred men come unto you to be instructed, will you forbear to instruct them?

Mrs. H.: As far as I conceive, I cross a rule in it.

Gov.: Very well and do you not so here?

Mrs. H.: No, sir, for my ground is they are men.

Gov.: Men and women is all one for that, but suppose that a man should come and say "Mrs. Hutchinson, I hear that you are a woman that God hath given his grace unto and you have knowledge in the word of God, I pray instruct me a little," ought you not to instruct this man?

Mrs. H.: I think I may. Do you think it not lawful for me to teach women, and why do you call me to teach the court?

MARY DYER IS MARTYRED

↦↤

George Bishop, *New England Judged by the Spirit of the Lord* (Philadelphia: T. W. Stuckey, 1885), pp. 98–103.

Massachusetts did not welcome dissenters of any stripe, but it dealt particularly harshly with Quakers. In part, this was because Quaker proselytizers were so persistent. Despite beatings and imprisonment, the same women and men frequently returned to the Bay Colony to preach a faith that orthodox Puritans considered too egalitarian with regard to both the promise of salvation in the next life and the rejection of social hierarchy in this one. When Quaker activist Mary Dyer returned to Boston after having been banished by the Bay Colony officials, the frustrated government ordered her hanged. But as Quaker commentator George Bishop recounts, Dyer was reprieved moments after the noose was tightened around her neck.

～

Not long after, viz., the 8th of the Eighth month following [1659], Mary Dyer, whom you had banished upon pain of death, and Hope Clifton, both of Rhode Island, came to Boston, on the first day of the week, to visit Christopher Holder [another Quaker], who was then in prison. On the next morning after they came in, they were espied, and carried by the constable to the House of Correction; who, after your worship was ended, came again, and charged the keeper, "body for body, life for life," with Mary Dyer, till further order. So Mary was continued without being sent for, but Hope Clifton was had before your deputy-governor the next morning, who recommitted her, and one Mary Scott, a daughter of R. and C. Scott, of Providence, aforesaid.

And now the time of the sitting of your Court drawing near, wherein you acted this bloody tragedy, W. Robinson and M. Stevenson, came to Boston, viz., on the 13th day of the Eighth month, and with them Alice Cowland, who came to bring linen wherein to wrap the dead bodies of those who were to suffer, and Daniel Gould, from Salem, William King, Hannah Phelps, the wife of Nicholas Phelps aforesaid, and Mary Trask and Margaret Smith, of the same town—all these, as one, came together in the moving and power of the Lord, to look your bloody laws in the face, and to accompany those who should suffer by them.

So your prisons began to fill, and on the 19th of the same month, W. Robinson, M. Stevenson, and Mary Dyer were had before your Court, and demanded of by you, "Why they came again into your jurisdiction, being banished upon pain of death?" To which having severely answered, and declared that the ground or cause of their coming was of the Lord, and in obedience to Him, your governor said, "That he desireth not their death," and "that they had liberty to speak for themselves, why they should not be proceeded with, as to the giving of sentence against them"; yet he bid the jailer take them away.

The next day after your worship was ended, being heated by your priest and prepared to shed the blood of the innocent, you sent for them again, and your governor, speaking faintly, as a man whose life was departing from him, for the hand of the Lord was upon him, said to this effect, "We have made many laws, and endeavoured by several ways to keep you from us; and neither whipping, nor imprisonment, nor cutting off ears, nor banishment upon pain of death, will keep you from among us." And he said, "I desire not your death"; yet presently he said, "You shall be had back to the place from whence you came, and from thence to the place of execution, to be hanged on the gallows till you are dead."

And, on the 27th of the Eighth month aforesaid, ye caused the drums to beat, to gather your soldiers together for the execution; and after your worship was ended, your drums beat again, and your captain, James Oliver, came with his band of men, and the Marshal and some others, to the prison, and the doors were opened. And your Marshal and jailer called for W. Robinson and M. Stevenson, and had them out of the prison, and Mary Dyer out of the House of Correction, who parted from their friends in prison full of the joy of the Lord, who had counted them worthy to suffer for His name, and had kept them faithful unto death. And having embraced each other, with fervency of love and gladness of heart, and peace with God and praises to the Lord, they went out of your prisons, like innocent lambs out of the butcher's cart, to the slaughter.

So being come to the place of execution hand in hand, as to a wedding-day, all three of them with great cheerfulness of heart, and having taken leave of each other with the dear embraces of one another in the love of the Lord, your executioner put W. Robinson to death, and after him M. Stevenson, who died, both of them, full of the joy of the Lord.

But as for Mary Dyer, after she had parted joyfully from her friends at the foot of the ladder, expecting to die, and seeing her two friends hanging dead before her, her arms and legs tied, the halter about her neck, and her face covered with a handkerchief which your priest Wilson lent the hangman, and was with the Lord in joy and peace, an order came for her reprieve, upon the petition of her son, and unknown to her; which being read, and the halter loosened and taken off her neck, she was desired to come down. Some came presently and took her in their arms, and sat her on horseback, and conveyed her fifteen miles toward Rhode Island, and then left her with a horse and man, to be conveyed further.

THE EXCOMMUNICATION OF MRS. ANNE HIBBEN

↔↔

The Records of the First Church in Boston (Boston: Colonial Society of Massachusetts, 1961), vol. 39, pp. 31–33.

Religious heresy was not the only grounds on which women could be excommunicated from the Puritan Congregationalist church. In the wake of Anne Hutchinson's trial, Massachusetts officials came to believe defiant, aggressive—in short, unfeminine— behavior should also be punished by church authorities. Mrs. Anne Hibben's confrontation with the First Church in Boston began when she persisted in accusing her neighbors of overcharging for carpentry performed on her husband's house, an accusation the church leaders considered unfounded. Not only did Hibben continue to complain, she also refused to acknowledge her "mistake" and openly criticized the church for reprimanding her. Her social behavior, not her religious beliefs, led the church to excommunicate her in 1640.

⁀

The 20th Day of the 7th Moneth 1640.

Mrs. Anne Hibbon our sister was by our pastor with the Consent of the Church, In the Name of the Lord Admonisht of her uncharitable Jealousies and Suspicions without sufficient Cause against sundry of the brethren that are joyners and other Neighbors of the same Calling as if they were of a Combination extortionously to sett high rates upon their worke, and for her obstinately persisting therein and impenitently against all the menes that were taken for her satisfying therein and also for many other disorderly things that passed from her Carryage therein. . . .

The 30th Day of the 12th Moneth 1640. . . .

Mrs Anne Hibbon our sister was by our paster, with the Consent of the Church, Excommunicated out of the Church, for her Irregular dealing with our brother John Davisse, in not Admonishing him according to Rule, for what she conceived to be a heynous sinne in him; and also for her Causeless unchartable Jelousies and suspicions against him and sundry of the brethren that are joyners, and other neighbors of the same Calling as if they were of a Combination, extortionously to sett high Rates upon their worke, and that against their Conscience they had over-valued some worke wrought in her husbands house by one John Crabtree a joyner; whereas the brethren did solemnly in the face of the Church take God to witnesse, that they did nothing therein against their Conscience, but according to the light thereof; Neverthelesse she persisted in her obstinate Judgeing and Condemning of them, leaving it to the Lord to bring out the Trueth of it. And like wise for sundry Untrueths openly proved by sundry of the brethren against her whereof, though she was Convinced, yet she made not any humble and penitentiall acknowledgement thereof; Moreover for the causeless Condemning of the Churches Censure of Admonition upon her to bee unjust, although she was privately admonished thereof by sundry of the brethren and sisters in private, noe nor yet to the whole Church in Publique.

The Wife of Henry Batchiler Stands Accused

⇥ ⇤

Ipswich Quarterly Court, March 1667, *Records and Files of the Quarterly Courts
of Essex County, Massachusetts. Vol. 3, 1662–1667* (Salem, Mass.: Essex
Institute, 1913), pp. 403–404.

*Seventeenth-century colonists considered witchcraft a plausible explanation for nu-
merous phenomena, including natural disasters, the sudden death of livestock, and
even a run of personal bad luck. While men could be accused of practicing the black
arts, women—especially the elderly, the poor, the solitary, and those with a reputation
for antisocial behavior—were considered more likely suspects when cattle died or
children grew ill. Midwives, who often entered homes to care for ailing mothers or
their infants, were susceptible to blame if their patients did not recover. The power to
heal, it seems, suggested the power to harm. In the case below, the wife of Henry
Batchiler stood accused because of the strange influence witnesses claimed she had on
animals.*

Joseph Medcalfe deposed, 30 : 1 : 1654, concerning the wife of Henry
Batchiler, that he met her near his farm, holding up her coats in an unseemly
manner, some pigs following her. She said she did not know whose they
were. A boy of Goodman Symonds also told him that he saw her upon a
Lord's day in his master's lot, etc.

James How, Thomas Medcalfe and Francis Bates deposed that Goodwife
Batchiler had several times said that some of Goodman Medcalf's and Goodman Howes' cattle would die, some would escape and others would live, and
it came to pass as she said, although they all seemed well when she told
it. . . .

James How, John Perly and John How and his wife deposed that during
the same summer the herd of cattle that Goodman How kept were exceedingly troublesome and acted in a strange and hideous manner several times,
as on a Lord's day morning "all the whole heard Brake out of a fenced yeard
and rann with such violence that it amazed all that looked out after them
makeing a hideous noyse lyke thunder with ratling of cheines to theyr seem-
ing but could p noe meanes be stopped." Also when they were counted there
would always be one over. Further Goodman Batchiler went to Goodman
How to borrow some draught cattle, but his wife said she was unwilling to
do so because she feared there was some evil practice in it. While they were
talking Goodwife Batchiler appeared and asked them why they were speak-

ing of her and seemed very angry, all of which made them marvel. James How, going to Rowley to load hay, put on half a load, with six bullocks to haul it, but coming home the cattle acted strangely, lying down often and at length would not draw the empty cart, etc.

GOODWIFE COREY DENIES ALL CHARGES

⇥ ⇤

Deodat Lawson, comp., *A Brief and True Narrative of some Remarkable Passages Relating to sundry Persons Afflicted by Witchcraft, at Salem Village, Which happened from the Nineteenth of March, to the Fifth of April, 1692* (Boston: Benjamin Harris, 1692), quoted in George Lincoln Burr, ed., *Narratives of the Witchcraft Cases, 1648–1706* (New York: Barnes and Noble, 1914), pp. 152–161.

The Salem witch-hunt of 1692 is the most famous episode of witchcraft accusations in American history. During six short months, more than 150 women, men, and children were arrested, most of them jailed, and many were tried, convicted, and executed. These events have been dramatized by playwrights and poets; the records of the trials and eyewitness accounts have been published and numerous scholarly and popular books written on the subject. Contemporary accounts like that by the Reverend Deodat Lawson, excerpted below, have proved to be remarkable sources for women's history. In them females, both accusers and accused, speak directly to the authorities and at the same time to their families, neighbors, and friends.

↜↝

On the nineteenth day of March last [1692], I went to Salem Village and lodged at Nathaniel Ingersol's near to the Minister Mr. P's [Parris's] house, and presently after I came into my lodging, Capt. Walcut's daughter Mary came to Lieut. Ingersol's and spake to me, but, suddenly after as she stood by the door, was bitten, so that she cried out of her Wrist, and looking on it with a Candle, we saw apparently the marks of Teeth both upper and lower set, on each side of her wrist.

In the beginning of the Evening, I went to give Mr. P. a visit. When I was there, his Kinswoman Abigail Williams (about 12 years of age) had a grievous fit; she was at first hurried with Violence to and fro in the room (though Mrs. Ingersol endeavoured to hold her) sometimes making as if she would fly, stretching up her arms as high as she could, and crying "Whish, Whish, Whish!" several times. Presently after she said there was Goodwife N. [Nurse] and said, "Do you not see her? Why there she stands!" And the said Goodw. N. offered her The Book but she was resolved she would not take it, saying often, "I won't, I won't, I won't take it, I do not know what Book it is. I am sure it is none of God's Book, it is the Divil's Book, for ought I know." After that she run to the Fire, and begun to throw Fire Brands about the house; and run against the Back, as if she would run up Chimney, and as they said, she had attempted to go into the Fire in other Fits.

On Lord's Day, the twentieth of March, there were sundry of the afflicted Persons at Meeting, as Mrs. Pope, and Goodwife Bibber, Abigail Williams, Mary Walcut, Mary Lewes, and Doctor Grigg's Maid. There was also at Meeting Goodwife C. [Corey] (who was afterward Examined on suspicion of being a Witch). They had several Sore Fits, in the time of Public Worship, which did something interrupt me in my First Prayer, being so unusual. . . .

In Sermon time when Goodw. C. was present in the Meetinghouse, Ab. W. called out, "Look where Goodw. C. sits on the Beam suckling her Yellow Bird betwixt her fingers!" Anne Putnam, another girl afflicted, said there was a Yellow-bird sat on my hat as it hung on the Pin in the Pulpit. But those that were by, restrained her from speaking loud about it.

On Monday, the 21st of March, the Magistrates of Salem appointed to come to Examination of Goodw. C. The worshipful Mr. Hathorne asked her, Why she afflicted those Children? She said, she did not Afflict them. He asked her, who did then? She said, "I do not know. How should I know?" The number of the afflicted persons were about that time Ten, viz. four married women, Mrs. Pope, Mrs. Putnam, Goodw. Bibber, and an ancient woman, named Goodall, three Maids, Mary Walcut, Mary Lewes at Thomas Putnam's, and a maid at Dr. Grigg's. There were three girls from 9 to 12 years of age, each of them, or thereabouts, viz. Elizabeth Parris, Abigail Williams and Ann Putnam. There were most of them at G.C.'s [Corey's] Examination, and did vehemently accuse her in the Assembly of afflicting them, by biting, pinching, strangling, etc. . . . [Corey] being asked about it, if she had any Familiar Spirit, that attended her, she said, she had no Familiarity with any such thing. She was a Gospel Woman, which Title she called herself by; and the Afflicted Persons told her, ah! She was a Gospel Witch. Ann Putnam did there affirm, that one day when Lieutenant Fuller was at Prayer at her Father's House, she saw the shape of Goodw. C. and she thought Goodw. N. praying at the same time to the Devil. She was not sure it was Goodw. N., she thought it was, but very sure she saw the Shape of G.C. The said C. said they were poor, distracted children, and no heed to be given to what they said. Mr. Hathorne and Mr. Noyes replied, it was the judgment of all that were present, they were Bewitched, and only she, the Accused Person said, they were Distracted. . . .

She was required by the Magistrates to answer that Question in the Catechism, "How many persons be there in the God-Head?" she answered it but oddly, yet was there no great thing to be gathered from it: she denied all that was charged upon her and said, They could not prove a Witch; she was that Afternoon Committed to Salem-Prison; and after she was in Custody, she did not so appear to them, and afflict them as before.

FRIGHTENED INTO FALSE CONFESSIONS
↔↔

"Recantation of Confessors of Witchcraft," *Collections of the Massachusetts Historical Society*, 2d ser., 3 (1815), pp. 221–225.

In the aftermath of the Salem witch-hunts, several ministers and judges publicly apologized for the roles they had played in the affair. Many of the accused also spoke out, publicly recanting their confessions of guilt. In the examples below, five women tell how pressures from family and authorities drove them to admit to crimes they had not committed and, worse, to doubt their own innocence for a time.

↜↝

Salem, Oct. 19, '92. The Rev. Mr. I. Mather went to Salem [to visit] the confessours (so called): He conferred with several of them, and they spake as follows:

Mrs. Osgood freely and relentingly said, that the confession which she made upon her examination for witchcraft, and afterwards acknowledged before the honourable judges, was wholly false, and that she was brought to the said confession by the violent urging and unreasonable pressings that were used toward her; she asserted that she never signed to the devill's book, was never baptised by the devill, never afflicted any of the accusers, or gave her consent for their being afflicted. Being asked, why she prefixed a time and spake of her being baptised, &c,: about *twelve years* since; she replyed, and said, that when she had owned the thing, they asked the time; to which she answered, that she knew not the time; but being told that she did know the time and must tell the time, and the like; she considered that about twelve years before (when she had her last child) she had a fitt of sicknesse, and was melancholy; and so thought that that time might be as proper a time to mention as any, and accordingly did prefix the said time.

Being asked about the cat, in the shape of which she had confessed the devill appeared to her, &c.; she replyed, that being told that the devill had appeared to her, and must needs appear to her, &c.; (she being a witch) she at length did own that the devill had apeared to her; and being press'd to say in what creature's shape he appeared in, she at length did say, that it was in the shape of a cat; remembering that some time before her being apprehended, as she went out at her door, she saw a cat, &c.: not as though she any whitt suspected the said cat to be the devill in the day of ——— but because some creature she must mention, and this came thus into her mind at that time.

Deacon Fry's wife said, that the confession she made she was frightened into, and that it was all of it false.

Mrs. Dean and Goodwife Barker said freely, that they had wronged the truth in making their confession; that they in their lives time never covenanted with the devill, or had seen him; that they were press'd, and urg'd, and afrighted; that at last they did say even any thing that was desired of them; they said that they were sensible of their great evil in giving way at last to own what was false, and spake all with such weeping, relenting, and bleeding, as was enough to affect the hardest heart; particularly G. Barker bewail'd and lamented her accusing of others, whom she never knew any evil by in her life time; and said that she was told by her examiners that she *did* know of their being witches and *must* confesse it; that she did know of their being baptised, &c.: and must confesse it; by the renewed urgings and chargings of whom at last she gave way, and owned such things as were utterly false, which now she was in great horrour and anguish of soul for her complying with.

Goodwife Tyler did say, that when she was first apprehended, she had no fears upon her, and did think that nothing could have made her confesse against herself; but since, she had found to her great grief, that she had wronged the truth, and falsely accused herself: she said, that when she was brought to Salem, her brother Bridges rode with her, and that all along the way from Andover to Salem, her brother kept telling her that she must needs be a witch, since the afflicted accused her, and at her touch were raised out of their fitts, and urging her to confess herself a witch; she as constantly told him, that she was no witch, that she knew nothing of witchcraft, and begg'd of him not to urge her to confesse; however when she came to Salem, she was carried to a room, where her brother on one side and Mr. John Emerson on the other side did tell her that she was certainly a witch, and that she saw the devil before her eyes at that time (and accordingly the said Emerson would attempt with his hand to beat him away from her eyes) and they so urged her to confesse, that she wished herself in any dungeon, rather than be so treated: Mr. Emerson told her once and again, Well! I see you will not confesse! Well! I will now leave you, and then you are undone, body and soul forever: Her brother urged her to confesse, and told her that in so doing she could not lye; to which she answered, Good brother, do not say so, for I shall lye if I confesse, and then who shall answer unto God for my lye? He still asserted it, and said that God would not suffer so many good men to be in such an errour about it, and that she would be hang'd, if she did not confesse, and continued so long and so violently to urge and presse her to confesse, that she thought verily her life would have gone from her, and became so terrified in her mind, that she own'd at length almost any thing that they propounded to her; but she had wronged her conscience in so doing, she was guilty of a great sin in belying of herself, and desired to mourn for it as long as she lived: This she said and a great deal more of the like nature, and all of it with such affection, sorrow, relenting, grief, and mourning, as that it exceeds any pen for to describe and expresse the same.

SARAH FISKE ACKNOWLEDGES HER ERRORS

↦ ↤

Sarah Fiske's conversion, from *The Notebook of the Reverend John Fiske,*
1644–1675 (Boston: Colonial Society of Massachusetts, 1974), pp. 33–47.

In order to gain admission to a seventeenth-century New England Congregational church, a prospective member had to testify to a transforming religious experience. Doubts about the validity of Sarah Fiske's conversion experience seemed to hinge on her failure to be a dutiful wife and her refusal to humbly accept the church's reproof. When Fiske showed herself properly repentant for both misdeeds, she was allowed to detail her conversion experience—which was typical in its progression from awareness of sin and damnation to a search for assurances from God, to self-loathing, to humility, and to reassurances and awareness of salvation.

↜↝

14 of 12t, [16]44. The case of the wife of Brother Phineas Fiske considered and reduced to two heads: whether any had caught against her conversation (private offenses excepted); who had caught for her. Two things were objected against her: her carriage towards her husband in accounting him an enemy and exclaiming against him commonly and saying he loved another woman better than his wife &c., and her miscarriage one Lord's day presently after a prayer and ordinance to challenge Sister White for a debt, which it was determined she should acknowledge in the public congregation.

Which, if she would promise to do and appear in some measure affected with and to speak to satisfaction to the brethren employed to acquaint her with the church's mind, the church determined to proceed no further with her. The brethren appointed by the church to show her the church's mind, and some days after she had duly considered of it to receive her answer, were Brother Read and Brother Geere.

20 of 3d. [16]45   At a church meeting the wife of Brother Phineas Fiske her case spoken to. The letter from Watertown was judged to clear our brother from the imputation cast on him by his wife. Concluded touching her that she should appear convinced of the evil of her accusations against her husband before we proceeded further with her. . . . And the evil that she is to be convinced of is especially, publishing what she should have concealed (had this been true) to the defaming of her husband. The evil from the mind of it. First, that twas done in way of extenuating her own evil. Secondly, that she said she was provoked to it. Thirdly, that she said there were some of the church that were not dealt with withall (which was conceived meant her husband). Fourthly, that he was the cause or occasion of her trouble. And fifthly, that she still justifies herself and these and such like. Considering her relation was an aggravation of her sin.

18th of 10t. 1645.   A church meeting. [Sarah Fiske] hoped to speak to satisfy the church. . . . And after she acknowledged she did evil in these particulars whereas she should have kept secret and as the duty of a wife . . . [and] It was asked her how she thought of the proceedings of the church toward her; she justified the church and acknowledged their faithfulness toward her and blesses God for it. So is the issue tending to put things to an end and to settle, if possible, a sweet accord betwixt [husband and wife]. It was asked of our brother whether he was satisfied in her acknowledgment and could pass by any offenses given on her part toward him. He answered affirmatively. It was then asked of him if he could find in his heart to desire of her to pass by his failing toward her. He answered affirmatively. Then the same things were likewise put unto her. She answered to both affirmatively. So it was agreed that we should proceed to propound her publicly for a church member. . . .

QUESTION: whether the wife of our Brother Phineas Fiske, having made her confession of these failings towards her husband in this church meeting, she should also acknowledge them in public. RESOLVED: she ought and should. . . .

30 of 11th. 1645.   At a church meeting. The wife of our Brother Phineas

Fiske called forth to declare to the church how God hath gone along with her in bringing her soul to Christ.

When she was a servant 22 years old, by Mr. Davis she heard there everyone gives account at the Day of Judgment for every work done in the flesh. She came to give account and said that she was guilty of two sins. . . . Then she prayed to God to show what sin was and whether the Lord spoke to her. To that answer that in John 3, the wind bloweth where it listeth &c. And if an answer to her that in Rev. 3, I counsel you to buy of me gold &c. She met with that and at once she came to see thence her one hope . . . but doubtful what effect on her. In that John 7, those that come to me I cast not away, and whereas she found that the Lord rejects not me &c. To that these words, none shall pluck them out of my hands.

. . . she saw that she is in a worse condition than any toad &c. Soon after the Lord spake to her (as twere a voice). Yet oftentimes she not resting content, but must look to God so she sought a place to pray and went trembling. And God gave her then a heart not to be satisfied till the Lord gave her some answer and given some assurance of His love in Christ. How she came out and He showed that nothing could help her but her hold of Christ and that if she has sins of 1000 worlds that was sufficient for her. And then she sought for a need of assurance and to that answered that in Rom. 8, shall I not with Him give all things. Yet she was not satisfied, but as Jacob wrestled . . . of Jacob to wrestle. And then Rom. 8, neither height nor depth, things present &c., and upon that went forth rejoicing and praising God, desiring the Lord to go on further with her. . . .

QUESTION: What evidence was there of God all this while for that time hitherto? ANSWER: She had a desire still continued to enjoy it, and she presumed she desired it the more. Whereupon she examined herself and found that it rested with God thus she had walked so unevenly. . . . And it came to her mind she. . . . and she found many temptations and trials, but could not be satisfied without them.

QUESTION: Hath the Lord helped you to see any such failings as whereby you justly may be hindered? ANSWER: She would set down if hindered.

QUESTION: But the Lord might be provoked and have occasion to glorify moreover in the knowledge of them. ANSWER: The Lord help you to see this failing. . . .

QUESTION: How came she to believe? ANSWER: By that first scripture &c.

QUESTION: But how came God your soul to rest upon? ANSWER: John 10, he that come to me I will in no wise cast off &c.

OBJECTION: But this scripture in order was alleged as a stay only and before the legal work was off. ANSWER: It was intended as that scripture and so that Matt. 11:28.

It was asked here if more had aught further to query or object. It was requested that testimony should be given of a life suitable to this profession and confession. Her brother G. testified to this effect that for the time he had observed her he had observed nothing, but human frailties, excepted, but what stayed with her profession and confession. This heard the second time: he stood to it. Then I replied I was condemned that twas an occasion of keeping her out hitherto for their offenses, which if but human frailties then I have done very evil in it. So her husband testified to the work his persuasion. Hereupon it was voted she should upon the Lord's day next make a public acknowledgment of her miscarriages particularly. It was moved that she show her assent to the church confession of faith. . . .

5 of 12t. 1645 . . . In the close of the day Brother Phineas Fiske's wife called and made her confession, particularly of the evil by her speeches of her husband and against the church and pastor. It was voted satisfactorily. . . . The covenant was administered to the wife of our Brother Phineas Fiske.

A WOMAN SPEAKS FROM THE GALLOWS
↔ ↔

"The Declaration, Dying Warning, and Advice of Rebekah Chamblit"
(Boston, 1733).

Eighteenth-century newspapers frequently carried the dying words of people about to face execution for a capital offense. In the following statement, a young woman convicted of infanticide sends out a warning, particularly to members of her own sex, against participating in "unclean" acts, that is, premarital sex. She also urges young people to be steadfast in their religious faith and in their attendance at church because her own descent into sinfulness came when her devotion faltered.

↪↩

. . . Being under the awful Apprehensions of my Execution now in a few Hours; and being desirous to do all the Good I can, before I enter the Eternal World, I now in the fear of God, give this Declaration and Warning to the Living.

I was very tenderly brought up, and well Instructed in my Father's House, till I was Twelve Years of Age; but alass, my Childhood wore off in vanity. However, as I grew in Years, my Youth was under very sensible Impressions from the Spirit of God; and I was awakened to seek and obtain Baptism, when I was about Sixteen Years of Age; and lived for some time with a strictness somewhat answerable to the Obligations I was thereby brought under. But within two or three Years after this, I was led away into the Sin of Uncleanness, from which time I think I may date my Ruin for this World. After this, I became again more watchful, and for several Years kept my self from the like Pollutions, until those for which I am now to suffer.

And as it may be necessary, so doubtless it will be expected of me, that I give the World a particular account of that great Sin, with the aggravations of it, which has brought me to this Shameful Death: And accordingly in the fear of God, at whose awful Tribunal I am immediately to appear, I solemnly declare as follows;

That on Saturday the Fifth Day of May 1st, being then something more than Eight Months gone with Child, I was about my Household Business reaching some Sand from out of a large Cask, I received considerable hurt, which put me into great Pain, and so I continued till the Tuesday following; in all which time I am not sensible I felt any Life or Motion in the Child within me; when, on the said Tuesday the Eighth Day of May, I was Deliver'd when alone of a Male Infant; in whom I did not perceive life; but still uncertain of Life in it, I threw it into the Vault about two or three Minutes after it was born; uncertain, I say, whether it was a living or dead Child; tho', I confess it's probable there was Life in it, and some Circumstances seem to confirm it. I therefore own the Justice of God and Man in my Condemnation, and take Shame to my self, as I have none but my self to Blame; and am sorry for any rash Expressions I have at any time uttered since my Condemnation; and I am verily perswaded there is no Place in the World, where there is a more strict regard to Justice than in this Province.

And now as a Soul going into Eternity, I most earnestly and solemnly Warn all Persons, particularly YOUNG PEOPLE, and more especially those of my own Sex, against the Sins which their Age peculiarly exposes them to; and as the Sin of Uncleanness has brought me into these distressing Circumstances, I would with the greatest Importunity Caution and Warn against it, being perswaded of the abounding of that Sin in this Town and Land. I thought my self as secure, a little more than a Year ago, as many of you now do; but by woful Experience I have found, that Lust when it has conceived bringeth forth Sin, and Sin when it is finished bringeth forth Death; it exposes the Soul not only to Temporal, but to Eternal Death. And therefore as a Dying Person, let me call upon you to forsake the foolish and live: Do not accompany with those you know to be such, and if Sinners entice you do not consent. I am sensible there are many Houses in this Town, that may be called Houses of Uncleanness, and Places of Dreadful Temptations to this and all other Sins. O Shun them, for they lead down to the Chambers of Death and Eternal Misery.

My mispence of precious Sabbaths, lies as a heavy burden upon me; that when I might have gone to the House of GOD, I have been indifferent, and suffer'd a small matter to keep me from it. What would I now give, had I better improv'd the Lord's Day! I tell you, verily, your lost Sabbaths will sit heavy upon you, when you come into the near prospect of Death and Eternity.

The Sin of Lying I have to bewail, and wou'd earnestly caution against; not that I have took so great a pleasure in Lying; but I have often done so to conceal my Sin: Certainly you had better suffer Shame and Disgrace, yea the greatest Punishment, than to hide and conceal your Sin, by Lying. How much better had it been for me, to have confess'd my Sin, than by hiding of it provoke a holy GOD, thus to suffer it to find me out. But I hope I heartily desire to bless GOD, that even in this way, He is thus entring into Judgment with me; for I have often thought, had I been let alone to go on undiscovered in my Sins, I might have provok'd Him to leave me to a course of Rebellion, that would have ripen'd me for a more sudden, and everlasting Destruction; and am fully convinc'd of this, that I should have had no solid ease or quiet in my mind, but the Guilt of this undiscover'd Sin lying upon my Conscience, would have been a tormenting Rack unto me all my Days; whereas now I hope GOD has discover'd to me in some measure the evil of this, and all my other Sins, enabled me to repent of them in Dust and Ashes; and made me earnestly desire and plead with Him for pardon and cleansing in the precious Blood of the REDEEMER of lost and perishing Sinner: And I think I can say, I have had more comfort and satisfaction within the Walls of this Prison, than ever I had in the ways of Sin among my vain Companions, and think I wou'd not for a World, nay for ten Thousand Worlds have my liberty in Sin again, and be in the Same Condition I was in before I came into this Place.

I had the advantage of living in several religious Families; but alass, I disregarded the Instructions and Warnings I there had, which is now a bitterness to me; and so it will be to those of you who are thus favoured, but go on unmindful of GOD, and deaf to all the Reproofs and Admonitions that are given you for the good of your Souls. And I would advise those of my own

Sex especially, to chuse to go into religious Families, where the Worship and Fear of GOD is maintained, and submit your selves to the Orders and Government of them.

In my younger Years I maintain'd a constant course of Secret Prayer for some time; but afterwards neglecting the same, I found by experience, that upon my thus leaving GOD, He was provoked to forsake me, and at length suffer'd me to fall into that great and complicated Sin that has brought me to this Death: Mind me, I first left GOD, and then He left me: I therefore solemnly call upon YOUNG PEOPLE to cherish the Convictions of God's Holy SPIRIT, and be sure keep up a constant course of fervent Secret prayer.

And now I am just entering into the External World, I do in the fear of GOD, and before Witnesses, call upon our YOUNG PEOPLE in particular, to se-cure an Interest in the Lord JESUS CHRIST, and in those precious Benefits He has purchased for His People; for surely the favour of GOD, thro' CHRIST, is more worth than a whole World: And O what Comfort will this yield you when you come to that awful Day and Hour I am now arriving unto. I must tell you the World appears to me vain and empty, nothing like what it did in my past Life, my Days of Sin and Vanity, and as doubtless it appears now to you. Will you be perswaded by me to that which will yield you the best Satisfaction and Pleasure here, and which will prepare you for the more abundant Pleasures of GOD's Right Hand for evermore.

> Sign'd and Acknowledg'd in the Presence of divers Witnesses, with a desire that it may be publish'd to the World, and read at the Place of Execution.
>
> SEPTEMBER 26TH
> Rebekah Chamblit.

A Slave Is Thankful for Christian Instruction

↦ ↤

Phillis Wheatley, "On Being Brought from Africa," 1773, in Margaretha M. Odell, ed., *Memoirs and Poems of Phillis Wheatley, A Native African and a Slave* (Boston: Isaac Knapp, 1838), p. 48.

Written sources by colonial African American women on any topic are rare, and religion is no exception. One of the few documents expressing an African American woman's religious beliefs comes from the poet Phillis Wheatley, who was brought to America as a slave at the age of seven. While Wheatley condemned slavery and wrote of the universal desire for liberty, she did not regret all aspects of her acculturation into white society. In this poem, she gives thanks for her conversion to a faith that promised salvation to people of all races.

✛

T'was mercy brought me from my pagan land
Taught my benighted soul to understand
That there's a God, that there's a Saviour too:
Once I redemption neither sought nor knew,
Some view our sable race with scornful eye,
"Their colour is a diabolic die."
Remember, Christians, Negroes, black as Cain,
May be refin'd and join the angelic train.

"AND HE MAKES NO DIFFERENCE IN THE SEED"

⇥⇤

Milton D. Speizman and Jane C. Kronick, eds., "A Seventeenth-Century Quaker Women's Declaration," *Signs: Journal of Women in Culture and Society* 1, no. 1 (1975), pp. 231–245.

The Quakers were notable, or notorious, for the prominent role women played in both their theology and their church organization. The following letter, from an established English Quaker women's meeting to fledgling meetings in the colonies, is a remarkable testament to Quaker women's belief in the spiritual equality of the sexes and their shared responsibility for sustaining the religious culture and community.

✛

From our Country Women's meeting in Lancashire to be Dispersed abroad, among the Women's meetings every where.
Dear Sisters,
In the blessed unity in the Spirit of grace our Souls Salute you who are sanctified in Christ Jesus, and called to be Saints. . . . To you that are of the true seed of the promise of God in the beginning, that was to bruise the Serpent's head, and which is fulfilled in Christ Jesus of which we are made partakers, which is the seed the promise is to; which the Apostle spoke of and said, God sent forth his Son made of a woman, made under the Law to redeem . . . To you all every where, where this may come, is this written. . . .
. . . And that every particular of us, may be ready, and willing to answer what the lord requires of us; in our several places and conditions . . . for we are all the children of God by faith in Christ Jesus, where there is neither

male nor female &c. but we are all one in Christ Jesus . . . So here is the blessed Image of the living God, restored againe, in which he made them male and female in the beginning: and in this his own Image God blessed them both, and said unto them increase and multiply, and replenish the earth, and subdue it, and have dominion over . . . the earth . . . And in this dominion and power, the lord God is establishing his own seed, in the male and female, over the head of the serpent, and over his seed, and power. And he makes no difference in the seed, between the male and the female. . . .

Soe all Dear friends and sisters, make full proofe of the gift of God that is in you, and neglect it not, in this your day, and generation; but that you may be helps meet, in the Restoration, and Resurrection of the body of Christ, which is his Church, and that every one may know their place and calling therein as the Godly women under the law did for all who were wise in heart, put their hands to the worke, about the tabernacle, and all the women whose hearts stirred them up in wisdome, had their several places to work in about the tabernacle as well as the men, for all the Congregation of the children of Israell every one both men and women whose spirits was made willing, they brought the Lords offering to the works of the tabernacle: as you may see. Exod: 35.25–26.

. . . And let us therefore . . . meet together, and keep our womens meetings, in the name and power, and fear of the lord Jesus, whose servants and handmaids we are, and in the good order of the Gospel meet.

1st   And first, for the women of every . . . monthly meeting, where the mens monthly meetings is established, let the women likewise of every monthly meeting, meet together to wait upon the lord. . . .

2ly   . . . If there be any that walks disorderly, as doth not become the Gospell, or lightly, or want only, or that is not of a good reporte: Then send to them, as you are ordered by the power of God in the meeting . . . to Admonish, and exhort them, and to bring them to Judge, and Condemn, what hath been by them done or acted contrary to the truth.

3ly   And if any transgression or Action that hath been done amongst women or maids, that hath been more publick, and that hath gott into the world, or that hath been a publick offence among friends; then let them bring in a paper of condemnation, to be published as far, as the offence hath gone, and then to be recorded in a booke.

4ly   And if there be any that goes out to Marry, with priests, or joineth in Marriage with the world, and does not obey the order of the Gospel as it is established amongst friends. then for the womens monthly meeting to send to them, to reprove them, and to bear their testimony against their acting Contrary to the truth, and if they come to repentance, and sorrow for their offence, and have a desire to come amongst friends again: before they can be received, they must bring in a paper of Condemnation, and repentance, and Judgment of their Action; which must be recorded in Friends Booke: And also to carry that paper to the priest, that married them, and Judge, and Condemn, and deny that Action, before him or any of the world before whome it shall come.

And dear sisters it is duely Incumbent upon us to look into our families, and to prevent our Children of running into the world for husbands, or for wives, and so to the priests: for you know before the womens meetings were set up, Many have done so, which brought dishonour, both to God, and upon his truth and people. . . .

5ly And also all friends that keeps in the power of God, and in faithfull obedience to the truth, that according to the order of the Gospell that is established, that they bring their Marriages twice to the womens meetings, and twice to the mens: the first time they are to come to the womens meetings that the women of the meeting, do examin both the man and the woman, that they be cleare and free from all other persons, and that they have their parents, and friends and Relations, Consent; And that enquiry be made of their clearness in each particular meeting to which they do belong, before their next appearance in the womens meeting.

And if nothing be found, but that they come in clearness to the next monthly meeting, then they may proceed according to the order of the Gospell, and perfect their marriage in the meeting of friends, as friends which they belong to sees it Convenient: But if any thing be found that they are not clear, but that others lay Challenge, or Charge to them, either by promise or otherwise that then they do not proceed, till they have given satisfaction both to the parties, and friends, concerning that matter, according to the order of the Gospell; and that if any thing be amiss concerning the woman, examin it, and look into it, which may not be proper for the men.

6ly And likewise, that the women of the monthly meetings, take care, and oversight of all the women that belongs to their several particular meetings, that they bring in their testimonies for the lord, and his truth, against tithes, and hireling priests once every yeare, Since the priests claimes, and challenges a tithe, which belongs to women to pay, as well as the men, not only for widdows, but them that have husbands, as piggs, and geese, henns and eggs, hemp and flax, wooll and lamb: all which women may have a hand in: Soe it concerns the womens meetings, to looke strictly to every particular meeting, that every woman bring in their testimony against tiths, and that those testimonies be recorded in the quarterly, or halfe yeares meeting book, once every year.

7ly   And at every monthly meeting, that they give timely notice, to every particular meeting, that they make ready their testimonies against tithes, be brought in at other Quarterly meetings, or half year as aforesaid. . . .

8ly   And also all friends, in their womens monthly, and particular Meetings, that they take special care for the poore, and for those that stands in need: that there be no want, nor suffering, for outward things, amongst the people of God, for the earth is the lords, and the fullness of it, and his people is his portion and the lot of his Inheritance, and he gives freely, and liberally, unto all, and upbraids none. . . .

And that all the sick, and weak, and Infirme, or Aged, and widdows, and fatherless, that they be looked after, and helped, and relieved, in every particular meeting, either with clothes, or maintenance, or what they stand in need off. So that in all things the Lord may be glorified, and honoured, so that there be no want, nor suffering in the house of God, who loves a Chearfull giver.

9ly   Also let Care be taken that every particular womens monthly meeting, have a booke to set down, and record their bussinesses and passages in, that is done or agreed upon, in every monthly meeting, or any service that any is to go upon, let the book be read, the next monthly meeting, and see that the business be performed, according to what was ordered.

And also that the collections be set downe, in the booke; and that the Receipts, and disbursments of every particular meeting, be set down in their booke, and read at their womens monthly meeting, that every particular meeting may see and know, how their collections is disbursed.

And that some faithfull honest woman, or women friends, that can Read, and write, keep the Book, and receive the Collections, and give a just and a true account, of the disbursments of them in the book, according as the meeting shall order, which must be Read every monthly meeting; And so give notice what is in stock; and when it is near out, to give notice that it may be supplyed.

10ly   And likewise that there be a general Book in every County, for their Quarterly, or half-years womens meetings . . . And that every Quarterly meeting, they call over every monthly, and particular meeting, to see if there be some of every meeting: and that they bring every particular womans testimony against tithes, from every particular meeting . . . And that all other businesses as is there presented, or that is done that day, may be recorded in that quarterly booke.

And so here in the power and spirit, of the Lord God, women comes to be coheires, and fellow labourers, in the Gospell, as it was in the Apostles dayes who entreated his true yoakfellow, to help those women that laboured with him in the Gospell, phill: 4.3. and also in his epistle to Timothy 5.3. he exhorted the elder women, that they should be as mothers, and the younger as sisters with all purity.

And in Titus: 2.3: the Aged women likewise that they be as becometh holiness, and teachers of good things; and that they teach the younger women to be sober, to love their husbands, to love their children, to be discreet, Chast, keepers at home, Good, Obedient to their own husbands; that the word of God be not Blasphemed.

So here was womens meetings, and womens teachings, of one another, so that this is no new thing, as some raw unseasoned spirits would seem to make it: So dear Sisters, in the everlasting truth, we conclude in the Apostles words, to his Brethren, in phill: 4.8.9. whatsoever things are just, whatsoever things are pure, whatsoever things are honest, whatsoever things are true, whatsoever things are lovely, whatsoever things are of good report; if there be any vertue, if there be any praise: think on these things, which yee have both learned, and received, and heard, and seen in me, and do them; and the God of peace shall be with you Amen.

And though wee be looked upon as the weaker vessels, yet strong and powerfull is God, whose strength is made perfect in weakness, he can make us good and bold, and valliant Souldiers of Jesus Christ, . . . and if he bring us unto his banquetting house, and spred his banner over us, which is love: there we can stand our ground, and fight our lords battel, boldly and valliantly. . . .

A WOMAN TAKES THE PULPIT

↬ ↫

Eunice Paine to Robert Treat Paine, Boston, July 21, 1769, in *Collections of the Massachusetts Historical Society* 88, pp. 447–448.

In 1769 Bostonians flocked to Faneuil Hall to witness a curious sight: a female Quaker preacher named Rachel Wilson. Clearly, religious tolerance had grown since the days of Mary Dyer's persecution and the condemnation of Anne Hutchinson for behavior unbefitting a woman. Nevertheless, Eunice Paine was astonished that a woman could keep her composure in so public a role, and several in the audience viewed Rachel Wilson as a humorous oddity.

⁂

Dear Brother

. . . Im very much fatigue'd having been to Faneuil Hall to hear the Female Quaker Preacher. 'Twas a very crouded assembly but Perfect order maintain'd. Everything was Novel to me—the approach of a woman into a Desk Dash'd me I cou'd hardly look up but I soon found She felt none of those perturbations from the Gaze of a Gaping multitude which I pity'd. Shes a Gracefull woman & has attain'd a very modest assurance. She spoke clear & Loud Eno' to be heard distinctly into the Entry. Her Language is very Polite & no doubt her mind is Zealously bent on doing good, her Exhortations to seek the Truth & Court that Light which Evidinceth the truth were Lenthy & towards the close workt up to Poesy & produced a tune Not unlike an anthem—her fluency gains the applause She receives for these, nothing like method, & many are her repetitions to my Ear tiresome. I learnt but one thing new which was an Exposition on the Parable of the woman who hid her Leaven in 3 measures of meal till the whole was Leavened this she says represent the Compound of man Soul, Body, and mind in which the spirit of God is hid & shou'd be kept Close, the man being inactive as meal till animated by the spirit as the meal with Leaven. After the Exhortation she rested, rose to Conclude with Prayer which was short & pertinent. She then thanked the Audience for their Decent atendance & reprove'd the Levity she observed in some few faces in a very Polite & kind manner & in the Apostles words Blessed the assembly & dismissd. us. A great Number of the Gentlemen of the town with their Ladys shook hands with her. Mr. Otis Desire'd the men to go out to Leave room for the women to retire Comfortably & that they would be orderly for the Honour of the town, twas done to his mind and Saving the Excessive heat of so crouded a place there was no inconvenience.

IF MAN IS SO MUCH SMARTER . . .?

↦ ↤

Judith Sargent Murray to her cousin Miss Goldthwait, June 6 1777, Judith Sargent Murray Papers, reel 1, vol. 1, Mississippi Department of History and Archives.

In the following letter, a prolific advocate of women's political and religious rights turns the issue of Eve's moral inferiority on its head by observing how easily Adam

157

was led astray. Murray's humor does not entirely hide her impatience with the custom-
ary appeal to Biblical authority in support of gender stereotypes.

~

Do you not know, my dear Girl, that every man is not an Adam—"True" you reply "but surely they ought to be unto their own Eves." Perhaps they ought. . . . That Eve was indeed the weaker vesel, I boldly take upon me to deny—Nay, it should seem she was abundantly the stronger vessel since all the deep laid Art of the most subtle fiend that inhabited the infernal regions, was requisite to draw her from her allegiance, while Adam was overcome by the influence of the softer passions merely by his attachment to a female—a fallen female in whose cheek "Distemper flushing gloomed": and you know, my dear, that by resisting the aberrating Fair One, Adam would have given the highest proof of manly firmness. But forgive this levity, it is seldom I allow my pen thus to wander.

CHAPTER FIVE

Politics and the Legal System

THE PROFOUND BELIEF that men and women had different capacities and characters, and that nature and the gods had assigned
them different destinies, played as significant a role in shaping political life as it did in shaping work roles. In both the "large politics" of
formal institutions and the "small politics" of community interactions,
gender was a key factor (although never the only one) in determining
a colonist's interests, access to power, and range of political rights,
privileges, strategies, and tactics.

Only among some Indian tribes, particularly the Iroquois nations,
did women enjoy a formal, institutionalized role in the governance
and the diplomatic policies of the community. Although Iroquois men
and women deliberated in single-sex councils, women's political authority was extensive. In most tribes whose territory fell within the
English colonial empire, however, women's political authority was
slowly eroded by the refusal of white government officials and traders
to acknowledge females as legitimate representatives in economic or
diplomatic negotiations. As Indians grew more dependent on Europeans as trading partners and suppliers of manufactured goods, they

came under the influence of white society's firm conviction that politics was a masculine domain.

In white colonial society, women were denied full political citizenship. A woman was not permitted to vote or hold office, regardless of wealth or social class. This exclusion was dramatically illustrated in the early seventeenth century when Margaret Brent, the richest landowner in Maryland, petitioned the colonial legislature to be allowed to vote and was denied on the basis of her sex. Property-holding women gained the vote in the first New Jersey state constitution, but this was the result of oversight rather than intention—and was soon corrected. Despite exclusion from formal politics, however, white women were part of a political community. They addressed the government directly through petitions, and many women were very effective in framing requests for privileges, assistance, and redress of grievances in petitions to colonial governors, assemblymen, and courts of law. Free white women were also able to establish an activist role in local political life. In colonial New England, women joined and sometimes organized food riots to protest shortages of staples or rising prices. They mounted campaigns against houses of prostitution and gambling and other sites of "vice." Women participated in intracolonial rebellions, arming themselves to fight with Nathanael Bacon against the tidewater planter aristocracy in seventeenth-century Virginia and supporting backcountry rebellions in the Carolinas and Pennsylvania in the eighteenth century. During the 1760s and 1770s, white women joined the prerevolutionary protests as members of mass demonstrations against Parliament's new stringent trade regulations and taxes, as organizers and supporters of tea boycotts, and as producers of cloth to compensate for the nonconsumption of British manufactured goods. During the home-front revolution that followed, women made public statements of political loyalties and acted on their own volition as spies for, and suppliers to, both the rebels and the Crown. Following the war, patriot and Loyalist women petitioned their governments for pensions, basing their claims not only on their husbands' loyalties but also on their own contributions to a political cause.

For black colonists, race trumped gender: neither male nor female

African Americans were permitted to participate in formal colonial politics or to claim basic political rights. But in the daily acts of resistance that were a political critique of slavery—some covert, such as destruction of farm equipment, theft of the master's property, feigned illness, work slowdowns, and escape from the plantations, some overt, such as the Stono Rebellion and Gabriel's Revolt—women were full political participants. During the American Revolution black women, like their white counterparts, declared and acted on their loyalties to the patriot cause or to the Crown.

Within the Anglo-European colonial world, women could not serve as judges or members of juries, just as they could not propose or enact legislation. Yet their presence was felt in the legal life of the community. Colonial women testified in court, gave depositions that influenced decisions for conviction or acquittal, and brought suit for debt, slander, theft, and assault. Men and women looked to one another to provide testimony to their deeds and testimonials to their character before the bench. The regular appearance of white and sometimes black women in civil and criminal court records attests to the fact that limited legal rights and powers did not mean exclusion from the legal process. Women were required to abide by the law and to pay penalties for its infraction; they were also allowed to seek redress of grievances when an injustice was done to them.

PRESCRIPTIVE DOCUMENTS

No Votes for Women, Infants, or Convicts

An Act for the Prevention of Undue Election of Burgesses, 1699, in William Hening, ed., *The Statutes at Large, Being a Collection of All the Laws of Virginia, from the First Session of the Legislature in the Year 1619* (Richmond, 1809–1823), vol. 3, p. 172.

Political participation was a privilege rather than a right of citizenship in colonial society. The privilege of suffrage, for example, belonged only to those men who exercised independent judgment, unhampered by economic dependency on others. Thus, servants and "infants," or minors, were excluded from the franchise. Gender disqualified women, whether sole or covert, as the following Virginia law illustrates.

+⌒+

For the prevention of undue election of Burgesses to serve in the general assembly in this his majesty's colony and dominion.

Be it enacted by the governor, council and Burgesses of this present general assembly, and the authority thereof, and it is hereby enacted, that no person or persons shall be enabled to give a vote for the election of a burgess or burgesses to serve in the general assembly hereafter to be called but those who are freeholders in the respective county or town for which the said burgess or burgesses shall be elected and chosen, and if any person shall presume to give his vote for the election of a burgess or burgesses in any county or town who is not a freeholder in such county or town he shall forfeit and pay the sum of five hundred pounds of tobacco for every such offence. *Provided always,* and it is the true intent and meaning of this act that no woman sole or covert, infants under the age of twenty-one years, or recusant convict being freeholders shall be enabled to give a vote or have a voice in the election of burgesses any thing in this act to the contrary notwithstanding.

WOMAN SUFFRAGE IN NEW JERSEY

↔↔

New Jersey Constitution, 1776.

New Jersey's constitution writers were so eager to ensure that suffrage was limited to independent property holders that they failed to stipulate the voter's gender. Thus, New Jersey became the first and only state in the new republic to allow women to vote. Political pundits mocked this glaring error, but politicians took it more seriously when Essex County women played a critical role in the election of 1797. In 1807 legislation was passed restricting suffrage to "free white male citizen[s] of this state."

+⌒+

All inhabitants of this colony of full age, who are worth fifty pounds proclamation money clear estate in the same, and have resided within the county in which they claim to vote twelve months immediately preceding the election, shall be entitled to vote for representation in Council and Assembly and also for all other public officers that shall be elected by the people of the country at large.

Born for Liberty

↦ ↤

Esther DeBerdt Reed, "The Sentiments of an American Woman"
(broadside; June 10, 1780), *Pennsylvania Magazine of History and Biography* 18,
no. 18 (1894), pp. 361–366.

*Perhaps no document better captures the rising political consciousness of women dur-
ing the American Revolution than this call to action penned by the thirty-three-year-
old matron Esther DeBerdt Reed. The author had lived in America for only a decade
when she issued her patriotic declaration and attached to it an ambitious blueprint
for a network of women's voluntary associations throughout the colonies. Just as the
Declaration of Independence laid out a detailed justification for the American revolt,
Reed's "Sentiments" justified women's mobilizing in support of a patriotic cause by
placing their activity in a historical context. When public crises demanded sacrifice
and activism, she observed, history had not deemed it unfeminine for women to respond to their country's needs. "Sentiments" prompted an immediate, and positive,
response across the nation.*

↜↠

On the commencement of actual war, the Women of America manifested
a firm resolution to contribute as much as could depend on them, to the
deliverance of this country. Animated by the purest patriotism they are sensible of sorrow at this day, in not offering more than barren wishes for the
success of so glorious a Revolution. They aspire to render themselves more
really useful; and this sentiment is universal from the north to the south of
the Thirteen United States. Our ambition is kindled by the fame of those
heroines of antiquity, who have rendered their sex illustrious, and have
proved to the universe, that, if the weakness of our Constitution, if opinion
and manners did not forbid us to march to glory by the same paths as the
Men, we should at least equal and sometimes surpass them in our love for
the public good. I glory in all that which my sex has done great and com-
mendable. I call to mind with enthusiasm and with admiration, all those acts
of courage, of constancy and patriotism, which history has transmitted to us:
The people favoured by Heaven, preserved from destruction by the virtues,
the zeal and the resolution of Deborah, of Judith, of Esther! The fortitude
of the mother of the macchabees, in giving up her sons to die before her
eyes: Rome saved from the fury of a victorious enemy by the efforts of Vo-
lunia, and other Roman ladies: So many famous sieges where the Women

have been seen forgetting the weakness of their sex, building new walls, digging trenches with their feeble hands; furnishing arms to their defenders, they themselves darting the missile weapons on the enemy, resigning the ornaments of their apparel, and their fortunes to fill the public treasury, and to hasten the deliverance of their country; burying themselves under its ruins; throwing themselves into the flames rather than submit to the disgrace of humiliation before a proud enemy.

Born for liberty, disdaining to bear the irons of a tyrannic Government, we associate ourselves to the grandeur of those Sovereigns, cherished and revered, who have held with so much splendour the scepter of the greatest States, The Batildas, the Elizabeths, the Maries, the Catherines, who have extended the empire of liberty, and contentd to reign by sweetness and justice, have broken the chains of slavery, forged by tyrants in the times of ignorance and barbarity. The Spanish Women, do they not make, at this moment, the most patriotic sacrifices, to encrease the means of victory in the hands of their Sovereign. He is a friend to the French Nation. They are our allies. We call to mind, doubly interested, that it was a French Maid who kindled up amongst her fellow-citizens, the flame of patriotism buried under long misfortunes; it was the Maid of Orleans who drove the kingdom of France the ancestors of those same British, whose odious yoke we have just shaken off; and whom it is necessary that we drive from this Continent.

But I must limit myself to the recolection of this small number of achievements. Who knows if persons disposed to censure, and sometimes too severely with regard to us, may not disapprove our appearing acquainted even with the actions of which our sex boasts? We are at least certain, that he cannot be a good citizen who will not applaud our efforts for the relief of the armies which defend our lives, our possessions, our liberty? The situation of our soldiery has been represented to me; the evils inseperable from war, and the firm and generous spirit which has enabled them to support these. But it has been said, that they may apprehend, that, in the course of a long war, the view of their distresses may be lost, and their services be forgotten. Forgotten! never; I can answer in the name of all my sex. Brave Americans, your disinterestedness, your courage, and your constancy will always be dear to America, as long as she shall preserve her virtue.

We know that at a distance from the theatre of war, if we enjoy any tranquility, it is the fruit of your watchings, your labours, your dangers. If I live happy in the midst of my family; if my husband cultivates his field, and reaps his harvest in peace; if, surrounded with my children, I myself nourish the youngest, and press it to my bosom, without being affraid of seeing myself separated from it, by a ferocious enemy; if the house in which we dwell; if our barns, our orchards are safe at the present time from the hands of those incendiaries, it is to you that we owe it. And shall we hesitate to evidence to you our gratitude? Shall we hesitate to wear a cloathing more simple; hair dressed less elegant, while at the price of this small privation, we shall deserve your benedictions. Who, amongst us, will not renounce with the highest pleasure, those vain ornaments, when she shall consider the valient defenders of America will be able to draw some advantage from the money which she may have laid out in these; that they will be better defended from the rigours of the seasons, that after their painful toils, they will receive some extraordinary and unexpected relief; that these presents will perhaps be valued by them at a greater price, when they will have it in their power to say: This is the offering of the Ladies. The time is arrived to display the same sentiments which animated us at the beginning of the Revolution, when we renounced the use of teas, however agreeable to our taste, rather than receive them from our persecutors; when we made it appear to them that we placed former necessaries in the rank of superfluities, when our liberty was interested; when our republican and laborious hands spun the flax, prepared the linen intended for the use of our soldiers; when exiles and fugitives we supported with courage all the evils which are the concomitants of war. Let us not lose a moment; let us be engaged to offer the homage of our gratitude at the altar of military valour, and you, our brave deliverers, while mercenary slaves combat to cause you to share with them, the irons with which they are loaded, receive with a free hand our offering, the purest which can be presented to your virtue,

By An American Woman.

DESCRIPTIVE DOCUMENTS

A WOMAN REBUKES THE AUTHORITIES

Minutes of the Orphan Masters of New Amsterdam, 1658–1659, in Berthold Fernow, trans. and ed., *The Minutes of the Orphan Masters, 1655–1663* (New York: Francis P. Harper, 1902), pp. 58, 68, 75, 77, 79, 138.

Unlike English law, Dutch law held that a wife and husband shared a "community of goods." Thus, widows were entitled to one half of the marital estate and had the right to administer the other half for the heirs. Although Geertje Hendricks's husband died intestate, he had appointed two guardians for his children. The local orphan's court (a watchdog for the financial interests and physical well-being of orphaned minors) expected Hendricks to cooperate with these men. In demanding that Geertje Hendricks share financial information with the guardians, the orphan masters were simply following a routine procedure. Hendricks, however, considered them meddlers and saw their demands as insults to her competence and honesty. It took the court months of prompting and threatening to get the necessary documents from the widow. At one point, the unruffled Hendricks rebuked the orphan masters, reminding them that "must is force," not justice.

↜

Geertje Hendrick, widow of *Andries Hoppe* dec'd., appearing states that her deceased husband has appointed as guardians of the children *Cornelis Aarsen* and *Lambert Huybersen Mol*, but has not made a testament. It is ordered, that said guardians shall inform the Orphanmasters by inventory of the estate of *Andries Hoppe* dec'd., real and personal debts and credits. . . .

Geertje Hendricks, the widow of *Andrees Hoppe*, coming in is asked, whether she had made an inventory of her deceased husband's property; she said, yes and the administrators have it. Then the following order was made: *Geertje Hendricks*, widow of *Andrees Hoppe*, is herewith directed, with the administrators to inform the Orphans Chamber of the estate of her late husband next Wednesday . . . under penalty of a fine. . . .

Geertje Hendrick, widow of *Andrees Hoppe*, was asked by the Board, whether she has the inventory; she answers No and says, Notary *Mattheus de Vos* has it, maintaining, that as long as she does not marry again, she need not report the estate of her late husband to the Orphans Chamber. She was told, that it was her duty to do it according to the customs of our Fatherland. She replies, she does not intend to do it and the Orphanmasters may do, what they please. Thereupon the Board decided to send the following order to the guardians of the children of *Andrees Hoppe* dec'd:

Whereas *Cornelis Aarsen* and *Lambert Huybertsen Mol* have been appointed by *Andrees Hoppe* before his death as guardians of his children, Therefore, having learned that an inventory has been made of the property of deceased, the Orphanmasters hereby direct said guardians to appear before this Board at the City Hall next Wednesday, February 26th, and to show by inventory the condition of the estate of said *Andrees Hoppe* dec'd, when such disposition shall be made of it, as shall be found proper.

Done etc. February 19th 1658. . . .

Geertje Hendricks, widow of *Andrees Hoppe,* appearing with the guardians, produces by them the inventory of the estate of her late husband and is asked, whether all debts and credits are entered: she says Yes and asked, whether she has agreed with the guardians about a settlement upon the children she answers, why should that be done before she marries again. She was told, she must do it. She answers "Must is force." Further asked, whether she was willing to make an agreement with the guardians, she says, she does not know any thing about it and is informed, that if she will not do it, she will be ordered. *Gertje Hendricks,* coming again with the guardians, is ordered to agree with them and promises to do so. The guardians are reminded, that the oldest child must remain with the mother. . . .

Geertje Hendricks comes with *Cornelis Aarsen* and *Lambert Huyberzen Mol,* the guardians of the children of *Andrees Hoppe* dec'd, and said guardians report, that they have agreed with the widow *Geertje Hendricks* about a settlement on the children of their paternal inheritance and 1000 fl., that is 200 for each child have been allowed, but the agreement has not yet been written out. They are ordered, to have it written and then hand it to the Secretary for record in the Orphans Book. . . .

Before us, the underwritten Orphanmasters of the City of Amsterdam in N.N., appeared *Geertje Hendricks,* widow of *Andrees Hoppe* dec'd., who stated, that she would give to her children, *Catrina, Wilhelmus, Hendrick, Matthys* and *Adolf Hoppe,* as their share of their father's estate the sum of 1000 fl. or 200 fl. to each child at once and not more, when they came of age or married, according to the agreement, made with the chosen guardians. . . .

Demanding Justice

↦ ↤

Mary Roffe's petition to the Ipswich Quarterly Court, March 1663, *Records and Files of the Quarterly Courts of Essex County, Massachusetts, vol. 3, 1662–1667* (Salem, Mass.: Essex Institute, 1913), p. 48.

In the prescriptive literature of the colonial period, husbands were instructed to speak for and protect their wives. In reality, women often had to do both for themselves. Mary Roffe's husband was absent when a suave gentleman named Henry Greenland began to sexually harass her, so she petitioned the court, asking that Greenland be brought to justice. Her demands were met and more than fifteen witnesses appeared before the jury, most corroborating Roffe's account of her own innocence and Green-

land's misbehavior. Eleven of those crucial witnesses were women, ranging in age from sixteen to fifty. Their testimony helped convict Greenland, who was ordered to pay a heavy fine or endure a whipping. Excerpted below is the petition that set this trial in motion.

～

I would desier the honord Court to here me a few words. I am a poor young woman and in an afflicted Condition. My husband not being with me: he Litl knowing the trubls I haue met with: being a verie Loving husband to me as anie young woman Can Expect and provided for me in his absenc tht I might live Cherfully as he thought and want for nothing therefor he went unto John Emeris house and got John Emeri and his wife to be willing to let ther daughter Elizabeth Webster to Com and live with me and to lye with me untill he Cam whom again: but by the prouidenc of god this fel out to be hurtfull to me. . . . I was occasioned to go often with hir to hir father Emeris house. . . . this Mr grenland Com to live in John Emeris house: and this becam a snare to me . . . but grenland have labored with manie of my naibours to posesse them that I am as guiltie as he and sais he can prove it. I hope it may apeer to the honored Court that not on[e] of my naibors in all the toune nether neer nor further of[f] Can say they saw anie uncivell Carridg or hurt by me in ther lives. . . .

SEEKING FREEDOM THROUGH THE COURTS
↔↩

Diary of John Adams, November 5, 1766, in *The Works of John Adams*, ed. Charles Francis Adams (Boston: Charles C. Little and James Brown, 1850), vol. 11, p. 200.

One hundred years after Mary Roffe petitioned the court to dispense justice, an anonymous slave woman went to court to protest the injustice of her enslavement. John Adams notes the suit but not the result.

～

[NOVEMBER] 5. Wednesday. Attended court; heard the trial of an action of trespass, brought by a mulatto woman, for damages for restraining her of her liberty. This is called suing for liberty; the first action that ever I knew of the sort, though I have heard there have been many.

WE WERE NOT SERVANTS
↔↩

Brom and Bett v. J. Ashley, Esq., 1781, in "Free Soil in Berkshire County," *New England Quarterly* 10, no. 4 (December 1937), pp. 783–785.

In 1781 an African American spinster and an African American laborer went to court to press charges against a white man for falsely claiming them as his bond servants. Their case was tried by white lawyers, before a white judge and jury—and was decided in the plaintiffs' favor.

◆

Commonwealth of Massachusetts

At an Inferior Court of common Pleas begun and holden at Great Barrington within and for the County of Berkshire upon the third Tuesday of August (being the 21st day of the same Month) in the Year of our Lord Christ, one thousand seven hundred and eighty one.

Present   William Whiting
Jahl. Woodbridge   Esquires
James Barker
Charles Goodrich

NUMBER 1: BROM AND BETT VS. J. ASHLEY, ESQ.

Brom a Negro Man and Bett a Negro Woman both of Sheffield in said County of Berkshire Plaintiffs against John Ashley of Sheffield aforesaid Esq. Defendent. In a plea of Replevin, wherein the said Brom and Bett prayed out of pleuries Writ of Replevin, signed by the Clerk of our said Court, dated the twenty eighth day of May, in the Year of our Lord one thousand seven hundred and eighty one which is as follows (to wit) The Commonwealth of Massachusetts. To the Sheriff of our County of Berkshire his under Sheriff or Deputy Greeting. When we have often commanded you that justly and without delay you should cause to be replevied, Brom a Negro Man of Sheffield in our said County Labourer, and Bett a Negro Woman of Sheffield aforesaid Spinster, whom John Ashley Esq. and John Ashley Junr. Esqu. both of Sheffield aforesaid have taken and being so taken detain (as it is said) unless they were taken by our special command, or by the command of our Chief Justice, or for Homocide, or for any other just cause, whereby according to the Usage of this Commonwealth they are not Repleviable, or that you should signify to us the cause, where fore the said John Ashley and John Ashley Junr. have taken, and, do detain the said Brom and Bett, and you having returned unto us that you have repaired unto the Houses of John Ashley and John Ashley Junr. Esqrs. to Replevy the said Brom and Bett according to the Tenor of our aforesaid Writ, but the said John Ashley Esqu. did not permit delivery of the aforesaid Brom and Bett to be made because he aserted the said Brom and Bett were his Servants for Life, thereby claiming a right of servitude in the Persons of the said Brom and Bett. We unwilling that the said Brom if he be a Freman, and the said Bett if she be a Free Woman, by such taking and claim should be deprived of the common Law, command you if the said Brom and Bett shall find you sufficient Security of being before our Justices of our Inferior Court of common Pleas to be holden at Great Barrington within and for our said County of Berkshire, on the third Tuesday of August next to answer unto the aforesaid John Ashley Esqe. if they shall find you such sufficient Security; then in the mean time that you cause to be replevied the aforesaid Brom and Brett according to the Tenor of our aforesaid Writs; and besides if the said Brom and Bett shall have made you secure of their complaint as aforesaid, then summon by good summoners the said John Ashley Esqu. that he be before the Justices of our said Court on the third Tuesday of August next to answer unto the said Brom and Bett of the takeing and claim aforesaid, and have there then the names of the Pledges in this Writ Tested by William Whiting Esqu. at Great Barrington the twenty-eighth day of May as aforesaid. The said Brom and Bett appear (by their Attorneys John Reeve and Theodore Sedgwick, Esqrs) and the said John Ashley Esqu. comes also (by his Attorneys John Canfield, Esqe. and David Noble, Gentleman) and says that the said Brom and Bett ought not to have and maintain their Suit aforesaid against him, but the same ought to be abated and dismissed, because he says the said Brom and Bett, are and were at the time of Issuing the original Writ, the legal Negro Servants of him the said John Ashley during their Lives, and this the said John is ready to verify, and hereof prays the Judgment of this Court, and that the said Suit may be abated. And the said Brom and Bett (by their said Attorneys John Reeve and Theodore Sedgwick, Esqrs.) say that their Suit aforesaid ought not to be abated, because they say they are not, nor are either of them, nor were they or either of them, at the time of the Issuing the original Writ, the Negro Servant or Servants of him the said John Ashley during their lives, and this they pray may be inquired of by the Country, and the said John Ashley (by his said Attorneys) likewise doth the same. And after a full hearing of this Case the evidence therein being produced, the same Case is committed to the Jury, Jonathon Holcomb, Foreman, and his Fellows, who being duely sworn return their Verdict that in this Case the Jury find that the said Brom and Bett are not and were not at the time of the purchase of the original Writ the legal Negro Servants of him the said John Ashley dureing life and Assess thirty shillings damages. Wherefore it is considered by the Court and thereupon by the said County adjudged and determined, that the said Brom and

Bett are not, nor were they at the time of the purchase of the original Writ, the legal Negro [servants] of the said John Ashley dureing life, and that the said Brom and Bett do recover against the said John Ashley the sum of thirty shillings lawful Silver Money Damages, and four pence like Money—And hereof the said Brom and Bett may have their Execution—The said John Ashley appeals from the Judgement of this Court to the Supreme Judicial Court to be holden at Great Barrington within and for the County of Berkshire upon the first Tuesday of October next; and John Ashley, Junior, Esqu. Recognized with Sureties as the Law directs for the said John Ashley his presecuting with effect this appeal at the said Supreme Court etc. as on File.

WOMEN ASSIST THE CORONER

→ ←

Mary V. Wats et al., "Report to the Court in the Case of Paul Carter," March 1679, *Virginia Magazine of History and Biography* 4 (1896–1897), p. 187.

Women did not serve as jurors, judges, or law enforcement officials in colonial society. Yet they could be empanelled by the courts to assist in the investigation of suspicious deaths, particularly when infanticide was likely. The twelve women called upon by this Virginia court conducted an "ordeal by touch," observing the response of the infant corpse when handled by suspects in the case. As their report to the court below indicates, when they exhumed Mary Carter's newborn child they observed changes in the corpse pointing to the guilt of Mary's stepfather, Paul Carter. (For additional documentation of this case, see pages 39–46.)

✦

Wee the subscribers being sworne to view the body of a dead bastard child confest by Mary the daughter of Sarah Carter to be borne of her body, wch said child we caused to be taken out of the ground in the garden where it was very shallow put in, then we caused Sarah the wife of Paul Carter & mother of the said Mary to touch, handle and stroake the childe, in which time we saw no alteration in the body of the childe; afterwards we called for Paul Carter to touch the s'd child and immediately whilst he was stroaking the childe the black & sotted places about the body of the childe grew fresh and red so that blud was redy to come through the skin of the child. We also observed the countenance of the said Paule Carter to alter into very much paleness; the childe also appearing to us to be very much neglected in several respects as to the preservacon of such an infant and we doe conclude if the child had any violence it was by the throat, wch was very black and continued so, though other places wch were black altered to red & fresh collered, to wch we subscribe our hands this first day of March, 1679.

Mary V. Wats,	Mary Mikell,
Elizabeth F. Cutler,	Mary Anderson,
Jane O. Taylor,	Amey Parker,
Mary Hill,	Mary × Sipple,
Margaret M. Jenkins,	Elener S. Calvert,
Matilda West,	Ann A. F. Fenn,
Wm. Custis, Coroner.	

A WOMAN RECEIVES THE DEATH PENALTY

↦ ↤

The Case of Maria Negro, Court of Assistants, Boston, 1681, *Publications of the Colonial Society of Massachusetts* 6 (1904), p. 321.

A woman convicted of a capital crime could expect no leniency because of her sex. While most were hanged, this African American woman, convicted of arson, was sentenced to execution by burning.

↦↜↤

At A Court of Assistants Held at Boston, 6 September, 1681

Maria Negro, servant to Joshua Lambe of Roxbury in the County of Suffolk in New England, being presented by the Grand Jury, was indicted by the name of Maria Negro for not having the fear of God before her eyes and being instigated by the Devil at or upon the eleventh day of July last in the night did wittingly, willingly and feloniously set on fire the dwelling house of Thomas Swann of said Roxbury by taking a coal from under a sill and carried it into another room and laid it on the floor near the door and presently went and crept into hole at a back door of thy master Lamb's house and set it on fire. Also taking a live coal between two chips and carried it into the chamber by which also it was consumed as by your confession will appear contrary to the peace of our Sovereign Lord the king, his Crown and dignity, the laws of this jurisdiction. The prisoner at the bar pleaded and acknowledged herself to be guilty of this fact. And accordingly, the next day being again brought to the bar, had sentence of death pronounced against her by the Honorable Governor, yet she should go from the bar to the prison whence she came and thence to the place of execution and there be burned.

Politics and the Legal System

Vigilante Justice

↔↩

New York Weekly Journal, May 5, 1735.

While the formal court sat in Chester County, a group of women organized their own informal court to deal with an abusive husband. The women who participated in the trial, conviction, and punishment of the offender were clearly familiar with the procedures they mimicked.

↩↪

We hear from Chester County, that last week at a Vendue held there, a Man being unreasonably abusive to his wife upon some trifling Occasion, the women form'd themselves into a court, and ordered him to be apprehended by their officers and brought to tryal; Being found guilty he was condemn'd to be duck'd 3 times in a neighbouring Pond, and to have one half cut off, of his Hair and beard (which it seems he wore at full length) and the sentence was accordingly executed, to the great Diversion of the spectators.

A Taxpayer's Complaint

↔↩

Letter to the editor, *New York Weekly Journal,* September 2, 1734.

It is impossible to tell if Deborah Careful actually existed or if someone in the assembly or the city government wrote this letter in an effort to expose a patronage scheme. Nevertheless, as a description of the difficulties facing a widow with property in New York City, the letter is accurate. Women of property did pay taxes, although they had no formal voice in determining how tax money was spent, and they were required to help provide civic services such as road mending and night patrols. Deborah Careful, like other widows, had to pay a man to perform these duties. In the letter below, the author reveals a sure knowledge of the legislation affecting her pocketbook, good investigative skills, and a keen sense of how to use the media for political ends.

↩↪

Mr. Zenger;

I am a poor widdow, who have a number of children to maintain, and have nothing to do it with but my own labour: I have often been summoned to watch, and have been forced to pay as much as the richest Man in town, tho' (God Knows) I can hardly buy my Bread; however I was told, I must do it, till there was an act of assembly passed to remedy the Evil. Some days Ago

I was sumoned to mend the roads, where I got a Man to work: I had a second summons, which I thought was very hard. I told the constable, that I could not see that this dry season there could be so much occasion to mend the Roads; Oh! say he, the roads are good, but they must be made strait, and we are to dig down Fresh-water Hill. I could not see by what Authority this was done, there being nothing in the act of Assembly, as I could see, about levelling mountains or digging through them. I was resolved to walk out on Sunday afternoon, to view this great and chargeable work, and took one of my little Boys with a string, and was so curious to measure, and found, if people went out of town through the road way, they saved about 150 foot; but if through the smith's fly; the other road was nearest. I wish those worthy gentlemen who have ordered this great work to be done, would acquaint the publick with the true motives of doing of it, for I never can be perswaded, that making the road strait can be the reason. And if still it must be done, I think by a generous subscription would be a better method than lodging the poor inhabitants with so heavy a tax.

I am yours,
Deborah Careful.

The Value of Reputation

Notice in *New York Weekly Journal,* November 26, 1750.

Reputation was important in a society that conducted much of its business in face-to-face transactions between friends, relatives, and neighbors. Even the rumor of dishonesty could ruin a colonist's livelihood. Cathrine Williams did not tell her newspaper readers how she earned her living, but she was adamant that gossip and false accusations had destroyed it. By issuing this notice, she showed herself willing to make a public statement and take an aggressive stand against her enemies.

This is to give notice that I Cathrine Williams, of the City of New-York, Widow, have long lain under the aspersion of several slanderous tongues, and that to my great Detriment, having thereby lost both my credit, my Livlihood, and good Name, which I defy the world & New York to deface, nay, they have even gone so far as to call me a wicked woman, and a Thief, which is not so, for I have lived in this city many years, always under the character of a good House-wife, an honest, and industrious wife, frugal and cleanly, and my honour un'tainted. Those aspersers are desired to make satisfaction, for taking away my name, my honour, and my livelyhood. They threaten me without Guiltiness, they shew their authority but know not for what, they have try'd all the Mysteries they could contrive, but they can't, for I have good courage and good knowledge to overcome their wicked Tricks and they have long sought to Ruin me, but they shan't, for satisfaction I will have between this and new Years my charge I demand for the loss of my name, my livelihood and my Honour, for which I insist upon the following,

<pre>
To the Loosing of my Livelyhood 5000
To the Loss of My character 6000
For fear of being Killed 1000
</pre>

in all £ 12000
Cathrine Williams

POLITICS DOES NOT BECOME THE LADIES

↔ ↔

Letter to the editor, <i>New York Weekly Journal,</i> August 19, 1734.

Factional politics was well developed in eighteenth-century New York, where supporters of the governor did battle with the "popular" party in every term of the legislature. The author of this anonymous letter to John Peter Zenger's newspaper clearly felt the contagion of politics had gone too far, affecting the behavior and permeating the conversation of the genteel women of the city. In urging the ladies to withdraw from partisan behavior, the author gives us a glimpse into the political engagement of elite women decades before the American Revolution.

ᡣᡩ

Mr. Zenger:
Insert the following into your journal, and oblige one of your readers.

Study the self, learn in what Rank and State
the wise Creator has ordain'd thy fate.

As Many of your Readers are of the female sex, I hope they wont take it ill, if they should be tho told, that politicks is what does not become them; the Governing Kingdoms and Ruling Provinces are things too difficult and knotty for the fair sex, it will render them grave and serious, and take off those agreeable smiles that should always acompany them.

It is with the utmost concern that I daily see Numbers of fair ladies contending above some abtruse Point in Politicks, and running into the greatest heats about they know not what. I must say that unluckily the other day I fell into company with some Ladies, and one of them said that for her part, she thought such a one was a very sad Creature. Another of the company said, she was of a different opinion, Being well acquainted with the lady and thought her to be a very discreet woman. Pray how can that be (says the 1st) when her husband has signed the Address to the Governour? Finding them to grow warm, I endeavored to Mitigate matters, and said, the woman might be a very discreet-Woman, that her husband had been so indiscreet as to do such a thing. But all I could say was in vain, and I luckily got clear without being scalded with the hot tea.

And what I think still worse, is they can't help showing their resentments in the publick streets. The other day I saw one of the courtiers walking along the streets and being obliged to pass by the door of one of the contrary Party, she speaks to her children who were with her, that at their perils they should not bow. When they pass'd by such a door, and when she got home could not help exulting at the great mark of disrespect that she had shewn, and how pretty the children had behaved.

Men indeed ought to exert themselves in Defence of their liberties, and shew a just Disregard for all those tools of Power that endeavor to contribute to their slavery; and had I the happiness of being a fair lady, I should always treat with contempt any man that appear'd a tool in any shape; Yet I think a woman never appears more agreeable than when she is discharging the Duties incumbent upon a mistress of a family, when through her Management her friends partake of a Genteel Frugality. I would not have you imagine I design by this to perswade the Ladies from reading your journals; by no means, let them read them, and teach their children the Principles of Liberty and Good Manners, which will redound much more to their Honour than by Discommoding their pretty faces with passion and resentment.

PROTEST AGAINST THE LIEUTENANT GOVERNOR

↦ ↤

Boston Gazette, August 19, 1765.

When Parliament passed the Stamp Act, few members were prepared for the hostile response from the colonists. Many colonial leaders were also caught by surprise. Prominent citizens in every colony accepted appointments as stamp distributors, among them the wealthy merchant Andrew Oliver, then secretary of the province of Massachusetts. A mass demonstration against Oliver and the Stamp Tax began on

August 14, 1765. The following night a crowd gathered to harass the lieutenant governor and chief justice, Thomas Hutchinson. However, the crowd dispersed upon learning that Oliver had resigned as stamp distributor. This brief newspaper notice reveals that women were active participants in the earliest phases of prerevolutionary protest.

This evening [August 15, 1765] about 9 o'clock, a great number of the Inhabitants of this town of both sexes, surrounded his honor's dwelling house at the N End. with loud Acclamations for Liberty and Property: after giving 3 cheers, they quickly dispers'd without doing any Damage to the house, having been told of Mr. Secretary's resigning of his stamp office as dangerous for him or any Man to accept. . . .

WOMEN MUST DEFEND LIBERTY

"The female Patriots, Address'd to the Daughters of Liberty in America," 1768 (Commonplace Book of Milcah Martha Moore, owned by Miss Sarah A. G. Smith, Philadelphia), quoted in "Trivia," *William and Mary Quarterly*, 3d ser., 34 (April 1977), pp. 307–308.

The author of this poem demonstrates her knowledge of current events as well as her impatience and disgust with colonial men who hesitated to take action against British "tyranny." She calls on women to enforce the boycott of British-made goods, designed to bring about the repeal of the Townshend Acts. In place of British cloth, paper, and paint, she urges white colonial women to wear homespun dresses, produce berry dyes, and write on leaves when their supply of stationery runs out.

Since the Men from a Party, on fear of a frown,
Are kept by a Sugar-Plumb, quietly down,
Supinely asleep, and depriv'd of their Sight
Are strip'd of their Freedom, and rob'd of their Right.
If the Sons (so degenerate) the Blessing despise,
Let the Daughters of Liberty, nobly arise,
And tho' we've no Voice, but a negative here,
The use of the Taxables, let us forbear,
(Then Merchants import till yr. Stores are all full
May the Buyers be few and yr. Traffick be dull.)
Stand firmly resolved and bid Grenville to see
That rather than Freedom, we'll part with our Tea

And well as we love the dear Draught when adry,
As American Patriots,—our Taste we deny,
Sylvania's gay Meadows, can richly afford
To pamper our Fancy, or furnish our Board,
And Paper sufficient (at home) still we have,
To assure the Wise-acre, we will not sign Slave.
When this Homespun shall fail, to remonstrate our Grief
We can speak with the Tongue or scratch on a Leaf.
Refuse all their Colours, the richest of Dye,
The juice of a Berry—our Paint can supply,
To humour our Fancy—and as for our Houses,
They'll do without painting, as well as our Spouses,
While to keep out the Cold of a keen winter Morn
We can screen the Northwest, with a well polish'd Horn.
And trust Me a Woman by honest Invention,
Might give this State Doctor a Dose of Prevention.
Join mutual in this, and but small as it seems
We may jostle a Grenville and puzzle his Schemes
But a motive more worthy our patriot Pen,
Thus acting—we point out their Duty to Men,
And should the bound Pensioners, tell us to hush
We can throw back the Satire by biding them blush.

A SLAVE ADDRESSES A KING

↦ ↤

Phillis Wheatley, "To the King's Most Excellent Majesty on his Repealing
the American Stamp Act," 1768, in Margaretha M. Odell, ed., *Memoir and
Poems of Phillis Wheatley, A Native African and a Slave* (Boston: Isaac Knapp,
1838), p. 50.

*Phillis Wheatley was a child when she was brought to America and sold to a family
in Massachusetts. Fortunately, the Wheatleys not only appreciated the girl's precocious
intelligence but also encouraged her to develop her talents. During the 1760s and
1770s Wheatley wrote poetry, much of it political commentary, that was greatly admired by the revolutionary elite. Wheatley received her freedom in 1778 and almost
immediately married a free black named John Peters. Despite having once journeyed
to England to meet the king and having received a letter of personal appreciation
from George Washington, Phillis Wheatley and her family sank into poverty and
servitude. She died impoverished in 1784. This poem, written to celebrate the repeal*

of the Stamp Act, illustrates her appreciation for a freedom she did not, at the time, enjoy.

๛

Your Subjects hope, dread Sire,
The crown upon your head may flourish long,
And that your arm may in your God be strong
Oh, may your sceptre num'rous nations sway,
And all with love and readiness obey.

But how shall we the British King Reward?
Rule thou in peace, our Father and our Lord!
'Midst the remembrance of thy favors past,
The meanest peasants most admire the last.

May George, beloved by all the Nations around,
Live with Heaven's choicest, constant blessings crowned.
Great God! direct and guard him from on high,
And from his head let every evil fly;
And may each clime with equal gladness see
A monarch's smile can set his subjects Free.

Renouncing Tea

↦ ↤

"A Copy of the Agreement of the Ladies in this Town, against drinking Tea, until the Revenue Acts are Repealed" (January 31, 1770), *Boston Gazette*, February 12, 1770.

Tea was the most popular drink in eighteenth-century colonial society, and the ritual of the tea table was among the most cherished in genteel circles. Nevertheless, white colonial women joined in the boycotting of tea after the passage of the Townshend duties in 1767. These Boston women took care to establish that their decision was arrived at independently and that their boycott agreement was not ancillary but co-equal to the agreement signed by the town's merchants. The women also demonstrated a sophisticated understanding of the purpose behind the new revenue acts and of the American protest tactics designed to defeat them.

๛

At a time when our invaluable rights and Priveleges are attacked in an unconstitutional and Most alarming Manner, and as we find we are re-proached for not being so ready as could be desired, to lend our assistance, we think it our duty perfectly to concur with the true friends of Liberty, in all the Measures they have taken to save this abused country from Ruin and Slavery: And particularly we join with the very respectable body of Merchants and other inhabitants of the Town, who met in Faneuil Hall the 23rd of this instant in their Resolutions, totally to abstain from the use of Tea: And as the greatest Part of the Revenue arising by virtue of the last Acts, is produced from the Duty paid upon Tea, which revenue is wholly expended to suport the American Board of Commissioners: We the subscribers do strictly engage that we will totally abstain from the use of that Article, (sickness excepted) not only in our respective families: but that we would absolutely refuse it, if it should be offered to us upon any Occasion whatsoever. This agreement we cheerfully come into, as we believe the very distressed situation of our country requires it; and we do hereby oblige ourselves religiously to observe it, till the late Revenue Acts are Repealed.

To this above agreement, the Mistresses of their respective families (only) are Come in, to the number of 100.

N.B. In the above number, the worthy Ladies of the highest Rank and Influence (that could be waited on in so short a time) are included.

"For the Publick Good"

↦ ↤

The Edenton Resolves, October 1774, quoted in Peter Force, comp., *American Archives* (Washington, D.C., 1834), 4th ser., 1, p. 891.

The Edenton Resolves were widely circulated in the patriot press of 1774 and 1775. This public political declaration by fifty-one women of Edenton, North Carolina, that they would act in the public interest was greeted with both praise and scorn. Loyalist writers scoffed and asked if a female congress had also been formed by patriotic ladies. Even in the revolutionary camp, some men were uneasy with women who spoke of personal commitments beyond the family.

↜

As we cannot be indifferent on any occasion that appears to affect the peace and happiness of our country, and as it has been thought necessary for the publick good to enter into several particular resolves, by meeting of Members of Deputies from the whole Province, it is a duty that we owe not only to our near and dear relations and connections, but to ourselves who are essentially interested in their welfare, to do everything as far as lies in our power to testify to our sincere adherence to the same; and we do therefore accordingly subscribe this paper as a witness of our fixed intention and solemn determination to do so.

Signed by fifty-one Ladies.

Renouncing Tea Once More
↔↩

"A Lady's Adieu to her Tea Table," *Virginia Gazette*, January 20, 1774.

In 1773 the British government revived colonial protest by the passage of the Tea Act. Although the new law actually lowered the price of tea, many Americans viewed it as the first step in a campaign to create a British monopoly on the American import market or as an effort to trick colonists into accepting the principle of Parliament's right to tax them. As in the past, women rallied to boycott the East India Company's tea. This verse gives a fine description of tea table equipment and of the gentrification of colonial social life among the prosperous classes.

↭

Farewell the Tea Board, with its gaudy Equipage,
Of Cups and Saucers, Cream Bucket, Sugar Tongs,
The pretty Tea Chest also, lately stor'd
With Hysen, Congo, and best Double Fine.
Full many a joyous Moment have I sat by ye,
Hearing the Girls' Tattle, the Old Maids talk Scandal,
And the spruce Coxcomb laught at—maybe—Nothing.
No more shall I dish out the once lov'd Liquor,
Though now detestable,
Because I'm taught (and I believe it true)
Its use will fasten slavish Chains upon my Country,
And LIBERTY's the Goddess I would choose
To reign triumphant in AMERICA.

An Appeal for Patriotic History
↔↩

Abigail Smith Adams to Mercy Otis Warren, August 14, 1777, in *The Adams Family Correspondence*, ed. Lyman H. Butterfield (Cambridge: Belknap Press of Harvard University Press, 1963), vol. 2, pp. 313–314.

In the 1760s Mercy Otis Warren wrote witty and pointed political satire on Massachusetts politics, portraying royal officeholders such as Thomas Hutchinson as self-aggrandizing enemies of liberty and assembly leaders such as her own brother James

Otis as champions of colonial rights. Both Abigail and John Adams admired her, although their friendship was strained in the 1790s, when John Adams became the Federalist president and Warren, a fervent opponent of the Constitution, wrote stinging criticisms of him. In the midst of the Revolution, when the outcome was much in doubt, Abigail Adams urged Mercy Otis Warren to write a history of the revolutionary cause from a patriot's perspective. More than twenty-five years later, Warren's three-volume history of the American Revolution appeared, making her the first historian of the War for Independence.

～

This is the memorable fourteenth of August. This day 12 years the Stamp office was distroyd. Since that time what have we endured? What have we suffer'd? Many very many memorable Events which ought to be handed down to posterity will be buried in oblivion merely for want of a proper Hand to record them, whilst upon the opposite side many venal pens will be imployd to misrepresent facts and to render all our actions odious in the Eyes of future Generations. I have always been sorry that a certain person who once put their Hand to the pen, should be discouraged, and give up so important a service. Many things would have been recorded by the penetrateing Genious of that person which thro the multiplicity of Events and the avocations of the times will wholly escape the notice of any future Historian.

ZEAL TRANSFORMS THE WOMEN

↦↤

Benjamin Rush to John Adams, Philadelphia, July 13, 1780, in *Letters of Benjamin Rush*, ed. L. H. Butterfield (Princeton, N.J.: Princeton University Press, 1951), pp. 253–254.

This letter from Rush to Adams illustrates the effects of women's wartime activism on male assumptions about women's natural "character" and their capacity for civic participation. After the war not all political leaders became advocates, as Rush did, of broad reform in women's education, but many supported a continuing civic role for women in the new republic.

～

Dear Sir,

The reduction (I will not say *loss*) of Charlestown has produced a new era in the politics of America, such as you and I saw and felt and admired in the years 1775 and 76. Our republics cannot exist long in prosperity. We require adversity and appear to possess most of the republican spirit when most depressed. The papers will inform you of the exploits of our governments, of our citizens, of our soldiers, and even of our ladies. If there is a single philosopher in the cabinet of St. James's, he will advise immediately to make peace with America. "The Romans govern the world," said Cato, "but the women govern the Romans." The women of America have at last become principals in the glorious American controversy.

Their opinions alone and their transcendent influence in society and families must lead us on to success and victory. My dear wife, who you know in the beginning of the war had all the timidity of her sex as to the issue of the war and the fate of her husband, was one of the ladies employed to solicit benefactions for the army. She distinguished herself by her zeal and address in this business, and is now so thoroughly enlisted in the cause of her country that she reproaches me with lukewarmness. Mr. Searle will inform you of what is going forward within doors. His zeal and integrity in the service of America, and of Pennsylvania in particular, entitle him to the good offices and regard of all the friends of liberty on your side of the water.—Adieu. From, my dear friend, yours most sincerely,

BENJN RUSH

A Soldier Commends a Camp Follower

↦ ↤

"Narrative of some of the Adventures, Dangers and Sufferings of a Revolutionary Soldier" (1830), in James Kirby Martin, ed., *Ordinary Courage: The Revolutionary War Adventures of Joseph Plumb Martin* (New York: Brandywine Press, 1993), p. 80.

Elite men were not alone in their appreciation of women's patriotism during the war. In this memoir by an ordinary infantryman of the Continental army, the author recollects the bravery of a female comrade-in-arms. Camp followers like this anonymous woman, who aided their husbands or lovers in loading the cannons and pouring water on them to cool them off, were known popularly as "molly pitchers."

↦↤

A woman whose husband belonged to the artillery and who was then attached to a piece in the engagement, attended with her husband at the piece the whole time. While in the act of reaching a cartridge and having one of her feet as far before the other as she could step, a cannon shot from the enemy passed directly between her legs without doing any other damage than carrying away all the lower part of her petticoat. Looking at it with apparent unconcern, she observed that it was lucky it did not pass a little higher, for in that case it might have carried away something else, and continued her occupation.

WOMEN WERE NOT DESTINED TO VOTE

↦ ↤

"A Friend to the Ladies," *Trenton True American*, October 18, 1802.

In the article excerpted below, an anonymous "friend" to New Jersey's women voters mounts an argument against woman suffrage. He bases his position on two assumptions: first, that women's true nature or character is not suited to political decision making; and second, that a woman is not an independent citizen and thus cannot cast an independent vote. The author's appeal to women to behave in accord with their delicacy and reserve foreshadows the nineteenth century's ideology of "true womanhood" among the genteel classes. His argument against women suffrage was echoed in the nineteenth-century opposition to universal male suffrage and the enfranchisement of African American men.

↦↤

Among the striking scenes which our election presents to the disinterested observer, none is more amusing than the sight of whole wagon loads of those "privileged fair," who for the lucky circumstance of being possessed of 50 pounds and of being disengaged at the age of 21 are entitled to vote.

What a blissful week has the preceding one been for them! How respectfully attentive each young Federalist and Republican has been to the fair elector! How ready to offer them his horses, his carriages, to drag them in triumph to the election ground! Oh sweet week! Why do you not last the whole year round!

However pleasing these reflections may be to the Ladies, it must be owned that the inconvenience attending the practice far outweighs the benefits derived from it. We may well be allowed to answer without being accused of detractions, that those votes are rarely, if ever unbiased. Timid and pliant, unskilled in politics, unacquainted with all the real merits of the several candidates, and almost always placed under the dependence or care of a father, uncle or brother, they will of course be directed or persuaded by them; and the man who brings his two daughters, his mother, his aunt, to the elections really gives five votes instead of one. . . .

When our Legislature passed the act by which the females are entitled to share in our elections they were not aware of its inconveniences, and acted from a principle of justice, deeming it right that every free person who pays a tax should have a vote. But from the moment when party spirit began to rear its hideous head, the female vote became its passive tools, and the ill consequences of their admission have increased yearly. This year their number arose to an alarming height; in some townships I am told they made up almost one fourth of the total number of votes, and we cannot blame the apprehensions of an old farmer who feared that the next election would be entirely left to the ladies.

Let not our fair conclude that I wish to see them deprived of their rights. Let them rather consider that female reserve and delicacy are incompatible with the duties of a free elector, that a female politician is often subject to ridicule and they will recognize in this writer a sincere

Friend to the Ladies.

A Female Soldier in the American Revolution

↦↤

The Petition of Deborah Gannett to the House of Representatives, Tuesday, November 28, 1797, recorded in *Journals of the House of Representatives*, vol. 3, p. 90.

Deborah Sampson Gannett served in the Continental army under the name Robert Shurtleff (or Shirtliffe) and sustained a wound while engaged in active service. Her petitions to state and federal governments for pension support were endorsed by leading patriots such as Paul Revere. Although the petition quoted below was denied, Gannett did receive funds from Massachusetts. Gannett is not the only woman on record who sought and received compensation for disabilities suffered in combat in the American Revolution, but she is the only one known to have enlisted and served as a male soldier.

↜↝

A petition of Deborah Gannett of the town of Sharon in the state of Massachusetts, was presented to the house and read, stating that the petitioner, though a *female*, enlisted as a continental soldier, for the term of three years, in the Massachusetts line, of the late American Army, by the name of Robert Shurtleff; that she faithfully performed the duties of a soldier during the time above specified, and received a wound while in the actual service of the United States, in consequence of which she is subjected to pain and infirmities; and praying that she may receive the pay and emoluments granted to other wounded and disabled soldiers.

Ordered, that the said petition; together with the petition of Andrew Pepin, presented the nineteenth of November, one thousand seven hundred and ninety-two, and the report of the Secretary of War thereon, of the second of March, one thousand seven hundred and ninety-three, be referred to the Committee of Claims.

[March 9, 1798] Mr. Dwight Foster, from the committee of claims, to whom were referred the petitions of James Brown, of Deborah Gannett, of John Smuck, one of the heirs of Francis Koonz, deceased, and of John Henry Zimmerman, made a report, which was read and considered: Whereupon,

Resolved, that the prayer of the petitions of the said James Brown, Deborah Gannett, John Smuck and John Henry Zimmerman, cannot be granted.

IN A TRADITIONAL POLITICAL VOICE

↦↤

"A Cherokee Women's Petition," May 2, 1817, in Theda Perdue and Michael D. Green, eds., *The Cherokee Removal* (Boston: Bedford Books of St. Martin's Press, 1995), pp. 124–126.

Despite their active role in support of the Revolution, women were excluded from the formal political life of the new nation. In the young republic of 1817, as in the old colonial society of 1717, women did not vote, hold elective or appointive office, or sit on juries or on the judge's bench. The Revolution had brought little change in the laws restricting married women's lives and few new economic opportunities for women. Gains had been made in women's education, but only in some regions and among the elite social classes. The petition continued to be women's primary access route to those with political and legal authority. As Indian women of the eastern seaboard were pressured to conform to traditional European gender roles, they too began to employ the petition as their most promising political tool. In the following appeal, Cherokee "ladies" speak to the male leaders of their tribe in the language of devoted mothers and dependent females.

᠅

The Cherokee ladys now being present at the meeting of the chiefs and warriors in council have thought it their duty as mothers to address their beloved chiefs and warriors now assembled.

Our beloved children and head men of the Cherokee Nation, we address you warriors in council. We have raised all of you on the land which we now have, which God gave us to inhabit and raise provisions. We know that our country has once been extensive, but by repeated sales has become circumscribed to a small track, and [we] never have thought it our duty to interfere in the disposition of it till now. If a father or mother was to sell all their lands which they had to depend on, which their children had to raise their living on, which would be indeed bad & to be removed to another country. We do not wish to go to an unknown country [to] which we have understood some of our children wish to go over the Mississippi, but this act of our children would be like destroying your mothers.

Your mothers, your sisters ask and beg of you not to part with any more of our land. We say ours. You are our descendants; take pity on our request. But keep it for our growing children, for it was the good will of our creator to place us here, and you know our father, the great president [James Monroe], will not allow his white children to take our country away. Only keep your hands off of paper talks for its our own country. For [if] it was not, they would not ask you to put your hands to paper, for it would be impossible to remove us all. For as soon as one child is raised, we have others in our arms, for such is our situation & will consider our circumstance.

Therefore, children, don't part with any more of our lands but continue on it & enlarge your farms. Cultivate and raise corn & cotton and your mothers and sisters will make clothing for you which our father the president has recommended to us all. We don't charge any body for selling any lands, but we have heard such intentions of our children. But your talks become true at last; it was our desire to forwarn you all not to part with our lands.

CHAPTER SIX

A *Changing Gender Ideology*

IN THE AFTERMATH of the American Revolution, political leaders and social reformers debated women's role in an independent republic. Out of this discussion came a new gender ideal, known as republican womanhood, and, with it, an elevated notion of women's intellectual and moral capacities that differed sharply from the assumptions of the colonial era.

The intellectuals who articulated these new ideas were members of a social elite, and their social class shaped and limited their vision. Although some argued for greater economic and legal autonomy for women, the majority continued to see the bonds of marriage and motherhood as the perimeters of any proposed change. Thus, their agenda quickly focused on women as supportive rather than fully participatory citizens in the new nation and on activities that did not, at least intentionally, challenge women's duties as wives and mothers.

To a great extent, women's contribution to the Revolution prompted and justified the intense discussion of political identity that arose after independence. During the war women had demonstrated their capacity for patriotism and political consciousness. After the war national leaders were uncertain how, and to what degree, this female patriotism should be acknowledged and encouraged to continue. The question came down to this: what was the appropriate role for women in the new nation?

The answer that emerged through public debate was republican womanhood. Republican womanhood was defined by a set of civic duties that could be executed from within the traditional female sphere. As mothers, women would be called upon to inculcate in their children those virtues and values believed to be critical to the republic's survival. They were to teach the secular faith of the day: that a republic depended upon the character of its people to ensure its success. Children would be taught that simplicity, honesty, and the willingness to sacrifice for the good of the nation were the cornerstones of national survival. As wives, women were to guard and sustain these virtues in their husbands.

This postwar ideology may have had little immediate impact on ordinary women, who were preoccupied with restoring homes, farms, and family life after almost a decade of war. Even among the elite, few women consciously modeled themselves on the new ideal. For several decades, greater wealth, more servants, and the convenience of manufactured goods had provided these women with more leisure time, and many had begun to devote that time to educating and socializing their children even before the Revolution began. In this sense, republican womanhood was political rhetoric that overlay a pre-revolutionary social trend.

But the impact of the new ideology cannot be measured by a head count of its self-conscious proponents. The concept of republican womanhood played an important role in weakening traditional notions of women's intellectual inferiority and in legitimating a vigorous campaign to expand women's education. The small but articulate group of American reformers who embraced Enlightenment ideas and endorsed the new ideology of republican womanhood published essays on both subjects. Essayists such as Judith Sargent Murray and Benjamin Rush argued that women's ignorance was the product of educational neglect rather than innate intellectual inferiority. They called for schools for young women with a curriculum similar to the course of study pursued in male preparatory academies. The creation of young ladies' academies was not only just, they declared, but pragmatic: a republican mother could not educate her children properly until she was educated herself.

These arguments constituted a radical agenda for American education. Until the postrevolutionary era, women had little access to any but the most rudimentary schooling. Fathers might choose, as Anne Hutchinson's did, to educate their daughters. Sisters might learn from sympathetic brothers, as Mercy Otis Warren did from James Otis, Jr. And the rare slave owner might see to the education of gifted female slaves, as Phillis Wheatley's Boston master did. But these were exceptions. In truth, while the majority of white female colonists in the mid–eighteenth century probably could read, fewer could write, and even fewer had any grounding in mathematics, the sciences, or the humanities. Not every influential colonist believed, as the seventeenth-century Massachusetts governor John Winthrop did, that excessive reading could drive a woman insane, but most considered formal education a frivolous indulgence for members of a sex that God, Nature, and society barred from occupations requiring such knowledge. By the 1780s, however, many Americans spoke of formal schooling for women as a national necessity.

Although critics warned that a formal education would produce masculine women and upset the natural relationship between the sexes, by the 1780s young ladies' academies had sprung up across the nation from New England to the Carolinas. These schools offered a rigorous curriculum that differed little from that encountered by male students. What did differ, however, was the ultimate purpose of education for the graduates of the young ladies' academies: to prepare them for their expanded duties as mothers and wives. These eighteenth-century women—and the men of their generation—would have been shocked by the unexpected consequences of this educational reform and the ideology of civic responsibility that it served. In the next century, a new generation of educated women would enter the public sphere as reformers and activists—and ultimately as feminists.

PRESCRIPTIVE DOCUMENTS
꙰

A CHALLENGE TO PATRIARCHY
꙰

Susanna Wright, "To Eliza Norris—at Fairhill," Library Company of
Philadelphia, quoted in Pattie Cowell, "Womankind Call Reason to Their
Aid: Susanna Wright's Verse Epistle on the Status of Women in Eighteenth-
Century America," *Signs: Journal of Women in Culture and Society* 6 (1981),
pp. 795–800.

*Even before the war began, women like Quaker Susanna Wright had begun privately
to question traditional notions of male intellectual and moral superiority as well as
the divine sanction of male dominance over women. In the poem quoted below, Wright
put these cornerstones of male privilege to the test of reason—and they collapsed.
Wright laid the blame for the continuing system of sexual inequality on the shoulders
of women as well as men. Borrowing from the rhetoric of the Revolution that brewed
around her, she reminded her own sex that tyranny thrives where there is acquiescence.*

꙰

Siner Adam, by our first fair mother won
To share her fate—to Taste, & be undone
And that great Law, whence no appeal must Lye
Pronounced a Doom, That He should Rule—& Die
The Patial Race, rejoycing to fulfill
This Pleasing Dictate of almighty Will,
(With no Superior virtue in Their Mind)
Assert Their Right to Govern womankind
But Womankind, call Reason to Their aid
And Question, when or where, that Law was made,
That Law Divine,—(A Plausible pretense)
oft urg'd, with none, & oft with Little Sense
from wisdom's source, no origin could draw
That form'd the Men, to keep The Sex in awe,
Say, Reason Govern, all the mighty frame
And Reason rules, in every one, the same
No Right, has man, his Equal, to controul,
Since, all agree, There is no Sex in soul;
weak woman, thus, in agreement grown strong,

shakes off the yoke, her Parents wore too long;
But He, who arguments, in vain, had tryed
Hopes still for Conquest, from ye yielding side
Soft Soothing flattery & Persuasin Tries,
And by a Feigned submission, seeks to rise,
steals, unperceived,—to the unguarded heart,
  And There Reigns TYRANT,— . . .

Till Then, my friend, the righteous claim forbear
Indulge Man in his darling vice of sway
He only Rules Those, who of Choice obey;
When strip'd of Power, & Plac'd in equal light
Angels shall Judge who had the Better right
All you can do,—is but to Let him see,
That woman still, shall sure his equal be. . . .

A Call for Reform

↦↤

Benjamin Rush, *Thoughts upon Female Education, Accommodated to the Present
State of Society, Manners, and Government, in the United States of America*
(Philadelphia: Prichard and Hall, 1787).

*British physicians and educators were leaders in advocating the gentle nurturing of
children in an intimate, affectionate family setting. Although their prescriptive literature influenced American educators, the didactic literature of the postrevolutionary
period also emphasized the relationship between child-rearing practices and the incul-
cation of republican principles such as virtue, independence, self-reliance, and re-
straint. Philadelphia physician and educational reformer Benjamin Rush was among
the first and most effective American advocates of formal education for the mothers
who would shape the character of a new generation of republican citizens. In this
address to the newly created Young Ladies Academy of Philadelphia, Rush lays out
his argument for the necessity and the value of female education.*

↜↝

Gentlemen:

I have yielded with diffidence to the solicitations of the Principal of the
Academy, in undertaking to express my regard for the prosperity of this semi-
nary of learning by submitting to your candor a few thoughts upon female
education.

The first remark that I shall make upon this subject is that female education should be accommodated to the state of society, manners, and government of the country in which it is conducted.

This remark leads me at once to add that the education of young ladies in this country should be conducted upon principles very different from what it was in Great Britain and in some respects different from what it was when we were a part of a monarchical empire.

There are several circumstances in the situation, employments, and duties of women in America which require a peculiar mode of education.

I. The early marriages of our women, by contracting the time allowed for education, renders it necessary to contract its plan and to confine it chiefly to the more useful branches of literature.

II. The state of property in America renders it necessary for the greatest part of our citizens to employ themselves in different occupations for the advancement of their fortunes. This cannot be done without the assistance of the female members of the community. They must be the stewards and guardians of their husbands' property. That education, therefore, will be most proper for our women which teaches them to discharge the duties of those offices with the most success and reputation.

III. From the numerous avocations to which a professional life exposes gentlemen in America from their families, a principal share of the instruction of children naturally devolves upon the women. It becomes us therefore to prepare them, by a suitable education, for the discharge of this most important duty of mothers.

IV. The equal share that every citizen has in the liberty and the possible share he may have in the government of our country make it necessary that our ladies should be qualified to a certain degree, by a peculiar and suitable education, to concur in instructing their sons in the principles of liberty and government.

V. In Great Britain the business of servants is a regular occupation, but in America this humble station is the usual retreat of unexpected indigence; hence the servants in this country possess less knowledge and subordination than are required from them; and hence our ladies are obliged to attend more to the private affairs of their families than ladies generally do of the same rank in Great Britain. "They are good servants," said an American lady of distinguished merit in a letter to a favorite daughter, "who will do well with good looking after." This circumstance should have great influence upon the nature and extent of female education in America.

The branches of literature most essential for a young lady in this country appear to be:

I. A knowledge of the English language. She should not only read but speak and spell it correctly. And to enable her to do this, she should be taught the English grammar and be frequently examined in applying its rules in common conversation.

II. Pleasure and interest conspire to make the writing of a fair and legible hand a necessary branch of female education. For this purpose she should be taught not only to shape every letter properly but to pay the strictest regard to points and capitals. . . .

III. Some knowledge of figures and bookkeeping is absolutely necessary to qualify a young lady for the duties which await her in this country. There are certain occupations in which she may assist her husband with this knowledge, and should she survive him and agreeably to the custom of our country be the executrix of his will, she cannot fail of deriving immense advantages from it.

IV. An acquaintance with geography and some instruction in chronology will enable a young lady to read history, biography, and travels, with advantage, and thereby qualify her not only for a general intercourse with the world but to be an agreeable companion for a sensible man. To these branches of knowledge may be added, in some instances, a general acquaintance with the first principles of astronomy and natural philosophy, particularly with such parts of them as are calculated to prevent superstition, by explaining the causes or obviating the effects of natural evil.

V. Vocal music should never be neglected in the education of a young lady in this country. Besides preparing her to join in that part of public worship which consists in psalmody, it will enable her to soothe the care of domestic life. The distress and vexation of a husband, the noise of a nursery, and even the sorrows that will sometimes intrude into her own bosom may all be relieved by a song, where sound and sentiment unite to act upon the mind. . . .

VI. Dancing is by no means an improper branch of education for an American lady. It promotes health and renders the figure and motions of the body easy and agreeable. I anticipate the time when the resources of conversation shall be so far multiplied that the amusement of dancing shall be wholly confined to children. But in our present state of society and knowledge, I conceive it to be an agreeable substitute for the ignoble pleasures of drinking and gaming in our assemblies of grown people.

VII. The attention of our young ladies should be directed as soon as they are prepared for it to the reading of history, travels, poetry, and moral essays.

These studies are accommodated, in a peculiar manner, to the present state of society in America, and when a relish is excited for them in early life, they subdue that passion for reading novels which so generally prevail among the fair sex. . . .

VIII. It will be necessary to connect all these branches of education with regular instruction in the Christian religion. For this purpose, the principles of the different sects of Christians should be taught and explained, and our pupils should early be furnished with some of the most simple arguments in favor of the truth of Christianity. A portion of the Bible (of late improperly banished from our schools) should be read by them every day and such questions should be asked, after reading it, as are calculated to imprint upon their minds the interesting stories contained in it.

Rousseau has asserted that the great secret of education consists in "wasting the time of children profitably." There is some truth in this observation. I believe that we often impair their health and weaken their capacities by imposing studies upon them which are not proportioned to their years. But this objection does not apply to religious instruction. There are certain simple propositions in the Christian religion that are suited in a peculiar manner to the infant state of reason and moral sensibility. A clergyman of long experience in the instruction of youth informed me that he always found children acquired religious knowledge more easily than knowledge upon other subjects, and that young girls acquired this kind of knowledge more readily than boys. The female breast is the natural soil of Christianity, and while our women are taught to believe its doctrines and obey its precepts, the wit of Voltaire and the style of Bolingbroke will never be able to destroy its influence upon our citizens.

IX. If the measures that have been recommended for inspiring our pupils with a sense of religious and moral obligation be adopted, the government of them will be easy and agreeable. I shall only remark under this head that strictness of discipline will always render severity unnecessary and that there will be the most instruction in that school where there is the most order. . . .

I cannot dismiss the subject of female education without remarking that the city of Philadelphia first saw a number of gentlemen associated for the purpose of directing the education of young ladies. By means of this plan the power of teachers is regulated and restrained and the objects of education are extended. By the separation of the sexes in the unformed state of their manners, female delicacy is cherished and preserved. Here the young ladies may enjoy all the literary advantages of a boarding school and at the same time live under the protection of their parents. Here emulation may be excited without jealousy, ambition without envy, and competition without strife.

The attempt to establish this new mode of education for young ladies was an experiment, and the success of it has answered our expectations. Too much praise cannot be given to our principal and his assistants, for the abilities and fidelity with which they have carried the plan into execution. The proficiency which the young ladies have discovered in reading, writing, spelling, arithmetic, grammar, geography, music, and their different catechisms since the last examination is a less equivocal mark of the merits of our teachers than anything I am able to express in their favor.

But the reputation of the academy must be suspended till the public are convinced by the future conduct and character of our pupils of the advantages of the institution. To you, therefore, YOUNG LADIES, an important problem is committed for solution; and that is, whether our present plan of education be a wise one and whether it be calculated to prepare you for the duties of social and domestic life. I know that the elevation of the female mind, by means of moral, physical, and religious truth, is considered by some men as unfriendly to the domestic character of a woman. But this is the prejudice of little minds and springs from the same spirit which opposes the general diffusion of knowledge among the citizens of our republic. If men believe that ignorance is favorable to the government of the female sex, they are certainly deceived, for a weak and ignorant woman will always be governed with the greatest difficulty.

I have somtimes been led to ascribe the invention of ridiculous and expensive fashions in female dress entirely to the gentlemen in order to divert the ladies from improving their minds and thereby to secure a more arbitrary and unlimited authority over them. It will be in your power, ladies, to correct the mistakes and practice of our sex upon these subjects by demonstrating that the female temper can only be governed by reason and that the cultivation of reason in women is alike friendly to the order of nature and to private as well as public happiness.

THE VIRTUES OF AN EDUCATED WIFE

↔ ↔

Susanna Haswell Rowson, "Women as They Are," in *Miscellaneous Poems* (Boston: Printed for the author by Gilbert and Dean and by W. P. & L. Blake, Corneill, 1804), pp. 105–115.

A Changing Gender Ideology

Susanna Haswell Rowson was an articulate spokeswoman for gender equality. In the poem below, written in the early nineteenth century, Rowson echoed the arguments of Susanna Wright and Judith Sargent Murray that nurture, not nature or divine injunction, created the inequality of the sexes in intellect and moral development. While Wright and Murray stressed the importance of education for women's sense of themselves and for the vitality of the nation, Rowson stressed the advantages husbands would enjoy in the private world of marriage if their wives were intelligent, virtuous companions rather than decorative dependents.

~

"Children, like tender osiers, take the bow,
And as they first are fashioned, always grow."

Thus spoke the bard; and 'tis a moral truth,
That precept and example, taught in youth,
Dwell on the mind till life's dull scene is past;
Clinging about us even to the last.
And women, pray for folly don't upbraid them,
Are just such things, as education made them.

The girl, who from her birth is thought a beauty,
Scarce ever hears of virtue, sense or duty;
Mamma, delighted with each limb and feature,
Declares, she is a fascinating creature;
Forbids all study, work, or wise reflection;
'Twill spoil her eyes, or injure her complexion.
"Hold up your head, my dear; turn out your toes;
Bless me, what's that? a pimple on your nose;
It smarts, dear, don't it? how can you endure it?
Here's some *Pomade Divine*, to heal and cure it."
Then, every little master, that comes near her,
Is taught to court, to flatter, or to fear her.
Nurse or Mamma cries, "See, my dearest life,
There's Charley, you shall be his little wife;
Smile my sweet creature; Charley, come and kiss her.
And tell me, is she not a pretty miss, sir?
Give her that orange; fruit, fine clothes, and toys,
Were made for little ladies, not for boys."

Thus, ere one proper wish her heart can move,
She's taught to think of lovers, and of love;
She's told she is a beauty, does not doubt it;

What need of sense? beauties can wed without it.
And then her eyes, her teeth, her lips, her hair,
And shape, are all that can be worth her care;
She thinks a kneeling world should bow before her,
And men were but created to adore her.
But call her to the active scenes of life,
As friend, as daughter, mother, mistress, wife;
You scarce can find, in the whole course of nature,
A more unfortunate or helpless creature.
Untaught the smallest duty of her station,
She stands, a cypher in the vast creation.
Her husband might perhaps expect to find
The angel's form contained an angel's mind.
Alas, poor man! time will the veil remove;
She *had* not fault. No! you were blind with love;
You flatter'd, idolized, made her your wife;
She thought these halcyon days would last for life.
At every small neglect, from her bright eyes
The lightning flashes; then she pouts and cries;
When th' angel sinks, I fear, alas, in common,
Into a downwright captious, teazing woman;
And if a reasonable friend was sought,
To counsel, sooth, or share each anxious thought,
Poor man! your disappointment I lament;
You've a long life before you—to repent. . . .

Methinks I hear some man exulting swear,
"Why, this is really "Women as they are."
Pardon me, sir, I'll speak, I'm not afraid;
I'll tell you what they are, what might be made.
When the Creator form'd this world in common,
His last, best work, his master-piece, was woman.
Ta'en from the side of man, and next his heart,
Of all his virtues she partakes a part;
And from that source, poor woman got a share
Of vice and folly, mingled here and there.
But would you treat us, scorning custom's rules,
As reasonable beings, not as fools,
And from our earliest youth, would condescend

To form our minds, strengthen, correct, amend;
Teach us to scorn those fools, whose only joys,
Are plac'd in trifling, idleness and noise;
Teach us to prize the power of intellect;
And whilst inspiring love, to keep respect;
You'd meet the sweet reward of all your care;
Find in us friends, your purest joys to share;
You then would own the choicest boon of Heaven,
The happiest lot that can to man be given,
To smooth the rugged path, and sweeten life,
Is an affectionate and faithful wife.

DESCRIPTIVE DOCUMENTS

EDUCATION IS A NECESSITY FOR ALL WOMEN

Anonymous, "On Educating Negro Women," 1827, quoted in Mortimer J.
Adler, Charles Van Doren, and George Ducas, eds., *The Negro in American
History* (Chicago: Encyclopaedia Britannica Educational Corp.,
1969), pp. 327–328.

*The architects of republican womanhood and the advocates of female education may
have had the wives and daughters of the "respectable classes" in mind, but the arguments they presented could be deployed by and for other women as well. In this anonymous letter to the African American* Freedom's Journal, *written in 1827, the author
challenges her readers to at last include African American women like herself in their
educational revolution.*

Messrs. Editors,

Will you allow a female to offer a few remarks upon a subject that you
must allow to be all-important? I don't know that in any of your papers you
have said sufficient upon the education of females. I hope you are not to be
classed with those who think that our mathematical knowledge should be
limited to "fathoming the dishkettle," and that we have acquired enough of
history if we know that our grandfather's father lived and died. It is true the
time has been when to darn a stocking and cook a pudding well was consid-

ered the end and aim of a woman's being. But those were days when ignorance blinded men's eyes. The diffusion of knowledge has destroyed these degrading opinions, and men of the present age allow that we have minds that are capable and deserving of culture.

There are difficulties, and great difficulties, in the way of our advancement; but that should only stir us to greater efforts. We possess not the advantages with those of our sex whose skins are not colored like our own, but we can improve what little we have and make our one talent produce twofold. The influence that we have over the male sex demands that our minds should be instructed and improved with the principles of education and religion, in order that this influence should be properly directed. Ignorant ourselves, how can we be expected to form the minds of our youth and conduct them in the paths of knowledge? . . . There is a great responsibility resting somewhere, and it is time for us to be up and doing.

I would address myself to all mothers, and say to them that while it is necessary to possess a knowledge of cookery and the various mysteries of pudding making, something more is requisite. It is their bounden duty to store their daughters' minds with useful learning. They should be made to devote their leisure time to reading books, whence they would derive valuable information which could never be taken from them.

I will not longer trespass on your time and patience. I merely throw out these hints in order that some more able pen will take up the subject.

Matilda

SOCIAL CLASS AND INTELLECTUAL LIFE

↔ ↔

Judith Sargent Murray to Winthrop Sargent, February 5, 1785, Judith Sargent Murray Papers, reel 1, vol. 2, Mississippi Department of History and Archives.

Massachusetts patriot Judith Sargent Murray was a prolific writer of religious tracts, political essays, poems, and plays. One of the central themes in her work was the social rather than divine or natural origins of male intellectual superiority. Although she believed educational opportunities would promote gender equality, she appreciated the role of race and class in determining a woman's access to and use of education. In the following letter to her brother, Winthrop Sargent, Murray fantasizes about the benefits of ease and luxury in pursuing a life of the mind.

↭

To My Brother

Gloucester February 5th, 1785

Had [I] been born a Lady, I could have enjoyed myself most delightfully. Do let me indulge imagination for a moment . . . a numerous train of well regulated and kindly disposed sevants, await my commands—I Have but to speak, and I am instantly obeyed—my retirement is not invaded, solitude may always be mine and my closet abounds with Authors of every description, and the most distinguished in every class—Here I can obtain solid advantage; Improvement, with dignified aspect, Figures majestically in the Classic Volumes; while during the moment so of rosy pleasure, amusement dressed by smiling fancy, courts my attention, and I luxuriate with inexpressible satisfaction . . . or, if arbitrary custom, which presumes to [present?] bounds to the progress of female education, hath obtained in regard to [man?] My Lord is a Man of Letters, and I live with him upon terms of equality he speaks, and investigation flows from his lips—by his interposition the doors of science are thrown open to me, and I enter with the Preceptor of my deliberate choice—Thus are my days sacred to wisdom, and I am exempted from every low born care—My housekeeper, at an appointed hour, enters my apartment every morning—she is dutiful, and affectionate—she receives the orders of the day, and I am sure to have . . . faithfully observed.

A GRADUATE SPEAKS HER MIND
↦↤

"The Salutory Oration of Miss Priscilla Mason," May 15, 1793, in The Rise and Progress of the Young Ladies Academyl of Philadelphia . . . (Stewart and Cochran: Philadelphia, 1794), pp. 90–95.

The Young Ladies Academy of Philadelphia opened its doors in 1787, offering courses in grammar, arithmetic, oratory, and geography no less rigorous that those available in the best male academies. This boarding school attracted the daughters of Philadelphia's elite families and the support of the city's most influential men, including Benjamin Rush. The academy provided its students with more than a fine education; it gave them membership in a female community that shared common experience outside the boundaries of family. Thus, lifelong friendships were formed and a sense of sisterhood was nurtured. In the speech excerpted below, Priscilla Mason boldly invites a "promiscuous," or mixed, audience of classmates, teachers, guests, and parents of the class of 1793 to abandon sexist educational traditions and embrace a philosophy more suited to a republic and its citizens. Her insistence that women deserve broader opportunities in the world outside the home illustrates the potential radicalism of the new gender ideology.

✳

. . . Respected and very respectable audience; while your presence inspires our tender minds with fear and anxiety, your countenances promise indulgence, and encourage us to proceed. . . .

A female, young and inexperienced, addressing a promiscuous assembly, is a novelty which requires an apology, as some may suppose. I therefore, with submission, beg leave to offer a few thoughts in vindication of female eloquence. . . .

Is a power of speech, and volubility of expression, one of the talents of the orator? Our sex possess it in an eminent degree.

Do personal attractions give charms to eloquence, and force to the orator's arguments? . . . Do tender passions enable the orator to speak in a moving and forcible manner? . . . In all these respects the female orator stands on equal,—nay, on *superior* ground. . . .

Granted, it is, that a perfect knowledge of the subject is essential to the accomplish'd Orator. But seldom does it happen, that the abstruse sciences, become the subject of eloquence. And, as to that knowledge which is popular and practical . . . who will say that the female mind is incapable?

Our high and mighty Lords (thanks to their arbitrary constitutions) have denied us the means of knowledge, and then reproached us for the want of it. Being the stronger party, they early seized the sceptre and the sword; with these they gave laws to society; they denied women the advantage of a liberal education; forbid them to exercise their talents on those great occasions, which would serve to improve them. They doom'd the sex to servile or frivolous employments, on purpose to degrade their minds, that they themselves might hold unrivall'd, the power and preeminence they had usurped. Happily, a more liberal way of thinking begins to prevail. . . . But supposing now that we possess'd all the talents of the orator, in the highest perfection; where shall we find a theatre for the display of them? The Church, the Bar, and the Senate are shut against us. Who shut them? *Man*; despotic man, first made us incapable of the duty, and then forbid us the exercise. Let us by suitable education, qualify ourselves for those high departments—they will open before us. They *will*, did I say? They have done it already. Besides several Churches of less importance, a most numerous and respectable Society, has display'd its impartiality—I had almost said gallentry [!] in this respect. . . . The members of the enlightened and liberal Church, . . . look to the soul, and allow all to teach who are capable of it, be they male or female.

But Paul forbids it! Contemptible little body! The girls laughed at the deformed creature. To be revenged, he declares war against the whole sex: advises men not to marry them; and has the insolence to order them to keep silence in the Church —: afraid, I suppose, that they would say something against celibacy, or ridicule the old bachelor.

With respect to the bar, citizens of either sex, have an undoubted right to plead their own cause there. Instances could be given of females being admitted to plead the cause of a friend, a husband, a son; and they have done it with energy and effect. I am assured that there is nothing in our laws or constitutions, to prohibit the licensure of female Attorneys. . . .

Heliogabalus, the Roman Emperor of blessed memory, made his grandmother a Senator of Rome. He also established a senate of women; appointed his mother President; and committed to them the important business of regulating dress and fashions. . . . It would be worthy the wisdom of Congress, to consider whether a similar institution, established at the seat of our Federal Government, would not be a public benefit. . . . Such a Senate, composed of women most noted for wisdom, learning and taste, delegated from every part of the Union, would give dignity, and independence to our manners. . . .